The Daddy of ALL Mysteries

by

Jess Welsby

The true story of my parents' secret love and the search for a father I never knew.

Best Wishes

Jess Welsby
(4)

AKA Monica
3 +

Published by M. McMullin

First Edition, January 2015.

Typeset: Jess Welsby
Cover Design: Jess Welsby

(Jess Welsby is the pen name of Monica McMullin)

Printed in the United Kingdom by Birkenhead Press

Published by M. McMullin
All enquiries email: monicamcmullin@mac.com

Follow me on Twitter and Facebook:

https://twitter.com/McWallaby
https://www.facebook.com/profile.php?id=100005630778262

ISBN 978-0-9931778-0-4

Author's Note

Although my birth was registered as Monica Welsby, my family's nickname for me was Jess. I used the pen name of Jess Welsby to write this book in honour of my family. If life had been different for my parents, my name would have been registered as Monica Freeman. In 1980 I married Brian and became Monica McMullin. So that's me; who I was, and who I am now. The story within takes care of the rest.

The Daddy of all Mysteries is my first attempt at writing. How this book came to be written is explained within the Acknowledgements. The Preface and Introduction will help you to get to grips with the entire story and research. All areas of a book that I usually skip. In this true story, they need to be read.

Researching, writing and the minefield of self-publishing have been a massive learning curve for me. I have included all my stupid mistakes and wrong assumptions. If *I* can do this — so can *you*.

The other reason I agreed to reveal such a personal story about my parents and their families, is best explained in the last few words on this page.

Proper writers; those who actually earn a good living from their work, often talk about 'finding your voice'. Well, I write in the same way as I speak... simply and plainly. My voice, I have given to my mum.

Reviews for - The Daddy of ALL Mysteries

The motivation for the authors search to find out more about the father she never knew was simple. It was not driven by where he was from or what he did for a living; it was to find out if he loved her mum. This book is more than a roadmap for anyone wanting to trace their roots. It's a warm, heartfelt account of a normal family, if there is such a thing, filled with wonderful characters and set against the backdrop of a Liverpool I remember from my childhood. I would highly recommend it. **Victor McGuire - Actor.**

Although this story could have turned into a bitter and depressing record of religious and moral ignorance, at no time was it a morbid read, with laugh out loud moments far outweighing the sad situation this family found themselves in. Jess is a natural storyteller whose warmth and humour oozes out of every page, her writing is simple and not forced and it was an unexpected delight that will stay with me and anyone else who has the privilege to read this story.
Angela Billing - Committee Member of Irish Centre, Liverpool.

This is a gripping real life story, written in an engaging, affectionate and humorous style, which uncovers a family history spanning almost 150 years and covering several continents. It shines a light on dark episodes of racial and religious intolerance and political and social history. I did not want to put the book down. The tenacity and scope of the author's detective work provides a textbook for aspiring genealogical researchers but more than that, it makes a strong case for banishing the bigotry, racial, moral and religious prejudices, which have caused so much fear, unhappiness and alienation within families in the past and remain a constant threat with today's increasing patterns of migration. **Shirley McDermott - Retired teacher.**

It is the Jewish heritage which emerges as a focus for Jess Welsby's search. This is the community Brian Epstein was a part of and which has an intriguing cultural link to the Dublin of James Joyce. You will be bowled along by the infectious, sensitive and emotional detective work as well as the considerable charm and insight which holds this inspirational narrative together.
Owen Hagen - Writer and avid reader.

The narrative unfolds at a delightful pace. While there is catastrophe, sadness and sorrow, there is great warmth conveyed in the words and feelings of the author. This book abounds with episodes that will bring a smile to the readers' face. Her relationship with her mother is beautifully described and in such an honest way. I hope I have conveyed the great pleasure I got from reading this book. I found it very hard to put the book down.
Joe England - Member of Irish Centre's book club.

A Tribute to a Lady

For all she suffered and the secrets that she took to her grave,

I write this book in memory of my mum.

Catherine (Katie) Welsby

Contents

Preface

Although I went to a Catholic school, I would sag off whenever I got half a chance, especially if religion was on the agenda. It's a subject that I've never had much interest in, and yet religion plays a big part in this book.

I spent much of my primary school years daydreaming my way through the weekly mundane routines of Saturday afternoon confession, followed by Sunday morning holy communion, which was monitored by my teachers first thing on Monday. My mum and nan had great faith in God, with hardly a sentence passing their lips without the mention of His holy name, but they couldn't have cared less about going to Mass, and left me to decide for myself.

Religion wasn't a subject that my mum talked about, while my nan saw prayer as a private conversation with God, rather than communal. Using her caustic humour to skit what she called, the fashion parade of church-goers who would sit jangling in the back pew before the body of Christ had barely the chance to pass through their system. Nevertheless, a set of rosary beads could be found in her pocket, accompanied by her hanky and snuffbox.

Conflicting information that made no sense to me and the lack of interest shown at home for any form of communal worship, eventually brought me to the conclusion that, if there was a God, surely it's not necessary to go through *any* third party to speak to him.

If you must put me into a pigeonhole, then the closest match should bear the heading 'humanist', but please leave the lid of the box open.

Acknowledgments

I owe a massive debt of gratitude to dead people. I didn't understand my late mum Katie; now I do, and everything fits into place. This book is for you, mum. Thanks for not parting with me. Heartfelt thanks to my late Uncle John for making me stand on my own two feet and to listen to what people *don't* say. My attitude to life I owe to my late nan, Annie Welsby who used her caustic humour to get herself through bad times. I can hear her now . . . 'There's always sumone else in life who's worse off than yerself.' I would also like to thank, my late cousin, Mary, for her loyalty to my mum and her Sunday roasts. My late Auntie Annie for her guts, polish and rhubarb pie. My late Uncle Tommy for that plastic globe, which gave me my travelling bug and my late Aunt Maggie for her keen eye for design. May they all rest peacefully and, if there is an afterlife, fingers crossed that it has a well-stocked library.

Now, I would like to thank the many stars of this story; the people who have helped, advised and supported me in my search for my late father and his family. I particularly want to show my gratitude and acknowledge every single one of these people, not only for their support and guidance throughout my research, but also for coaxing me, manipulating me and bulldozing me into writing this book, and for not taking a blind bit of notice of what I've since been told was the literary equivalent of stage fright.

However the problem I've been faced with in acknowledging and giving these people the credit that they so deserve is that . . . I don't have a clue who most of them are!

I know only their usernames and a few snippets of information I've learned about them during my research. These invisible people have been my educators, my mentors and my inspiration. To this day, I have never met them and I know very little about them. These people are my online or e-friends. Many have read my thread or the many messages I have left on the countless family history websites and have actively helped, advised and followed my mum's story to help piece together the life of a father who I never knew.

So this long list of names is mostly a list of usernames, which people use so as not to reveal their true identities online. They are not *real* names but they are real people, and these people are scattered around the four corners of the globe. I have never met them and I may never do, but without their help and guidance I would never have found my late father and my lovely new family or the roots that seemed to have been buried deep within my subconscious all along. Without them, this book would not now be resting in your hands . . .

OC: Maudarby (Moggie); Annswaby; Tilly Mint; Night Owl; Peppie; Niaomiatt; Watson; JayG; Margaretmarch; Margaret in Burton; KarenS; Borobabs; Mary from Italy; Clematised; Gerry; Kit; Christine in Herts; Maggie4_7_; Chrissy Smiff; Jill on the A272; Don; Janet in Yorkshire; BigOoms; Breckland Jane; Merry Monty; Jessbowbag; Muggins in Sussex; Wanda Houghton; All the members, administrators and moderators of familytreeforum.com: From websites; genealogistsforum.co.uk; JewishGen.com; British-Jewry.com; Dublin.ie; Great War Forum; 1914-1918.net; I would also like to thank; Joel Levy, UK; Barbara Zimmer, Virginia USA; Edward David Luft, Washington DC; Rabbi Zorack Meir Salasnik, Bushey Synagogue; Stanley Diamond, Montréal, Canada. Executive Director, Jewish Records Indexing, Poland; Saul Marks, professional genealogist and lecturer in Jewish ancestry brotherswish.com; Dr Mervyn Kingston, Chairman of Merseyside AJEX; Archivists at Liverpool Records Office; Charles Tucker, archivist to the Chief Rabbi's office; United Synagogue; Justin Levy, Dublin; Steven Smyrl, Massey and King, Dublin; Aideen Ireland, National Archives, Ireland; Arnold Lewis, Liverpool Jewish Community Archivist; Anne Lapedus Brest, Shalom Ireland; Stuart Rosenblatt P.C. FGSI, Jewish Genealogical Society of Ireland: Steven Zuckerman, USA; Chaim Freedman Israel; Murray Freedman, Leeds; Naomi Ogin, Australia; Belinda Kaye, UK; Hanne Stinson Chief Executive The British Humanist Association; Susan Brugnoli, Liverpool; Janet Scott and Fatima Williams, wardens at Rose Bush Court; Edward Lewison, Baltimore; Stephen McCormac, Archivist, The Royal Hospital Donnybrook, Dublin; Allan Freedman UK; Maurice Freeman, Melbourne; Selwyn and Lynn Neiman, London; Ruth Fogelman, Jerusalem Ron Freeman and his wife Mary Lacy Porter, Baltimore USA; Ged Fagan, inercityliving.com; Simon Ryan, Archivist at Merseyside Fire Service: Esther (Hershman) Rechtschafner, Israel; Major I.L Riley TD.MA.FSA Scot, Honorary Secretary, Liverpool Scottish Regimental Museum; Jean Crimmins, Merseyside Fire and Rescue Service; Ralph Saliger, Israel; Lauren Newby UK; Vera Lourie and Nicky Begent, The Friends of the Royal Free Hospital; Shani Struthers, UK; Rachel Perez-Arwas, South Hampstead Synagogue; Sylvia and Stephanie Garshag, USA; Sylvia Seddon UK; Stan Rose UK; Jean Emmerson and Cormac at Birkenhead Press.

Finally, I would like to thank the people whom I *can* name. People I have known for most of my life, who are a part of my life; people I could never imagine my life without. At the top of this list is the most important person in my life; my better half Brian, thanks for not divorcing me. Eternal gratitude to my mum's nephew Brian Hennessy for his invaluable memories. My mother's great-niece Mary Fortune for her encouragement. Special thanks to my father's three nieces Shirley, Joyce and Margaret and their families for welcoming me so warmly and introducing me to my late father. Also to my father's great-niece Natalie and great-nephew Arthur. I would also like to thank Joanie for the laughs we shared throughout our early childhood. Linda, for listening to me, on the few occasions I managed to get a word in edgeways. Jo and Lisa, the daughters we never had. And to Shelagh, Vic and Shani for their support. All my friends and anyone who has put up with me in my search for my roots.

Introduction

Life is so different today, but in the inner-city slums of Liverpool during the early part of the 1950s, for an unmarried, penniless Catholic woman to give birth to a child at nearly forty-one years of age, was an absolute disgrace. My mother had broken all the rules and the consequences were cruel and often brutal. She experienced bigotry and ridicule on a grand scale and was ostracised by many in the community. She would never reveal my father's identity to a soul, which led to further speculation. It was not until after her sudden death in 1989 that I found a letter which led me to uncover the reason for all the secrecy. A further twenty years of my life would pass before I finally discovered who my father had been.

Tucked away in the bottom drawer of my mother's old mahogany dressing table, I found a letter. It was in the custody of my childhood teddybear, wrapped in a blanket of pink tissue paper as if they were both cherished and belonged together. I recognised my mother's shaky handwriting on the small, blue, Basildon Bond self-addressed envelope. The letter, which was dated the 18 September 1987, was written from the warden of Rose Bush Court, a retirement apartment complex in Parkhill Road, Hampstead in London. It appeared that my mum had written to the warden enquiring about a man who had lived at the apartments. The letter gave my mother the news of his death.

It was this letter that instigated my search and eventually led me to a discovery that has left me wondering if there is some memory locked away, hidden deep within our DNA; because, instead of finding the scandal that I had expected, I found a heart-warming story that slowly revealed itself from an unmarked grave in a Hertfordshire Jewish cemetery.

For my mum to be enquiring about *any* man, let alone a man who'd lived in London, was totally out of character for her, as apart from dreaming about her screen idol Tyrone Power, I never remember my mother ever bothering with men. Somehow, I instinctively knew that this man had to be my father. Now, I had a name and an address and it was from then that my parents' story began to slowly unfold. Being nothing more than an ink blot on my birth certificate, my father had always been a closely guarded secret, which I would later discover that my mother had kept since she was barely fifteen years of age; a secret she had taken to her grave.

Essentially, this story is about my search for that mystery man revealed to me in the letter, the father I never knew. But as I researched and gathered information about both my parents and their families, this book has evolved into far more. It's about the people who struggled and paved the way for us to live a far better life than they had to endure. It's about how they needed to duck and dive just to merely survive, eking out a life for themselves and often burying their children along the way. It's about a generation who fought in two world wars, and yet they were given little support from the country they fought for and were often forced to rely on charity in the form of the workhouse. Above all, this book has evolved into a nostalgic journey of discovery; discovery about myself and about a way of life in the Liverpool that was. It's also about bigotry, tenacity and above all, hope; and all the struggles, fears, laughter and tears of a generation now dead and gone.

1 Little Italy

John was my nan's blue-eyed boy. But that didn't stop her calling him a feckin' gobshite under her breath whenever he made a holy show of her with his high-minded, heathen questions that no living soul could answer. He was my nan's youngest surviving son and my mother's younger brother. He was also the only father I ever knew.

I was raised by my mum and nan until John returned home to live with us. We were a household of odd-bod leftovers. My widowed nan, Annie. Her unmarried nephew, Paddy. My unmarried mum, Katie. And my unmarried uncle, John. I called him John, not Uncle John. He usually called me by an odd nickname of his choosing, which was Jess. I never thought to ask him why he called me Jess, it was just the way things had always been. He also had an assortment of other pet names for me including Wallaby, The Worm or Bloody Nuisance, depending more on my mood than his, as I spent my entire childhood tormenting the life out of him with a million questions the minute he walked through our door.

My nan didn't allow swearing under her roof. She herself only cursed the Irish way, which, in her mind, didn't count. And she only cursed under her breath, accompanied by a squiggled self-blessing before she clasped her hands and glanced up to heaven. It was as if she thought that God himself was stone deaf or too far away to be listening. 'Feckin' eejit' could usually be read on her lips, especially when doing battle with Mick the coalman or calling John fit to burn. Consequently, I was able to lip-read before I was able to book-read.

The community where I lived with my odd-bod family in 1950s inner-city Liverpool was known as Little Italy because of the many Italian immigrants who had settled there, along with hordes of Irish immigrants who had left Ireland during the 1840s potato famine. Religion and poverty united them, and they all got on well together. Ninety-nine per cent of our neighbours were either Catholic Italian or Catholic Irish. We were all left-footers, as us Catholics were called, and we all lived in varying degrees of 1950s working-class poverty.

We shopped at Paddy's Market in Cazneau Street, where Cilla Black's mum had her market stall and which later relocated to Great Homer Street. And most of us either purchased or pawned our few meagre possessions from what had been the community's lifeline for more than a hundred years – Berry's pawnbrokers.

I doubt my mother would have survived without Berry's; it served as her bank and department store. I'll never forget the coils of sticky flypaper, encrusted with the bodies of dead flies, dangling from the cobwebbed ceiling like macabre, silent wind chimes as they turned slowly, driven by the draught from Berry's door. I can still picture the bare 40-watt light bulb, which shed a glimmer of light onto the rack of overcoats and suits that had been previously pawned and were hanging up for sale. The smell of the stale, musty odour from their previous owners desperately clinging on, just as desperate as their owners had been. Life was cheap in those days. We were all in the same boat – the HMS *Destitute.*

Asian door-to-door hawkers would call with their little leather suitcases packed with odd pieces of cheap knitwear, household items, children's clothes and other peculiar items that could be bought for just a few coppers 'on the weekly'. We called these hawkers the door-knockers.

I remember my mum opening the door one cold December day and a large statue of Our Lady was pulled from a suitcase. My mother nearly hit the lad over the head with it. Unperturbed, he dived back into his suitcase and produced a full crib, complete with the three wise men, each carrying their gold, frankincense and myrrh, and their donkeys were thrown in for free. This must have been the beginning of buy-one-get-one-free.

'God . . . luv . . . trier,' he said in his broken English and a cheeky grin. Then he stuffed the three wise men back into his suitcase and tucked Our Lady under his arm.

'Yer, 'e luvs a trier, so go an' *try* sumwhere else, lad.'

The door-knockers tried to sell everything to us Cat'licks. Then, there was the Jew-man, as he was known, who would call to offer you a ticket, which gave you credit at the many clothes shops around the London Road area. You could spend the value of the ticket, treating yourself to a new frock or coat from their ready-to-wear, or off-the-peg as it was then called, or you could have something designed and made to measure at one of the many excellent tailors' shops in the area – Liverpool's very own *haute couture.*

The Jew-man would then call to collect his money every Friday night, usually a shilling or two each week until the debt was paid off. Then, when you had fully paid up, he would try to coax you into another ticket. But my mother didn't like being in debt and always preferred to leave off *before,* rather than to pay off *after.* Often she would say to me, 'whether it's second'and or bran' spankin' new, it's paid for wit' luv frum me t' you.'

The tenement flat that was our home through the 1950s was furnished with bits and pieces of bizarre furniture from Harden House, an auction room run by the Salvation Army, while bigger pieces of furniture were purchased from the all-year-round Christmas club at Stanley's furniture store. Whatever Stanley couldn't sell, usually because it was so grotesque that even the desperate turned their noses up to it, Stanley would slash the price down to get rid of it quickly and you could bet your life that this would be the item that my mother would buy. She would usually leave about 2/- (two shillings) off each week until it was fully paid, and then whatever rubbish she had bought would be delivered.

I was playing in the street one day and I will never forget Stanley's furniture van arriving and the doors being flung open to reveal what me and my mates first mistook for a fairground ride. But when it emerged from the darkness of Stanley's rusty old van, I could see it was a three-piece suite, covered in luminous, purple plastic wrapping. It was the kind of colour that reflected on anything that came within its vicinity, like some kind of scientific experiment that had gone badly wrong. As it floated past me, carried high upon the heads of the delivery men, I realised that the fairground ride wasn't wearing any wrapping. My mates creased up. And, as a large crowd gathered around waiting to be entertained, I laughed too. While we all stood there watching this colourful spectacle being paraded across the street, we began taking bets on who, in their right mind, could have handed over their hard-earned money for this monstrosity. The smirk was soon wiped from my gob when this fairground waltzer twisted and turned up the steps and then disappeared into our flat!

We were stuck with this abomination for donkey's years, and I would dread visitors. Not that people ever mentioned it, but it would always be the first thing their eyes would fall upon when they walked through our door. Then they would look away quickly, trying their best to hide their amusement, only to then feast their eyes upon the rest of our colourful, eccentric interior. Purple was probably the only colour that was missing from our flat, so my mother's purchase fitted in perfectly with the rest of the eclectic mess that we called home.

My mum chose things because they were cheap. It didn't matter to her what they looked like. It didn't cross her mind that we had orange psychedelic curtains – which my confused nan called psychiatric curtains – blue psychedelic oilcloth covering the floor and red flock wallpaper covering the walls. To keep out the cold, new wallpaper would always be layered on top of the old wallpaper. This was our cavity wall insulation and over the years it became so thick on the walls that there was no longer any sign of a skirting board to be seen, and the old round dolly light switches were embedded into the wallpaper like cherries on the top of a cake.

Never dreaming of buying what she couldn't afford, my mother scrimped and saved what little she had. Making use of the tiny brass ornamental jars that were placed along the mantelpiece of the black cast iron fire grate, she saved her joeys, pennies and ha'pennies in the end brass jar. When she had enough, she changed the copper into a sixpence and moved it along to the next jar, and when she had two sixpences she changed them into a shilling. Some shillings were saved for the gas and leccy meters, and some would be changed into half-crowns. When she had eight half-crowns she changed them into a pound note, which was then added to the tiny bundle she kept hidden under the palliasse, carefully wrapped in lazzi bands and placed inside one of my little white ankle socks.

This was how my mother scraped through the grey, depressing 1950s. Apart from moneylenders, there was no other way for people like us to borrow money and so people lived within their means, saved every penny or pawned what little they had. Neighbours were much closer, they needed each other and looked after each other. Doors were left unlocked, and children safely roamed the streets playing the simple games of kick-the-can, hoppy and hide-and-seek. Games that cost no money to buy.

The majority of people were good-natured, hard-working and genuine, but like most communities, it was a melting pot of saints and sinners. Some people could be insular and intolerant of anybody who they saw as different. Although happy to trade with Asians, Jews and outsiders, they didn't mix with them. An invisible line was drawn by *both* sides.

We were all petrified of what we didn't understand. It was the fear of the unknown. So we stayed in our little groups. It wasn't until I grew up and started my first job that I first met and had a conversation with a black person. And when I worked with a girl who I really got on well with, I was absolutely flabbergasted to be told that she and her family were . . .

'Wha'! Yer family are Martians?'

'NO! Mormons.'

She might as well have told me that her family were Martians, for all I knew of this religion. Yet she was no different from me or from anyone else for that matter, and we stayed good friends for many years. I soon realised that deep down we were all just the same. Whether black or white, Catholic or Jew, Muslim or Mormon and most probably Martian too. The difference between us was only in the mind of the individual.

My mother couldn't very well hide the fact that I was illegitimate. It was common knowledge throughout the entire community, and I remember it often being the subject of malicious gossip, mostly aimed at my mum. Relentless ridicule and mocking silent glances followed her as she walked along the street. Some people just didn't speak to her, or if they did, it was with an air of contempt. I was far too young back then to fully understand the uncomfortable feelings that crept over me if my mother stopped and talked to some of our neighbours. Sometimes the atmosphere was so heavy that it could be cut with a knife.

People were less informal in those days and even people who had lived alongside each other for many years respectfully referred to each other as Mr or Mrs, rather than by their first names. My mother referred to herself as Mrs Welsby in a feeble attempt to hide the terrible shame she always felt being an unmarried mother. That shame never left her. Always being a very private and unassuming person, she was extremely self-conscious and would drain of what little confidence she possessed whenever she was placed in unfamiliar company. As a child I took no notice, but when I think back, I never knew my mum to bother with men. I don't remember her ever getting dressed up to go out anywhere to meet anyone, and yet she was not accepted by many of her generation, not even with the passing of time.

The photograph on page 5 of this book was taken when she was only about twenty years of age. I'm told that she was as beautiful then as she appears in her picture, and always dressed and looked elegant, even in her hand-me-downs. However, the mother I knew was very different. Rarely did she spend any money on herself. Throughout my entire childhood, I can remember her using the same old stick of Max Factor Panstick make-up, In the same old broken white plastic container, which she hurriedly applied. Then, without a second glance, she would lick her finger and smooth her eyebrows. Both winter and summer she wore the same old checked coat and little woolly hat and while I would be left at home with my nan, my mother went to work, running from one office cleaning job to the next and then the next as she tried to earn some money to make ends meet.

Throughout the 1950s, the Catholic Church continued to hold a powerful influence over the Catholic community. In Liverpool, as with many other cities, it was still the norm to place unmarried mothers into mother and baby homes, and they were pressured into giving their babies up for adoption. The Magdalene reform homes typified the mentality of the Catholic Church and the authorities of the day, and this influenced peoples' attitudes towards illegitimacy. The stigma, which having a child 'out of wedlock' carried back then, was perceived by most of society as justified, given the political and religions clout that supported it. Consequently, with the evidence of mere whispers and rumours, some people appointed themselves both judge and jury. The sentence was passed in unspoken words. The guilty individual was shunned and there was no pardon.

The philosophy of the notorious Magdalene homes was to reform and cleanse these so-called penitents of their sins and help them to return to God's grace through hard work and prayer. These institutions profited from the laundry service that they supplied to hospitals, prisons and hotels using unmarried mothers as unpaid labour. Such establishments were not *all* run by the Catholic Church, but most of them were registered charities, which for many years didn't come under factory regulations. In the days before IVF treatment was available to childless couples, many of these charity-run mother and baby homes accepted donations from couples seeking to adopt a child.

The Magdalene homes were strewn, not only across Ireland, but could also be found as far away as Australia. The Convent of the Good Shepherd was one of many mother and baby homes in Liverpool. It was close to Ford Catholic cemetery and closed its doors in 1965. The best part of thirty years would go by before Ireland's last Magdalene laundry closed in 1996. Named after Mary Magdalene, the biblical so-called fallen woman, it seemed irrelevant whether these unmarried mothers were the products of prostitution or destitution.

Guilt. Accompanied by the fear of hell and the inherent belief that a Catholic parish priest actually had the power to wash away your sins was embedded into devout Catholics. This fuelled a kind of religious one-upmanship. A pious upperclass of church-goers among the customers of Berry's Pawnbrokers, who looked down upon their neighbouring sinners. The G-word was controlling and powerful. It gripped and instilled such fear into the faithful. The judgmental flock who did no wrong.

I may never know the full details of my mum's personal experience of coping with the authorities, Catholic Church and a judgmental society when, at the age of nearly forty-one, she gave birth to me back in 1953. From memory and the information I've uncovered during my research, I know that my mother stood up against the many problems that she faced; raised me and loved me more than I ever appreciated when she was alive.

I clearly remember her many desperate attempts to gain acceptance with people. Forever armed with her self-effacing humour, she would try her best to make people laugh. As I got older, I noticed that the people who liked and had time for my mother were usually genuine and strong-minded. Sometimes they would be social outcasts themselves, perhaps having experienced some difficulties within their own lives.

My relationship with my mother was not always smooth. In fact, she could be hard work at times, and I often behaved like a little brat. She was always well-guarded, secretive and mistrustful and I would often lose patience with her because of her ways. I just didn't see the need for all the secrecy and I can see now that this caused a rift between us when I was growing up. But my mother could also be quite comical and often had me completely demented, because most of the time she just lived in a world of her own.

I remember in my teenage years going shopping together one day and, as was often the case, we were having two entirely different conversations. She was ranting on and on, complaining about the cheek of the butcher with the fatty mutton he was trying to pass off as lamb and, as usual, she wasn't taking a blind bit of notice to me. I thought she was behind me when I hopped on to the 14A and paid the driver for two adults. I sat down in a window seat, deeply engrossed in my *Jackie* magazine, and a checked coat topped with a woolly hat sat down beside me and began rummaging through her handbag as usual, in search of her Woodbines and matches. The bus moved on, and as it stopped at the next set of traffic lights, I glanced out of the window – just in time to catch a glimpse of my mum still standing in the street. My head spun around like an owl to the checked coat and woolly hat sitting next to me, who thought I was a good little girl for paying her fare! I dived off the bus at the next stop and found my mum still calling the butcher fit to burn and totally oblivious to the fact that I'd been missing. I have countless similar memories of my mum, which I have placed throughout the pages of this book. Even without trying, she could be so hysterically funny. But all this humour was nothing more than a negation. Just a mask she wore to conceal the truth and the sadness that she kept hidden beneath. It's only now, as I put my memories down in black and white on the pages of this book, that I realise my mum was one of the loneliest people ever to walk the face of this earth. Over twenty-five years after her death, I've been able to get to know that beautiful young woman whose photograph adorns page 5 of this book, the mother who always wore that same old checked coat and little woolly hat and ran from one job to the next. The person I knew all my life as . . . me mam.

2 Fine Irish

My mother's family were among the thousands of poor, working-class people who lived in the inner-city slums of Liverpool before the First World War. My nan, Annie Welsby née Hill was born in Liverpool in the year 1885 of Irish parentage, while my grandfather William Henry Welsby was from an old Liverpool family whose ancestors could be found living and working on the many farmlands within the Liverpool area as far back as the year 1573. Although Liverpool was in the county of Lancashire back then, the city became a part of Merseyside after the boundaries were reshuffled back in 1974.

Our Welsby name, which I was given, was fairly unusual, being an old Anglo-Saxon surname, which apparently means 'the people who lived by the holy well', or so I've read. Although my goal was to find information about my father, I first traced my mother's family, because I knew that the Welsby name would be relatively easy for a novice researcher, like I was myself at that time, to practice on with there being so few of them about and I found many experienced genealogists who were keen to generously share their findings. In fact, any descendants I found bearing my mother's family name seemed absolutely delighted to find one another still *above* ground and still breathing.

I found my Welsby ancestors were stonemasons, market gardeners and farmers; peasants who worked *on* the land, but never owned the land. To search further back than 1573 would be difficult, as I would then be delving beyond the time when churches began recording the births, marriages and deaths of the peasants of the parish. This was a time when Elizabeth I sat upon England's throne and back in those days only records of royalty, nobility and landowners were important. We were a family of no importance.

I never met my mother's father, who was known as Will. He was born in 1879, son of stonemason, William Welsby and Mary Welsby née Kelly. His birth certificate states that the family then lived at no. 61 Sawney Pope Street, which was later renamed Alexander Pope

Street. Will was just four years of age when he lost his father, and after his death, his mother, Mary, moved my grandfather Will and his four sisters into the courts of East View. My grandparents married in 1904. Will was then twenty-five years old and my nan, Annie, was just eighteen. After slum-hopping from one unsanitary court slum to the next, they settled in the back-street courts off Comus Street, located behind Richmond Row, midway between St Anne Street and Byrom Street. Sadly, not a single photograph has survived of my grandfather, so before I began my research I had no idea what Will looked like. However, I **did find a 1915 Christmas card from France, where he served as a private w**ith the Liverpool **King's Regiment and become a champion boxer known as Bomb – a nick**name his army **mates gave to him. They claimed a month's army pay could be easily lost** betting against **Bomb, because he could unexpectedly explode, when he appeared to be out** for the count.

Left and Below:
Front and reverse of
my Grandfather Will's
First World War
Christmas card from
the Western Front - 1915

My grandfather's Christmas card looks like it had been through its own personal war, but the faded ink, now close to a century old, is still visible. Being part of the first generation of working-class children to benefit from compulsory education, Will's message was simple, and yet eloquently written. With every stroke of his pen, I could almost feel his loneliness and concern in every written word; anxiously worrying for their welfare, wishing them a safe and Merry Christmas, sending all his love and finishing with a kiss for each and every one of his young family.

Before the Great War my grandfather worked as a licensed luggage porter, or badge porter at the docks. A badge porter was licensed by the railway or docks, but relied on the generosity of passengers' tips to earn a living. Will also worked at Lime Street Station and for a while at the Adelphi Hotel. This magnificent building was then newly built and it stood on Ranelagh Place, where it still stands today, a short walk along from the station, nestling among some of the finest architecture that can be found in this country. Will often brought home autographs of the guests staying at this prestigious hotel and I remember my mum often reminiscing about the bitter-cold winter nights of her Comus Street childhood, when her father would come home from work and, after he had finished his supper, he would sit himself down beside the fire in his old rocking chair. Then, while my nan made a pot of tea, my mum and her siblings would scramble to claim the best speck on the floor around their father's feet and, once everyone had settled, Will would light his pipe and delight his family with stories of the rich and famous. Of course, many of the tales he told were all me eye, purposely manufactured purely for their entertainment.

Although my grandfather survived the war, his health never fully recovered and he died just a few years later, in February 1924, leaving my nan to raise their young family alone. Following an inquest, my grandfather's death certificate gives the cause of his death as: 'Myocardial Degeneration – accelerated by being gassed in the late war.'

In exchange for a husband and father, a war widow's pension was then 13/9d per week for a private, topped up with a few extra coppers for dependants. In the early 1920s, long before the welfare state existed, poor families had little to live on if they couldn't work, so my nan joined the ranks of thousands of other war widows who got down on their knees and scrubbed the decks of the hundreds of cargo ships and liners that docked at Liverpool.

In those days, back-breaking work like this, taking in washing, sweeping the streets or hawking flowers and fruit was the only honest work that could be found for war widows. However, their efforts did not go unnoticed; these women earned the respect of shipowners, dockers and even the local councillors of that time. With the meagre wage my nan earned from her hard labour, she tried to feed and clothe her young family as best she could, and with the few measly coppers that she was left with, she drank herself into total oblivion. This was the only way that she could numb the pain of losing her beautiful Will, the name she called her dead husband, who had been laid to rest in a public grave at Ford Catholic cemetery, alongside countless others.

'We're only mere mortals,' she would say, as she sat by the fire watching the remains of the fading embers as they slowly turned into ash, singing her sorrowful love song, all alone, in her drunken, semiconscious state.

It would always be this same old song, 'Are yer lonesome t'night, d' yer miss me t'night, are yer sorry we drifted apart . . .' And when her song ended she would whisper low, 'Ah, me poor beautiful Will.' Then she would sob, quietly, until she fell asleep in Will's old rocking chair, and once asleep, her two young daughters – my mum Katie and her elder sister Annie – who were only ten and twelve years of age when their father passed away, would come down from their room and put her into bed, there in the kitchen next to the fire.

My nan could have taken an easier route; few would have blamed her, but she didn't. She didn't steal, she did harm to no one; she just sat in a quiet corner of the snug at the Morning Star and, keeping herself-to-herself, she drank the couple of bottles of Guinness to numb the pain and to take her memories away, for one night at least, only for them to be waiting for her when morning came. Not being used to drink, a couple of bottles of the black stuff were all she needed and all she could afford.

Before I began researching my family's history I was only aware of my grandparents having had six children in all, with only four of the six surviving. But my research uncovered a shocking family secret; two more children who had never been spoken of. I discovered that no fewer than four of their eight children had died - three of them in infancy, while two more hovered on the brink. Perhaps it was too painful for my grandparents to talk about.

Bronchial pneumonia was the most common cause of infantile fatalities in the early 1900s and it was this that claimed the life of their firstborn, Mary. Their little girl was born on the 23 February 1905 and died at the Liverpool Workhouse on the 28 November 1909. She had not yet had her first day at school. The only thing that has survived of Mary is the simple handwritten card from her flowered wreath. Although now so faded that it is barely legible, I was still able to recognise that same handwriting from the Christmas card, which my grandfather had written six years later from the Western Front.

Their son Tommy was next. Born on 23 September 1906, he grew to be 6 feet 2 and as broad and as strong as an ox. Tommy was a shy man, a man of few words. He had joined the merchant navy as soon as he came of age. When his father died, Tommy was seventeen, and he was thousands of miles away from home on his very first voyage to the Indian Ocean.

My research uncovered another sad story – that of a son, William-John Welsby, who I knew nothing about. He was born on the 1 February 1909, and less than fifteen months later, William-John was also laid to rest. An inquest was held, perhaps because he had died only six months after his sister Mary had passed away. William-John's death certificate revealed that bronchial pneumonia had struck for a second time.

On Valentine's Day in 1911, Annie arrived on the scene, and she was a born survivor. Unlike her elder brother Tommy, Annie was anything but quiet, with always plenty to say. Taking herself very seriously, Annie was scared of nothing and nobody. Her father would often say, 'If them Germans would've 'ad our Annie, we'd 'ave been stuffed!'

Stories of my Auntie Annie are legendary, and her introduction into this book almost deserves a drum roll. Strong and overflowing with confidence, Annie was both the boss and the hero of the family.

My mum Catherine was called Katie, and she arrived on the 19 February 1913, two years after her bossy sister. She was delicate and shy, which she hid by acting the clown. With fair skin, millions of freckles, brown eyes and chestnut hair, my mum was one of the two who hovered on the brink. After narrowly escaping death from meningitis when she was a young teenager, she then suffered a brain haemorrhage just a few years later. Lacking in confidence, my mum was always bossed about by her big sister Annie, who took charge of every situation, asserting her assumed authority. Annie had a thick mop of fiery red hair and, like my mum Katie, she also had millions of freckles. But in complete contrast to my mum, Annie oozed dominance and she had a way with words. In fact, she rarely needed to say much at all; just a look was enough to give her opponent the message that, it wasn't worth challenging Annie Oakley. Of course, Oakley was not our family name, but a nickname given to my mother's bossy and courageous older sister. Nobody in his or her right mind would dare mess with Big Annie Oakley.

Two years after my mother, William-Henry Junior was born on the 29 April 1915. Will's army service records revealed that he had returned to France two days later on 1 May, which was my grandparents' wedding anniversary. Will's 1915 Christmas card provided some vital information. It gave his army service number along with his battalion: Private

10912, B Company, 4th battalion of the Liverpool King's Regiment. I later also found my grandfather's attestation records from when he first enlisted into the militia on 8 July 1896. These earlier records were interesting. From the information given in the notes it appears that my grandfather changed his mind about joining the militia, and a few months later he enlisted into the regular army. These attestation records of 1896 also gave me a description of a grandfather who had died nearly thirty years before I was even born. He was then just a skinny, eighteen year-old kid, 5 feet 6 inches tall, weighing a mere 114 pounds, with a fresh complexion, brown eyes and, it made me smile to read that my grandfather had sandy hair. Apart from me, we were a family of mostly gingerbread people, so now I know who to blame for that colourful DNA. The record also mentioned more than a few scars, which were listed as distinguishing marks, perhaps earned from his budding boxing career. Never having seen a photograph of my grandfather Will, I found all this information absolutely fascinating. Obviously Will could not have had an inkling just how important his Christmas card would become nearly a century later, to the granddaughter who he never lived to meet.

I found that Will had enlisted for the First World War on the 3 September 1914. He was relatively old at thirty-five years. The 4th battalion of the Liverpool King's Regiment were pre-war special reservists, part-timers who became full-time at the outbreak of war. From many helpful members of the Great War Forum website, and information I also found from following my grandfather's battalion on The Long, Long Trail website (1914-1918.net), I learnt that Will's battalion actually arrived at Le Havre a few weeks before my grandfather, on the 6 March 1915. So it appears that Will followed on after the main battalion's crossing. I can only guess that he was maybe given a few days grace to stay until my nan gave birth.

I read that the 4th Battalion of the Liverpool King's Regiment was based at Seaforth and became a part of the Sirhind Brigade in the Lahore Division, which was mostly Indian army, based at Robecq. Engaged in the Western Front, the 4th Battalion was involved in many of the most notorious, savage battles of the First World War.

I was remarkably lucky to find Stephen Nulty, owner of the prescot-rollofhonour.info website and who has the Battalion War Diary for the 4th LKR, which records a weekly list of men being added or deducted from the strength of the battalion. This diary revealed that Private 10912 William Welsby was taken to hospital on the 17 April 1916. The battalion was in trenches at Auchy at that time. The diary gives no mention of any gas attack that day. Will's exposure to gas must have come later. It's more likely that Will was either sick or wounded by the heavy salvos fired by the enemy mentioned in the report transcribed next.

Three Days in the History of the Great War.

15th April 1916, Trenches, Auchy left sub sector:

In trenches. Fine day. 2 officers and 90 men employed on working parties with Trench Mortar Battery. Two mines were exploded between MINE POINT CRATER and R.W.F. CRATER by our miners. This was followed by our artillery and Trench Mortar fire, to which enemy retaliated. Following the explosion, two raiding parties of 2nd Argylls went out and entered enemy's tranches where they found many articles of value and identification. Our companies in trenches co-operated in the action but were not called on to assist. 2 men from hospital. Lieut L C SNODEN & 4 men wounded. One man killed (No 14062, Pte J KELLY).

16th April 1916, Trenches, Auchy left sub sector:

In trenches. Fine day. 1 officer and 20 men employed with Trench Mortar Battery. Nothing unusual occurred. 2nd Lieut R McCRAE rejoined from Lewis Gun course. One man killed (No 11587 Pte J BROWNHILL). 4 men wounded.

17th April 1916, Trenches, Auchy left sub sector:

In trenches. Dull, windy and showery. Lieut J S HUTCHINGS went to Lewis Gun Course. 2nd Lieut G S HORBUEY rejoined from Lewis Gun course, CAMIERS. Lieuts A H SHARPE and D H BANGHAM joined from base. **2 men to hospital,** 3 men wounded. Enemy fired heavy salvos on our support & reserve lines, doing little damage. Hostile machine gun fire at night.

Above: A Transcript from the Original War Diary - 4th Battalion, King's Liverpool Regiment. A Poignant Reminder of what our Grandfathers and Gt. Grandfathers Sacrificed for us. Courtesy of Stephen Nulty. prescot-rollofhonours.info

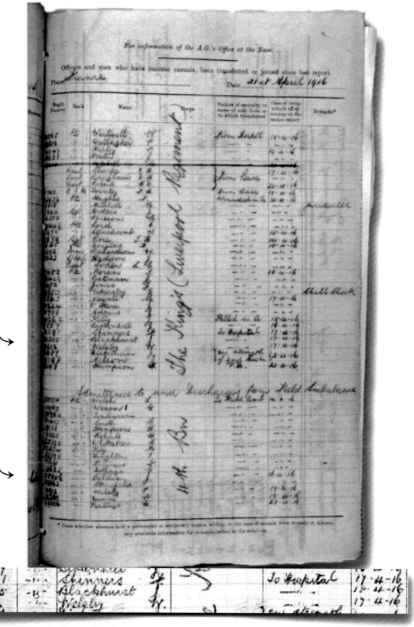

Above: An Image of a Page taken from the War Diary of the 4th Battalion, Liverpool King's Regiment. My Grandfather Will (Private 10912 Welsby) is listed twice, being taken to field ambulance, and then further down being taken to hospital on 17 April 1916. Written at Auchy, France. Image Courtesy of The National Archives: Ref:WO/95/2427. Image Reference: 455.

There's no record of William Welsby coming back on strength, as it was called, so perhaps my grandfather was in hospital for some time or given leave and came home. He was later transferred to the Labour Corps, where he was given the service number Private 410798. Given that the Labour Corps was not formed until 1917, it seems that Will's service with the LKR was a number of years. Perhaps after the effects of being gassed he was no longer fit for front-line duty, but was perhaps still of some use to the infantry maybe digging trenches, or whatever the army needed at the time. His medal entitlement was the 1914-15 Star, the British War Medal and Allied Victoria Medal. Commonly known as 'Pip, Squeak and Wilfred'.

Meanwhile, my nan was left to raise their young family: Tommy, then nine years old, Annie four, my mum Katie, who was just two, and her newborn son, William-Henry Jr.

My mother was close to her younger brother, I remember she spoke about him often. To distinguish him from his father he was known as Billy. I can still see his sepia photograph, which hung on the wall in our flat until we moved. He was a good-looking lad with grey eyes that were half-hidden beneath bushy, blond eyebrows and a mop of sandy hair. He was just shy of his ninth birthday when his father passed away. Thankfully, my nan could not have known then, that her handsome son's life would also be cut short. Billy later died of TB when he was just twenty-two years of age.

My nan's son. William Henry Jr. aka Billy.
Died of TB in 1937. Aged twenty-two.
This is the only photograph I have of him.
Circa early 1930s.

After the First World War was over Will returned home and, unaware that his days were numbered, my grandparents got on with their lives and added to their family. Born five years after Billy in January 1920, my nan's blue-eyed boy John, aka feckin' gobshite, was another child who hovered on the brink. He was barely four when his father died, and again, pneumonia was to blame for bringing John close to death before he'd taken his first steps. Complications set in and John was given the last rites, but somehow he managed to scrape through, although he was left with damaged bronchial tubes which plagued him throughout the rest of his life.

I remember my mum telling me that they would be taken to New Brighton every year on Whit Sunday by the League of Well-doers, a charity formed by Lee Jones, the son of an American cotton planter, who took all the poor kids for a day out. They marched to the Pier Head in time to the beat of a big drum and caught the ferry across the Mersey to New Brighton fair. The kid who marched at the front of this colourful, rather noisy procession would be given a big banner to carry, and John, who would only have been about six at the time, wanted to be the standard-bearer. His elder sister Annie didn't think twice about going up to some big tough kid and snatching the banner out of his hands to give to her little brother John. It was well known and accepted by all that whatever Annie wanted, Annie got. Unless you wanted seven shades of the brown stuff knocked out of you.

On the 10 October 1921, my nan completed her family when she gave birth to James. Eleven days later, acute bronchial pneumonia and cardiac failure ended his brief little life. His death certificate told a sad story. Not only had my nan registered her son's death herself, but she had been present when he died and she had registered his death on that *same* day. It amazes me how she found the strength after giving birth to him only eleven days earlier. Mary's death had been registered by Will, and I found the Workhouse admission records, which showed that it was my grandfather who had taken Mary to the Workhouse Infirmary, where she died a few days later. So I can only guess that perhaps my grandfather was too ill by this time to relieve my nan of such a heartbreaking task. James had never been spoken of.

People didn't talk about such tragedies back then, and my family were no exception. So I knew very little about my nan's life. She was so tiny, and, as many people were in those days, equipped with only the most basic education. But even tragic stories such as this can defuse over time and quite easily go into one ear and out the other. They can become just another of the countless sad stories in life. It's only when holding the records in your hands that our ancestors and their stories become tangible. Little scraps of paper are the only proof we have left that these tragedies happened to our grandparents. Many children died before they had the chance of life and my nan's heartache was not uncommon. At least now, the children she bore and buried; Mary, William-John, Billy and James Welsby, along with their siblings who somehow managed to survive, are recorded within the pages of this book. They were a part of my small family – the Welsby family, and they will not be forgotten.

As for my nan, her wits and humour became important weapons after she lost Will, and with them she raised her five remaining children alone. With her troubles far from over and remaining tight-lipped about her losses, Annie Welsby survived.

Out of her mind with the worry that John could soon make that same journey to an early grave, she wrapped him up in cotton wool. Even though she needed to beg the Lord's forgiveness for the many colourful terms of endearment that she used for her youngest lad, she adored him. Like his elder brother Billy, John spent a lot of his younger years in hospital and convalescent homes around the Colwyn Bay area of North Wales, and he missed a lot of his education because of his health. But John was intelligent and his thirst for knowledge prompted him to educate himself. He read anything and everything he could lay his hands on and he questioned everyone. Always wanting to know how things worked, particularly machinery, which fascinated him. As if she didn't have enough on her plate, John tormented the life out of his mam with millions of questions which she didn't have the answers to.

'Mam . . . where's me dad gone?'

'Mam . . . 'ow does a clock work?'

'In da name o' God, do I look like I know 'ow a feckin' clock works! Get frum under me friggin' feet, wit' yer, mam, mam, mam.'

To get rid of him from under her 'friggin' feet', she would send him out for her snuff: 2 oz of Fine Irish, bought from The 98 Shop, the local tobacconist run by an Irish family. Named after the 1798 uprising in Ireland, The 98 Shop sold things of Irish interest along with snuff, which looked like heaps of ground cinnamon but smelt nothing like it. Snuff was both the pleasure and the medicine of my nan's era and Fine Irish was the blend that she swore kept her alive. She would always have a pinch of snuff in her fingers – 't'clear me 'ead,' as she would say – and her clean white hanky was waiting on standby for a sneeze so loud that it could wake the dead.

On St Paddy's Day, The 98 Shop sold big bunches of fresh shamrock displayed in buckets of water on the pavement outside the door. God knows what the Poles did with it. They bought it in such abundance that, I think they thought it was cress.

3 Pockets of Humanity

When my grandparents began their married life back in the early 1900s, Liverpool's docks were a hive of activity, handling no less than forty per cent of the world's trade. The city was a place were money could be made for the upper classes. But this also had its consequences; Liverpool's population was bursting at the seams when immigrants began pouring into the city in search of work. For the lower classes, such as my grandparents, life was not good. Housing for the seething masses was still in Victorian court dwellings, the kind of habitat depicted within the pages of Dickens. Three-story, gas-lit boxes housed pockets of humanity; one tiny room to each floor, no sanitation or indoor plumbing whatsoever and a dank cellar. Their only fresh water was drawn from a communal outside tap in the middle of the court. The sickening stench of rotting sewage from the shared outside lavatories permeated the air, catching the backs of their throats and clinging to their clothes as it overflowed in to the courts where the children played. Being the perfect breeding ground for disease, TB and pneumonia were rife. Consequently, Liverpool had one of the highest infant mortality rates in England, with one third of children dying before they had their first day at school, while those who were lucky enough to survive often faced a lifetime of poor health.

Home to fleas, rats, cockroaches *and* working-class families, nobody ventured into these courts unless they had to. Accessed through narrow alleyways, the courts were well hidden from view behind the cobbled streets, attractive to those who wanted to hide away; the notoriously, violent street gangs who lurked around corners.

Three stone steps outside each front door were all the separation and privacy a family could expect from the outside world. But those three stone steps displayed the pride of every family home and were scrubbed white with a donkey stone until they sparkled.

The descendants of African slaves had already formed a close-knit community within the Toxteth inner-city area following the abolition of slavery, from which the city had grown wealthy. Images from this barbaric trade can still be found carved into the exterior masonry of many of Liverpool's grand buildings.

Pockets of Welsh, Scots, Poles and Germans were also scattered around the city. But it was the thousands of Irish who had left Ireland over sixty years earlier during the 1840s potato famine, to join their predecessor who had already integrated into the community, which pushed the numbers of Irish settlers to over twenty per cent of the population, and Liverpool became known as the capital of Ireland. Settling mostly around the Scotland Road area of the inner-city, the Irish had a lasting impact on the port, especially on the Catholic community. You would be hard pressed to find a Catholic priest in any Liverpool parish without that all-too-familiar warm Irish drawl, *and* without a drop of Irish in his hand.

Many Italian and eastern European immigrants came looking for work, and as they congregated together, communities were formed and became known as Little Italy or the Jewish Quarter and the city also became home to the oldest Chinatown in Europe.

The areas of Liverpool each had their own markedly individual character, much like the boroughs of New York, Liverpool's twin city. The Italian immigrants were especially full of character, and they brought along with them the very essence of their homeland, with homemade ice cream to die for and many wonderful Italian dishes that were affordable and nourishing to poor families. These three cultures had much in common, and a fusion of quirky Irish mannerisms, mouthwatering Italian food, together with cheeky Scouse humour, made for a rich, vibrant tapestry.

* * *

The years went by, and in 1929 my mum's sister Annie married William Hennessy and moved out to the newly built council houses in Huyton, a suburb about six miles east of the city and close to the River Alt.

In 1932 her elder brother Tommy married Margaret Allison and he stayed in the merchant navy throughout his working life. Margaret was from the east end of London, and it was there that they settled in Woolwich and raised three sons; Tommy Jr, Billy and Jimmy. I called her Aunt Maggie, and we all loved her dearly. My mum called her Coco, because she always dressed elegantly, and in her younger years she resembled Coco Chanel. She had exquisite taste and wore stylish clothes, with many vintage pieces, which she would buy from flea markets or Petticoat Lane and transform into something that would grace any catwalk. She wore antique jewellery made of jade, amber and pearls, which Uncle Tommy bought for her on his many travels to China, Singapore and the many countries of Europe.

I remember my mum's friend Angie Volante creasing up when I proudly informed her in my childish voice, 'Me Uncle Tommy's gone on a slow boat t' China!' I was about four years old.

I longed to go with him on these trips, and he promised that he would take me with him one day. He gave me a little plastic globe to show me where he'd been and where he was going to next, and I carefully marked each country with blobs of pink chewy which I'd rolled into tiny balls. Then I learnt as much as possible about whatever country he'd sailed off to, as I knew he would ask me questions. I was too young to be able to pronounce half of the names, but I had long-term plans to earn my own money and visit these far-off lands one day, and my biggest blob of pink chewy was stuck on Russia. For some reason, it was Russia that fascinated me the most. I longed to see the Onion Cathedral, the name my Uncle Tommy gave to St Basil's, and I wanted to see it in the snow because my mum told me that the Snow Queen lived there. Pulling my leg, she told me that it was impossible to see her because of the iron curtains. Knowing nothing of the political curtain, my four-year-old imagination pictured our orange psychedelic curtains stretched tight across St Basil's windows.

On one of my Uncle Tommy's visits, he took me to see his ship – *Empress of Canada*, when it docked at Liverpool, and I remember the sailors gave me pear drops and dandelion and burdock. I was introduced to the captain who was lighting his pipe at the time. Taking it from his mouth, he looked down at me through clouds of smoke. I've always loved the smell of pipe tobacco ever since. He shook my hand as if I was a grown-up and he had ringlets all over his white beard as if he twisted it into rags each night. I remember he said to me:

'Well, hello there young lady. Where did you get those big brown eyes from?'

I said nothing, but thought to myself: *I wish I knew!*

After failing the medical for the Second World War, my nan's blue-eyed boy, John, took an engineering apprenticeship and went to work in Luton. So, throughout the war years there was only my mum left at home looking after my nan, who by then had become frail. I'm told my nan had been pretty in her youth with enormous grey eyes, and she was always slim and petite. But the many trips to Ford cemetery had taken their toll and now history was repeating itself and she worried about her eldest son Tommy, who by then had joined the Royal Navy. She knew he was in Europe but didn't know where, and it was a while since she'd had a letter from him.

'Echoes o' da past,' is what she would often say. 'We're only mere mortals . . . echoes o' da past.' Tommy had been wounded and spent months in hospital. It was not until the war had ended that his family would hear that he was safe and well.

With Irish roots being difficult to trace, I've hardly scratched at the surface of my nan's family tree. Although I was aware that she had a younger brother also named John, I have since learnt that she was the eldest of four surviving children, with another brother, Patrick and a sister, Bridget. The 1911 census shows her parents James and Mary Hill had six children in all, but two had already died prior to the census being taken. I remember my mum telling me that when she was a child herself, she often stayed at her grandmother's house and ran errands for her grandmother because she was blind. She told me that her grandmother's name was Bridget and was called Biddy. I now know that my nan's mother's maiden name had been Mary Walsh and my grandfather's mother's maiden name had been Mary Kelly. The only Bridget in the family was my nan's sister. Family stories are often wrongly remembered. In this case, it seems that my mum was confusing her grandmother, with her mother's sister. It's more likely that Bridget was Biddy, and maybe she was blind.

Like many, my grandparents moved from one unsanitary court slum to the next, in a desperate attempt to find healthier living conditions in which to raise their young family. I found them living in Bevington Street in 1909 and my nan's parents, James and Mary Hill, had also lived in the same street when my nan Annie was born. My nan's birthday was always celebrated in the middle of August. I remember John organised a surprise party for her eightieth birthday. Uncle Tommy and Aunt Maggie came from London with their sons. My Auntie Annie, her husband Bill, their children and their families. Friends and neighbours all came to celebrate her birthday... in August. Except, my nan's birthday was not in August. I found that my dear nan was actually born on the 6 October 1885. There were no less than four Annie Hills born around the same time in the same area. So that birthday party was two months early!

Electoral rolls list my grandparents living in Peover Street in 1915, before they settled at no. 8 House, no. 8 Court, Comus Street, which was their home for more than twenty-five years. Will's elder sister and my nan's parents, lived a few doors away in the same court, which ironically, is shown on page 36 in the 1927 photograph. I wonder if the children shown playing in the photograph were my mum or her siblings?

After my grandfather's death in February 1924, my nan struggled on through the Great Depression, remaining in the same court house in Comus Street until 1935 when she, along with my mum, were rehoused to Back Salisbury Street, another back-street slum in the parish of St Francis Xavier, known as SFX, which is located in the Everton district, an elevated area of the city with some streets having views down to the River Mersey.

Electoral rolls show that, for some reason, my nan didn't stay long in Back Salisbury Street and soon returned to her old neighbourhood, this time settling at no. 40 Comus Street itself, rather than the back-street courts. It was here at no. 40 Comas Street in 1937, that her son Billy lost his fight with TB. His death certificate gives graphic details of the cause of death; 'cardiac failure and acute caseous phthisis.' An archaic term for advanced TB of the lung. Often referred to as galloping TB. According to Billy's death certificate, my nan was by her son's side when he died at the age of twenty-two, and again, she had registered his death.

Perhaps it was the declining health of her son that prompted my nan to move from Back Salisbury Street so quickly. Maybe moving from the court houses of Comus Street, she had jumped from the frying pan into the fire.

According to family lore, my nan moved again somewhere within the Little Italy area just before the outbreak of the Second World War. The people of inner-city Liverpool were always ready to move quickly at this time, but it's impossible to confirm her address during the war as no electoral rolls were taken. In any case, wherever she moved to, she wasn't there for long when one night, fate changed everything. It was during one of the many air-raids on Liverpool that she returned home from the air-raid shelter to find that her few meagre possessions, along with most of the street where she lived, had gone.

I remember her talking about a week of hell. I can only guess that she was perhaps referring to the May Blitz. The seven nights of bombings that began on 1 May 1941, when 2,895 lives were lost and thousands of families were made homeless, when close to 2,500 explosive and incendiary bombs were dropped on the city My nan and mum were probably among the homeless. It's times like this when I wish I had paid more attention on the rare occasions when my nan opened up and talked about the old days. Instead, my naive lack of understanding of war and hardship, allowed her stories to go in one ear and out the other.

It's well documented that a staggering ninety per cent of troops and provisions that were brought into Britain passed through Liverpool's quays and how heavily the city was bombed. The docks were only a few streets away from the clusters of tiny inner-city homes. But Liverpool's docklands were not the only target. I've read that the Queensway Tunnel, which opened in 1934, was also targeted. The entrance and toll booths to this four lane, two-mile-long road link under the River Mersey to Birkenhead, which we nicknamed the Mersey Tunnel, sat opposite St John's Gardens at the end of Byrom Street, where it is today. I remember its toll booths were always a handy, reliable source for shillings for the leccy meter. An indication of its closeness to our flat.

Right:
No. 8 Court, Comus Street.
Where my nan raised her family.
I wonder if any of these children
were my mum or her siblings.
Photograph is dated 1927.
Courtesy of Liverpool Records Office.

Left:
Byrom Street branching to Scotland Place.
The Morning Star is the building on the left.
The 98 Shop is the white building at centre.
Photograph Circa 1952.
Courtesy of Liverpool Records Office.

Right:
Berry's Pawnbrokers
Richmond Row. Est. 1850.
Anything bought, anything sold.
Photograph Circa 1950s.
Courtesy of Ged Fagan
inacityliving.piczo.com

Opposite the tunnel, the streets branch into William Brown Street, which is today a part of Liverpool's World Heritage site. Home to the irreplaceable listed buildings of the Walker Art Gallery, the County Sessions House, Picton Reading Room and Hornby Library, which come under the umbrella of Liverpool Central Library. Standing at the top of the hill where William Brown Street meets Lime Street, is the city's crowning glory; St George's Hall.

In stark contrast, many homes around Little Italy stood in the long shadows cast by these giant masterpieces of lime and sandstone. Running beneath the foundations of Little Italy, the Wapping Tunnel was thought to have been another target. This was one of the first, if not *the* first tunnel ever to be dug under a city. Serving the port possibly since as early as the 1830s, this freight rail link ran from Edge Hill station, some 1.6 miles down the steep hill to Liverpool's docklands. Munitions and supplies were transported to and from the docks via this rail link, and the tunnel's Byrom Street portal was visible. Thousands of families lived in the midst of all these targets and despite heroic efforts of Liverpool's fire bobbies, the city and its eleven miles of quays were ablaze, with many homes and public buildings being damaged or destroyed. For security reasons, the damage Liverpool and Birkenhead docks sustained was kept quiet. By the end of the Second World War, the death toll stood at close to 4,000. Annie Welsby's spirit was so typical of the widows of the First World War. These women had already lived through hardship and had seen the effects of war before.

It wasn't long before more tragedy struck for my nan, when her brother John died. He and his family had also lived in Comus Street, but they had been rehoused into the newly built tenement flats that flanked Byrom Street. Sadly, they never got a chance to enjoy their new home when his sons, John Jr, Paddy and Jimmy Hill, were left to fend for themselves.

Tragedy upon tragedy, yet my nan's losses were no worse than the losses of many. Stories such as this were ten-a-penny in Liverpool, across England and no doubt it was just as tragic throughout the countries that were caught up in the mindless destruction of the Second World War. This is the story of one small family.

After her brother's death my nan moved into the tenement flat to look after her three young nephews, and I'm sure she was also thinking of a new home for herself and my mum. It was this sequence of events which flung my odd-bod family together, and overnight their lives were miraculously transformed. It's often said that good things can come from bad, and for my nan, this was the turning point. At last she had landed on her feet.

This was the psychiatric tenement flat – as my nan used to call it, which I was later raised in. It was equipped with all the mod-cons of postwar Britain; a living room, known as a kitchen, and a kitchen, which was more like a scullery and called a back-kitchen. It had the luxury of an indoor bathroom, electricity and gas. For my mum and nan it must have seemed like they were moving into a palace. The filth and stench of the court slums were left behind, and had become nothing more than a bad memory to mingle with the ghosts of the past.

Long before war intervened, Liverpool City Council had already started building tenement flats in the footprint of many of the Victorian court dwellings as part of their slum clearance programme. So families who had lived in courts moved into blocks. But at least communities were held together. Hitler merely helped to speed the demolition job along.

My mum and nan shared a bedroom, while my nan's three nephews, John Jr, Patrick and Jimmy Hill, scrapped over who was to have the other big room and who was to have the tiny box bedroom, which was also the coldest of the three bedrooms. These issues were trivial in comparison to the overcrowding and sanitation problems that they had left behind and life in the modern Art Deco style tenement flats was at last worth living. Less than fifteen years later, the novelty of the tennies, as they became known, would wear off. They became less desirable places to live and were perceived in a similar light to the court slums that they had replaced. A rough neighbourhood, best given a wide berth. I suppose this was true, but tough communities prepare you for anything and everything that life throws at you. *Where* you were raised is unimportant. What matters is *how* you were brought up.

As their lives continued on throughout the bleak war years, like everybody else in Liverpool and the rest of the country, my mum and nan rolled up their sleeves and quickly adapted to their new circumstances. Every morning my mum caught the six o'clock tramcar to make the slow ten-mile journey north to Kirkby in the blackout to work at the munitions factory, while my nan scrubbed the church steps at St Joseph's instead of the ships' decks.

Ever inventive, my dear nan devised her own method of health and safety in the workplace by adding a few scoops of holy water to her bucket from the font. She figured that the holy water, having been previously blessed, would help to protect people from slipping on the soapy steps, and she swore blind that those few drops of holy water also made the steps sparkle and that they stayed cleaner for a little longer.

I remember my mum telling me about the day when Father Maloney copped my nan scooping the holy water from the font into her bucket. Father Maloney was always up for a laugh; he and my nan were like a comedy double act when they were together. He stood and watched for a while and then, scratching his head in sheer bewilderment, he asked:

'Annie . . . what on earth would yer be doin' wit' God's 'oly wata?'

My nan used to call him Farder Bunloaf – not behind his back, but straight to his face. While continuing with her scrubbing, she glanced up at him with her usual couldn't be arsed attitude and mimicking his warm southern Irish drawl, she replied wryly:

'Be Jaysus, farder, I's surprised yer find da need t' ask me a question wit' such an ob'ious answer! Didn't yer know . . . it makes da steps sparkle!'

Farder Bunloaf took the carrot and replied, 'Ah, Annie, da yer' not tink it'll be da drop o' bleach an' not God's 'oly wata workin' tha' lickle miracle?'

My nan had a drop of Irish blood in her own veins, accompanied by a very dry sense of Irish humour. Up on her feet, she leaned on her mop and explained to him slowly, as if he was as thick as two short planks.

'Yer see farder, yer 'ave t' 'ave faith! Sure, not a soul's fell 'cos I always adds a lickle drop o' God's 'oly wata t' me bucket. So, 'aps if yer bless da bleach, then I won't need t' use up all o' God's 'oly wata!'

'Ah, God bless yer, Annie. I don't tink yer need either da bleach or de 'oly wata! Sure, yer make dem steps sparkle wit' yer own bare 'ands, so yer do.'

Her plain, simple logic never ceased to amaze him. He enjoyed all the *craic* and leg pulling that went on between them, and chuckled to himself as he blessed Annie and her little bucket of hot, soapy holy water.

4 The Telly knob

By the beginning of the 1940s my mum's sister, Big Annie Oakley, had a family of her own. My Aunt Annie had six children in all, three of each. From the eldest in descending order, they were: Billy, Mary, Tommy, Brian, Kathleen and Ann. But by the time I came along in '53, they were all grown up with children of their own, and seemed more like aunts and uncles than my first cousins. They had grown up in a nice new home, with a front and back garden, and pink rambling roses arched their way around their front door, carefully trained so as not to conceal my aunt's doorbell. Her washing and bed linen always smelt fresh from being dried on the line in her garden, where she grew rhubarb and vegetables behind her shed. In front of the shed was a tiny square patch of grass surrounded by a narrow border where a solitary iris stood alone like Billy-no-mates. Neatly clipped privet hedges surrounded the front garden of each house in the road, and an array of white lace curtains were proudly draped across the windows, displaying the pride of every family home.

My Aunt Annie always seemed rich, sophisticated and posh to my childish mind, and I enjoyed going to visit her. I can remember the wonderful cooking smells that drifted from her kitchen, where an enormous white fridge stored all kinds of homemade goodies like bread pudding and rhubarb pie. Her thick mop of curly, red hair always looked as if it had just been set at the hairdresser's. She wore nice new clothes, painted her nails and always wore lipstick and 4711 *eau de cologne,* and her gold-framed glasses were actually bought on a private prescription! If she was alive today, she would be bending my ear with claims of being related to Grace Kelly. Her only scrap of evidence to latch onto the Hollywood movie star was that Will's mother Mary was from Ireland, her maiden name had been Kelly and my aunt had been told a long time ago that some of her Kelly family had also gone to America. Reluctant to reveal the source of her information, my aunt was quite happy to delude herself with ideas of grandeur at the notion of being a distant cousin to Princess Grace of Monaco.

I was close to my cousin Mary, who was my Aunt Annie's eldest daughter. Being twenty-three years my senior, she seemed more like an aunt to me, and I always looked up to her when I was growing up. Mary adored my mum and followed her everywhere when she was a child. After my mother's death, it would be my cousin Mary who would eventually tell me about my father. I hounded the life out of my mum to tell me about my dad when I was growing up:

'Mam, who wus 'e?'

'Mam, wha' wus 'e like?'

'Mam, would yer just tell me 'is name?'

When I was about six, I overheard my nan telling our neighbour that my father was Taboo. My mum had always stuck to the same story of him being killed in the war, and I swallowed it. My childish mind tried to put all this together and concluded that Taboo must have been shot in the war. Taboo was a war hero!

I never met anyone else who didn't have a dad. There were very few kids in our neighbourhood without a father in those days, or at least they kept their mouths tight shut. There were a few kids at school whose fathers always seemed to be away at sea and were never seen or talked about. Then one day they mysteriously died, but there would be no funeral because they had been buried at sea. I'd believe anything when I was little.

In the early fifties, only one in about twenty-five kids was born out of wedlock, as it was called, as if it was something dirty. So I was a novelty. Especially with a mum who was a similar age to most of my classmate's grandmothers. Some kids at school plagued me about my dad, always wanting to know who and where he was. I would tell them he'd been killed in the war, which is what I'd been told and had always believed. Until one day I was baking scones in my first ever cookery class and a girl I was sharing an oven with began to probe.

'Me mam said 'e wus killed in da war.'

I'll never forget the look on her face. In a loud voice, in front of the entire class, she said to me, as if I was thick.

'But, da war finished in 1945. Years before yer were born!'

This minor technicality had never dawned on me before, because I'd always believed what I had been told and thought no more about it. Of course, it was now blatantly obvious, and I felt such an idiot, especially with the other kids sniggering behind my back. There was no question of any other war as my mother only ever talked about the Second World War, and besides, we kids were only ever aware of the First and Second World Wars at that age.

So after that day, I never asked my mother anything about my father ever again. Of course, as I got a older, I realised my mum was a master of red herrings and would tell me anything, the first thing that came into her head, just to shut me up and give her a bit of peace.

I can't remember when it was that my nan's blue-eyed boy John returned home from Luton to live with us. There was never any talk about him, at least not in front of me. The only thing that my mum ever told me as a child was that things were hard for us until John came home. She never went into detail or complained much. But back then, the government didn't provide financial support for unmarried mothers in case it encouraged them to have more illegitimate children. So my mum was not entitled to any maternity or child benefits; no rebates, not even a council flat of her own. So money was scarce and the hostility of some people in the community was difficult.

My life was grey until John came into it. My earliest memory of him was when he took me to the Co-op in Byrom Street. The Co-op was not like it is today. It was a huge store that sold food, clothes, toys and furniture. It was just around the corner from the old Mersey Tunnel and also from where we lived. It was Christmastime and the whole store was filled with Christmas trees decorated with lights, glass baubles and tinsel. Giant holly wreaths tied with red velvet ribbon hung on doors and pillars, and on every counter, Christmas stockings filled with Everton mints, butterscotch and cinder toffees were displayed in wicker baskets. I remember being fascinated by the chains that were strung across the ceiling which carried small, shiny brass cylinders that were the shape of jam jars. This antiquated system, which looked like a Heath Robinson contraption, was used to transport money from the tills up to the cashier's office. When the chain was pulled the cylinders would glide across the ceiling making a swishing noise above our heads.

I remember my Uncle John had hold of my hand and he said to me:

'Well Jess . . . does anything catch your eye?'

Having never heard this saying before, I didn't have a clue what this meant and thought to myself: *Dus anythin' catch me eye! What's tha' mean?* I confused it with the old saying: It's all me eye, which meant; it's all kidology or it's all baloney. I didn't have the words to ask him what he meant and so I just rubbed my eyes and stared up at him blank and fish-faced, as my nan would always say of anyone expressionless. John turned to the shop assistant:

'Excuse me, dear. Do you have anything for my little niece? Perhaps a doll or teddy?'

I thought: *God . . . tha's wha' 'e meant! 'e gunna buy me somethin' frum da Co-op!*

My mum would take me window-shopping, which we often did after the shops were closed, and I really enjoyed this, especially at Christmastime when we would wrap up warm and walk up to Lewis's department store to see their animated Christmas window displays. Street decorations would be lit and a huge Christmas tree stood in Clayton Square with a crib beneath. Carol singers were accompanied by the Salvation Army's brass band and the mouthwatering smell of **roasted chestnuts filled the air.**

I was far too shy **to ask for anything that day in the Co-op, but I remember being** completely mesmerised **by a little white straw basket, which was shaped like a fire bucket** with lids at both ends an**d paper, yellow sunflowers decorating the sides. It was only a few** coppers and so John boug**ht me a little brown teddy bear too.**

*Me aged four years-old **at the** Christmas grotto **in the** Byrom Street **Co-op.** Circa **1957***

It's funny the things that **stick in your mind. I remember I felt as if someone had given me a** million pounds that day, **and so after seeing Father Christmas, I walked home swinging my** white straw basket with **Ted tucked safely inside, holding my Uncle John's hand. That day** was one of the happiest **days I can ever remember as a child. I was always so proud to walk** anywhere with John. He **was so polite and respectful to everybody, and people had such a lot** of respect for him too. Unlike my mum, nobody ever treated him badly. He had this rich, deep, velvety baritone voice, which reminded me of Bing Crosby whenever he spoke or sang, which he often did at get-togethers at my Aunt Annie's house on New Year's Eve.

John had a laid-back personality and a slightly different way of expressing himself, a different vocabulary, and most of the time I didn't understand a word he said. Although he had a Liverpool accent, which he always told me to be proud of, his accent wasn't as thick or as rough as ours sounded. He was always confident but in a quiet way. John was a thinker, a background person who talked to everyone, even to posh people who my mother found intimidating. Nobody intimidated John, and my life would have been empty without him.

Having not had much schooling because of his health, John was mostly self-educated. His bedroom was filled with books on every subject under the sun. My nan would say:

'Oh, tha' lad. 'e's like a friggin' walkin' 'plopedia!'

He came home one day with a secondhand radiogram to play his huge collection of 78 rpm records, filling the house with the music of Gershwin, Louis Armstrong, Bing Crosby and Maria Callas.

'God bless us an' save us! Da state o' 'im an' 'is posh music! Tha' Maria Collins girl sounds like she needs a good dose o' syrup o' figs!'

A secondhand Baird telly was, for me, a more exciting purchase. I used to sit in front of it watching the little girl on the test card for hours, waiting for the programmes to begin. Then it changed from the test card to fish swimming about on the screen and more boring posh music, which didn't impress my nan.

'Well, in da name o' God. Wha' d'we want wit' a telly box usin' up all da leccy, t' watch fish! When we've go' a goldfish der in da bowl, swimmin' round fu nothin'. Tha' lad's gone soft in da 'ead!'

But once the programmes began, with *The Woodentops*, *Bill and Ben the Flower Pot Men* and then the BBC news, my nan was mesmerised. Whenever we went out of the kitchen she used to peep behind the telly trying to see where the pictures went in. She soon had her favourite programmes and loved *The Army Game* and *Cheyenne*, that 1950s cowboy series – John Wayne and cowboys-n-injins, as she called the Westerns. She had no trust in anythin' leccy, but once she realised there was BBC *and* ITV, she took complete control of the knob. Until, one day, the knob came off in her hand.

She didn't know what to do with it and so she gave it to me to play with, so that when John came home from work she could blame me, because John wouldn't tell me off.

'Tell 'im you did it. 'e won't shout a' yer.'

But I started crying, so she took the Bakelite knob back off me and gave me a cup of warm milk to shut me up. ''ere, stop cryin'. Jesus, anyone would think yer'd been murdid!'

Her day had begun in flames. She had spread a sheet of the *Liverpool Echo* across the fire to give it a kick start, and as usual, she had left it there until the paper began to scorch. But that morning she had not been quick enough to pull the paper away from the burning coals before it caught fire and when I went into our kitchen I walked in to a storm of burning ash with fragments drifting up to the ceiling and floating back down to settle everywhere, including the goldfish's bowl. My nan was dancing around the kitchen trying to put out the flames. Ignoring her screams to get out of the room before I was burnt alive, I used Ted, my teddybear, to swat any burning pieces of newspaper that drifted my way. The white hankies that had been hanging on the mantlepiece to dry were now black with soot, and so was Ted. So while my nan got to work cleaning up the kitchen, I stood on a chair at the back-kitchen sink and tried to wash the soot off Ted. A couple of hours later, my nan put Ted in the bread oven of the fire grate to dry and we both settled down to watch the telly as if nothing had happened. It was when she changed the station from BBC to ITV that her day went from bad to worse. Now, the telly knob was like a hot potato in her hand and John would be home any minute. By now, I was highly amused at the day's excitement. It had all been like a game to me and so I sat drinking my cup of warm milk and suggested places to hide the knob. With her nerves still on edge, she got into a panic and flung it over the landing wall, down to the street below. But unfortunately Father Bunloaf was doing his rounds.

'Oh, sufferin' Jesus!' She said under her breath, as she ducked behind the landing wall before he could see her. Nonchalantly, she stood up and put her hand out, as if to feel if it was raining. Then, as if she'd only just that second noticed him, she shouted down to him:

'Oh, muther o' God! Are yer all right der, farder? Da kids roun' 'ere are feckin' lickle demons! May God fugive thum, an' me fu cursin'. Put a drop o' 'oly wata on it when ye get back t' St Joseph's, farder. It works betta thun witch 'azel, so it does.'

John came home from work and while he tucked into his tea, he listened patiently to my nan as she explained why the kitchen ceiling needed 'a lick o' paint.' Then, as he walked over to turn the telly on, my nan sloped off to the back-kitchen, and kept her mouth shut:

'Where's the knob?' he said.

'Wha' knob?' she said.

A new knob was painstakingly crafted from a white ping-pong ball and black sticky tape and life went on. For some reason, a 14-inch, brown Bakelite television with a ping-pong ball stuck to the front didn't look out of place in our kitchen – in fact, it fitted in rather well with the rest of our eclectic mess. Convincing herself that she had convinced John that she'd never noticed that the telly had a knob, she breathed a sigh of relief. Reaching into her pocket for her Fine Irish, she glanced at me wryly and gave me a sly wink. Then she settled down to watch her idol, Rudolph Valentino. John settled down to read the *Liverpool Echo*, and peace and calm were restored. Reaching across the table for his cup of tea, John looked over his glasses at me, chuckled and gave me a sly wink . . . he knew his mam so well.

Television brought some quality into her life, and she was able to see a few of the **changes that were beginning to take place in a world that she would soon be leaving.**

Above: My dear nan, Auntie Annie and me.
Mum always cut my fringe. I think she used a bread knife.
Circa 1960s.

5 That's the Story of Me Life

My nan could quite easily have stepped from the pages of that much-loved, Liverpool classic, *Her Benny*. She talked and dressed in the old Liverpool way, with winceyette bloomers that stretched right down to her knees, where they rendezvoused with her 60-denier stocking. Then, over an ankle-length skirt, she wore the most important garment of all; her pocket. Her pocket was tied around her waist, like an apron is worn today, and this was where her rosary beads, hanky and snuffbox along with her few coppers where safely stashed away. Once the morning ritual of washing and dressing was complete, she tackled her long silver hair, which, after applying a splash of bay rum, she parted on one side and, without the use of a mirror, twisted it up into a loose knot, securing it with hairpins at the nape of her neck. With one solitary tooth centred on the bottom row, she was then ready to face the world.

Granny Clampett from *The Beverly Hillbillies* always reminds me of my nan, but with a Liverpool accent from days gone bye, unless she was conversing with Father Bunloaf or arguing, as she often did, with Mick the coalman – then she would fall into an Irish accent at the drop of a hat. She never allowed her family to forget their roots, and woe betide you if for one minute you got above yourself. An abrupt reminder would be received in the form of a clout around the ear, which would quickly be followed by her down-to-earth philosophy:

'Honesty an' modesty is Our Lord's policy. Yer impudent little mare!' CLOUT!

Before I began school, my nan was diagnosed with colon cancer and had a section of her colon removed. She was in her mid-seventies at the time and although I know the details of her illness now, the word 'cancer' was never mentioned back in those days. The operation was then still in its infancy in the mid-50s, and her doctor was delighted with her recovery, so much so that the success of her surgery was newsworthy and she got a tiny mention in the *Stop Press* section of the *Liverpool Echo*, as everything functioned as normal, without the need for any accessory.

After being processed through the hated Saturday night routine of being scrubbed pink with carbolic soap and inspected for nits, I would be plonked onto our big oak kitchen table and my long, dark hair would be twisted into rags while still damp to make ringlets. Then, on Sunday afternoon John would take me to visit her in Walton Hospital.

My nan soon bounced back and got on with her life. It was nearly nine years later, around the Easter of 1967 when the beginning of the end began. My mum noticed that my nan had taken a Beecham's Powder earlier that morning, and for most of the afternoon she had been sitting quietly reading, with one hand holding onto her broken NHS specs, and the other hand resting across her stomach. She was unusually quiet, and when my mum asked if she was okay, I overheard her whispering that she felt as if the nerves in her stomach were jumping about. When she moved her hand away, I could see this, and I felt like I wanted to be sick. The cancer had returned, and this time there was nothing that could be done.

She had always shared a bedroom with my mum and me, but our bedroom was so cold that during wintertime the inside of the windows turned into sheets of ice. So the purple couch was moved out of the kitchen and her single bed was moved in. An all-night burner was fitted to the fire so that the coals could burn low and last throughout the night.

It was to be my first ever experience of death. Listening to our neighbours telling old wives' tales made me stiff with fear, and I was absolutely petrified of what was to come. For my mother, it was a difficult time. For over six months she cared for my nan single-handedly, right up until her death. There was nothing that my mum did not do for her. In those days it was a daughter's duty; John could only look on.

Although she had the occasional district nurse, there were no Macmillan nurses or financial support back then, and so despite several visits from the school board's attendance man, I stayed off school and did my mum's string of office-cleaning jobs while she looked after my nan for what were to be the last few months of her difficult life. With that type of casual work there was always someone ready to snatch your job if you couldn't do it, and whoever paid your wages didn't care who did the job, as long as the job got done.

I have to say that as a thirteen-year-old I just didn't appreciate anything that was happening at that time. Gripped by a permanent state of sickening fear, I was glad to get out of our flat to do my mother's work. Polishing the endless brass doorknobs and letterboxes on the big office doors in Dale Street and Moorfields and mopping the miles of corridors and staircases at least allowed me to forget about the nightmare of all I had seen at home, and I felt grown-up to be going to work and doing something that seemed so important.

It was the way my mum spoke of my nan to other people that showed the love and respect that she held for her. From a young age my mum had witnessed the life of hardship that my nan had endured and she had never forgotten. Now, when I cast my mind back to those dark, difficult days, to the horror of all that I remember, of all that I just wanted to run away from, those memories that haunted me for so long have now been replaced by pride. Pride for my mum, for what she did and for how deeply she cared. In those days, before all the support and drugs that are available today, neither the living nor the dying was easy.

The night before my nan died she spoke at great length about her beautiful Will. She told us that she had seen him standing at the foot of her bed. She said that he never uttered a single word, but just kept smiling down at her, just like his old self. By this time she was so thin and weak, yet she took her time to explain every tiny detail of my grandfather's visit.

All this talk terrified the life out of me, and so I lay awake throughout the entire night with one eye open, waiting for daylight and listening for the slightest noise, but the flat was so still and unusually quiet that night, with the only sound being from the ticking of the old mantle clock that struck out each hour and half-hour. I remember I was bursting for a wee, but there was no way I was going to walk across the dark hall, so I held out.

The next morning without any fuss, this brave little old lady quietly went to meet her beautiful Will. It was the 26 November 1967. How unfair for her to end her days in this way after the hard life she'd had. Like so many others of her generation, my nan deserved more.

I still have the tiny, gold sleepers she wore in her ears, which were her only jewellery. Her wedding ring had been pawned many years before, and Berry's had sold it on when my nan didn't have the coppers to retrieve it before the pawn ticket ran out. She often said: 'That's da story o' me life! Yer life goes in t' one door o' Berry's an' it's sold on out de otha.'

And that was so true. Berry's pawnshop epitomised that degrading way of life for that entire war generation, and the humiliation could be read on peoples' faces and in their body language as they snuck into that corner door to pawn their few meagre possessions. How life has changed; how lucky we are.

My nan's single bed was taken away and replaced by her tiny coffin. I remember it was so small that it looked like a child's coffin. Neighbours prepared our flat for her wake. Mirrors were covered and white sheets were pinned up across the windows, blocking out the daylight, and my mother surrounded her coffin with vases of beautiful white calla lilies. This was a traditional Catholic funeral. This was how things were done back in those days. Old customs brought comfort in times of loss.

The next few days and nights brought along a steady stream of family, neighbours and friends from near and far to pay their respects. Many placed Mass cards at my nan's feet as she lay in her open coffin. Father Bunloaf, now himself old and frail, brought with him a little bottle of holy water, which he warmed before anointing her and administering the last rites.

'Ah, Annie always liked 'er 'oly wata warm, so she did. May she arrive at da gates of 'eaven 'alf an 'our before da divil knows she's dead. An' may da Lord 'ave mercy on 'er soul for she did 'arm t' none.'

I actually quite enjoyed my first wake. It was not the sombre occasion I'd expected; in fact, it was just the opposite. People we hadn't seen for many years came to visit, and memories and funny stories were exchanged until the small hours. It was quite bizarre, with my nan lying there in her open coffin in the midst of us all. On a small table next to her coffin was a little drop o' stout, which was never allowed to go flat. My nan was never once left out of the conversation. It was almost as if people expected her to wake up and take part in all their storytelling. Her outspokenness, wry humour and sharp eye inspired heart-warming, funny stories which entertained us and took our minds off the previous difficult months. I heard tales about the day she came home from cleaning the ships' decks with a tattoo on her arm and about her legendary tap-dancing. My Aunt Annie told us the hilarious story of a coal dispute that she remembered my nan having with Mick the coalman when he tried to convince her that he'd delivered two-hundred-weight of coal, when he knew quite well that he'd only dropped the one. Taking centre stage, my dear aunt acted out the coal dispute like Mrs Bouquet, aka Mrs Bucket, in a scene from *Keeping up Appearances*. Impersonating my nan down to the finest detail, she narrated the tale.

'Oh, so yer've dropped two 'undred o' coal, 'ave yer now! Well 'ow's it tha' two 'undred o' coal always fills me coal 'ole, an' me coal 'ole's still 'alf empty? As da furries bin durin' da night an' made me coal 'ole bigga? Yer must tink I's as green as a feckin' shamrock!'

My aunt had now morphed into my nan and she stood there in silence; shoulders back and arms folded, as she mimicked my nan glaring up into Mick the coalman's face, waiting to hear his pathetic reply.
Now, playing the part of the coalman, my aunt plea-bargained,

'Well, yer see, Annie, da coal's a lot smalla this week, so it is.'

Then, my nan again, 'Ah, go an' shite – if it's a lot smalla, it'll be easier t' pick it up agen an' pu' it back on yer wagon.'

Mimicking her walk, my aunt played her final scene, toddling off to the back-kitchen, cursing under her breath, just like my nan used to do, with a squiggled self blessing, a clasp of her hands and a glance up to heaven.

After enjoying the round of applause, my dear Aunt plonked herself down next to Father Bunloaf, and while topping up his glass and bending his ear with her fabricated story about her nearest and dearest cousin Princess Grace, my mum took over the storytelling. Sounding more like my nan than my nan did herself, my mum ignored her big sister's glares and took her turn mimicking my nan's satirical assault on my posh aunt's airs and graces. While everybody roared laughing, my aunt smouldered in the corner with a face that could stop a clock. As the laughter died down, Father Bunloaf rounded off the night with what had to be the best tale of all. It was the comical story about a flying telly knob. . .

'It cum hurlin' through da sky! An', but for da grace of God, it nearly took me 'ead frum me shoulders, so it did. Like a lickle miracle, Annie appeared as if frum nowhere an' advised 'oly wata to be da best remedy . . . for da swellin'. A marvel of a woman, so she wus.'

With a smile curling around his lips, Father Bunloaf stared over towards our telly, then, raising his glass in honour of my nan, he took a swig of his whiskey and said goodnight. The crafty old bugger must have clocked the ping-pong ball stuck to the front of our old set and he had put two and two together. Yet, he had never cracked on in all those years that he had known all along, that it was my nan who had been the culprit.

Of course, our old telly had conked out many years before and had been replaced by a new one, rented from Radio Rentals, a firm who hired radios and televisions and repaired or replaced them when a clout to the side of the set failed to stop the picture from rolling.

So, that was my nan's wake. Although she believed in God, religious paraphernalia was not high on her list of importance and Father Bunloaf was aware and understood that. This time, he had come to pay his respects as a friend and, no doubt a little drop of Irish too; he was only human after all. It was a good send-off that celebrated my nan's life, her canny wits and caustic humour. She was Annie Welsby. A little woman who had survived against all odds and I would not be sitting here writing this book but for her.

Above: My nan Annie. Welsby. b:1885 - d:1967.

Taken at her 80th birthday party in August 1965, which was two month's early.

That's Uncle Tommy's arm around her. Whoever took the photograph has decapitated him.

6 Me Son's a 'eeeeathen!

Although my body made the occasional guest appearance, my mind never returned to school after my nan's death. I had handed over every penny of my mum's wages to her, when I took over her work while she cared for my nan, and she gave me pocket money in return. But although I earned no real money, I'd had a taste of what became one of the most important things in my life; independence, and for me, there was no going back.

On Halloween 1968, I turned fifteen and left school the following Easter without any qualifications. A few years later, Easter leaving was stopped and the age for pupils leaving school increased to sixteen. I had scraped through and was excited to join the working ranks. I loved everything connected to design, display and especially architecture. I first trained as a window dresser, working in various shops and department stores, including Lewis's department store, creating the window displays I had so admired as a child. My first wage was six guineas and I gave half to my mum.

Just like my mother, I had an assortment of different jobs, but soon realised that it wasn't money that motivated me. It was independence. I wanted the luxury of choice. To choose who I worked with and make my own decisions. For me, money was just the vehicle to take me where I wanted to be. So I educated myself on a need-to-know basis, through books and endless night-school courses. Inner-city living had its advantages. My nearest library was a five minute stroll around the corner from our flat, to the Picton Library, which provided me with an education and fuelled my interest in architecture. This stunning building became my classroom and its books were my teachers. With an encyclopaedia and dictionary to hand, I hid in a corner reading for hours, looking up the words that I didn't understand. But anaemia plagued me through my younger years making it hard to focus and I tired quickly. But at least the lessons were of my choosing and I didn't have condescending teachers, breathing down my neck and tutting at my every mistake.

The exterior of the old tenement flats looked cold, austere and unwelcoming and my classrooms at primary school, which was built in the 1600s, had been much the same. But sitting in the circular reading room at Picton Library, I was transported to another world. William Brown Street had been my summer playground throughout my earlier childhood, and these buildings were so familiar to me. During summer school holidays, I often spent warm, sunny days playing on the steps of the Walker Art Gallery, with my best friend Joanie, drenching one another with spray from the Steble fountain or giving one another a leg-up to sit on the backs of the lions as they lay guarding St George's plateau. During our pre-school years, we spent many afternoons giggling at Judy while she beat the living daylights out of Punch under the giant columns of St George's Hall.

The biggest influence of my entire life was my nan's blue-eyed boy John, who is largely responsible for shaping the person I am today. He brought quality to my life and showed me that there was more, if you were prepared to work hard. He spent a great deal of time with me when I was growing up and taught me things without me realising I was being educated. When I was little, we had this game where he would ask me ten questions on general knowledge. It made the cold winter nights more interesting, and when he came home from work I would pester him to 'ask me a question'. Then he would mimic my words back to me, imitating my childish voice. I loathed school. I dreaded the sound of the one o'clock gun, which was my cue to return after lunch, but John was interesting and I wanted to learn from him, because everything he taught me made sense. He explained things to me as if I was on his level, as if I had a mind of my own, unlike many of the teachers at school who talked down to me. John taught me things by example. He built a story around the most boring subject and this made such subjects interesting, so I listened and I learnt.

John was well aware of his working-class background and he was proud of it. He knew exactly who he was and what he was, and what he was not and would never be. John was a realist who, unlike his big sister Annie, had no interest in material things and poked fun at his sister's highfalutin ideas of grandeur. He never boasted, and he had opinions that others were interested to hear. People often stopped him in the street just to talk to him, as opposed to my mother who they would only talk about after she had walked on by.

When Father Bunloaf was doing his rounds, he would often knock at our door, then just walk straight into the kitchen without being invited; back then, doors were never locked in Little Italy. My mother would make a pot of tea and respectfully call the priest, 'Farder'. But when John came home from work, the atmosphere quickly changed. Catholic priests got no special treatment from John, and he would never dream of changing his routine for them. He didn't disrespect them. He wasn't rude to them. He just didn't share their beliefs and he wasn't afraid to tell them so. He would do so with the greatest of respect, but they would be told nevertheless. So the priests of the parish usually gave John a wide berth.

When my nan was alive her eyes would roll up to heaven and she would throw her arms up in the air and call him for everything.

'Me son's a ' eeeeathen! May God fugive yer. What'll Farder Bunloaf tink o' me now? Yer feckin' gobshite. Yer've made an 'oly show o' me. with yer 'eathen questions an' ideas!'

John would laugh and mimic her words back to her, imitating her old way of talking. But John had a mind of his own and analysed everything. He would never blindly follow anybody's say-so. He would talk to a priest like he was no different from himself or from anyone else. He never liked patronising people who rammed their opinions down his throat or passed their opinions off as facts, and neither did I. So this made me analyse and question everything too.

As I got older, when John went on holiday I loved to sleep in his room. It was the only time I ever had my own bedroom. Although my nan's nephews John and Jimmy Hill had both married and left when I was a toddler, her nephew Paddy remained single and never left us, and so I still shared a bedroom with my mum and counted the days to John's annual holiday. His room was carpeted and felt warm and cosy. It was like sleeping in a reference library, with shelves full of books on every subject under the sun, from engineering to evolution. He'd buy them from secondhand book shops. Some were about far-off lands like China, America and Russia, and I would look at my little plastic globe to find where in the world these countries were. I loved reading books about far-off lands and watching movies such as *Lawrence of Arabia* and later *Doctor Zhivago*. I had little interest in fiction. True stories about people from far-off lands were what kept me quiet for hours. I was fascinated by these countries, but out of them all, it was Russia that intrigued me the most, with its beautiful buildings and their funny-shaped onion domes. I often stayed up reading John's books until it broke daylight. If I didn't understand a big word, he had a dictionary to help and an encyclopaedia to explain. John's books were my education as well as his.

Primary school was so mind-numbingly boring. It taught me all the Catholic stuff, and I could recite the catechism before I could recite my tables, but then I'd go home and read the theory of evolution and my naive childish mind would try to make sense of it all. I would think to myself, *'ang on a minute. Wha' 'appened t' little baby Jesus an' da Virgin Mary?*

My head was full of questions that nobody could, or would, answer or bother to explain. When I finally plucked up the courage to ask Miss O'Toole why monkeys were never mentioned in the Bible, I got chastised in front of the entire class:

'We are Catholic, and this is what Catholics believe. Have you no faith, child?'

Her condescending lecture was then followed by the usual three tuts that earned her the nickname of 'Old 3-Tuts Tooie'. She made me feel like I was a complete waste of space. Faith; I was too little to understand what the word meant. So I didn't know if I had it or not! I would think to myself, *I only asked a feckin' question! Why tell me off? Why not just explain?*

When I told my best friend Joanie about the stuff I had read, she was gobsmacked. Joanie did not share my doubts, and was absolutely mortified at the mere thought that I was questioning the teachings of the Catholic Church:

'Me Auntie Josie said she'd make a friggin' monkey out o' yer when she gets 'er 'ands on yer. An' yer'll go t' 'ell, yer will! Yer 'eeeeathen!'

Then she dragged me off to Mass and scooped the holy water out of the font and threw it over me and stood there in silence watching me, waiting to see if I went up in a puff of smoke. When we went to confession, I could hear the little cow snitching on me to Father Bunloaf! I remember sitting in the pew outside the confessional box, waiting for my turn to go in, and Joanie was in there for ages, telling Father Bunloaf everything I had told her about the evolution stuff I'd read. I remember the church was so ghostly quiet that you could hear a pin drop, and I could hear Joanie's baby voice echoing from the confessional box as she mentioned my name over and over again. Then, when Father Bunloaf was finally able to get a word in edgeways, I heard him saying to Joanie:

'Oh, she did, did she now? Good God almighty! I shall 'ave t' 'ave anuder word with tha' child. Is she outside?'

Before he managed to squeeze himself out of his box, I'd legged it past every patron saint and apostle and was halfway home.

I suppose Old Tooie had hit the nail on the head. My problem *was* a complete lack of faith. Nothing about religion made any sense to me whatsoever, and I just couldn't get my head around it. I could never understand a single word the priest preached when he got up into the pulpit, and so I didn't see any point in listening to him. So I didn't bother. He seemed to adopt an entirely new personality and a different way of talking once he climbed up onto his perch. It was almost as if someone or something had taken possession of him, and I could never understand what the hell he was on about, but *hell* was usually it!

Then there was Holy Communion. You needed to fast before receiving the body of Christ, and at nine o'clock Mass we would drop like flies, fainting from the hunger. Brenda Kelly dropped flat on her face one morning, without any warning whatsoever. One minute she was singing away like a delicate little angel to a chorus of rumbling stomachs, then, BANG – she was out like a light, and when somebody picked her up she had a conk on her head the size of a golf ball. Of course, we would see the funny side of everything back then, so we were wetting ourselves.

Holy Communion on an empty stomach always made me feel faint. The thin, dry wafer stuck to the roof of my mouth like a flying saucer, but without the sherbet inside, and we were not permitted to chew or touch it with our tongue; instead, we were only allowed to let it slowly melt, which just seemed to take forever. It was like having a piece of blotting paper stuck to the roof of your mouth, and it seemed to soak up every bit of moisture until you were gasping for a drink.

Joanie had a good mind. She was clever and well-behaved, even though she messed about, she wanted to believe in . . . *something*. I was not well-behaved, and I wanted proof. The evolution theory made much more sense to me. I liked the honesty in John's books. They didn't have all the answers to all the questions. They *asked* questions rather than answered them, questions that I couldn't put into words. These books made me stop and think, and I realised at a young age that a person's religion is a person's belief and we should all have the freedom to believe or *not* to believe as long as we don't harm anyone.

I became more open-minded about everything in life. I never practised my religion once I left school; I never practised it much *in* school either, but I never lost my respect for it, and I took an interest in other people's beliefs, as long as they didn't ram their opinions or faith down my throat.

Joanie and I often had these childish, heated debates about God, heaven and hell, monkeys, and who the hell my dad could be! But we were never serious for long and would soon find something comical to giggle about. Joanie was always wild and hysterically funny. She denied any connection to monkeys, but then rolled around the floor like a demented chimp, making unrepeatable comments about Farder Bunloaf's hairy legs.

'Well . . . when did yer get t' see Farder Bunloaf's 'airy legs?'

'At nine o'clock Mass last Sundey mornin' – 'e wus 'alf asleep, an' 'e went fu' a burton on de altar steps when 'e wus dishin' out 'oly communion. If yer'd gone t' Mass . . . then, yer'd 'ave seen 'im too. But yer didn't go did yer? Yer 'eeeeathen!'

Ignoring the cross she'd made with her two index fingers, which she then shoved in to my face as if I was the devil's disciple, between giggles I asked for further details of Farder Bunloaf's comical misadventure.

'An' wha' 'appened t' God, when Farder Bunloaf fell over?'

'God fell too! 'e rolled down de altar steps. It looked like someone 'ad dropped a big bag o' flying saucers. Yer missed Ash Wednesdey too! Oh, yer've 'ad it when Old Tooie sees no ashes on yer 'ead tomora! Yer'll be da only one in da classroom without ashes! Yer can't wash dem off, cos' that's a mortal sin. So yer'll after think of anutha excuse. Yer 'eeeeathen!'

Looking over at the half-dead plant on Joanie's mother's windowsill I said,

'Oh, I'll think of sumthin'.' Then, nonchalantly, I enquired,

'Wha' colour vestments did Farder Bunloaf 'ave on this mornin'?'

Joanie thought for a second and then replied, 'Errrrm . . . Purple.'

The next morning I toddled off to school complete with ashes on my forehead, like a good little girl, and Old Tooie asked the usual string of question. It was then that I found out the lying cow had, yet again, dropped me right in it. Everybody, apart from me, answered in unison:

'Greeeeen, Miss.'

While I said, 'Puuuurple, Miss.'

It took Miss not much longer than three seconds flat to find out where the 'Purple, Miss' had come from, and by this time her gob was the same colour.

'OUT! Get – out – of – my – sight! Not only do you not go to Mass . . . but, you then tell me liiieees about not going to Mass! That's two mortal sins in one day!'

I tried to dig myself out of a hole by pleading innocence, but Old Tooie didn't buy it.

'Ahhhh, b-b-but Miss . . . I thought yer meant *lassst* Sundey.'

'That's three! OUT! And if you think, for one minute, that you're kidding me with that soil you've smudged across your forehead . . . well, you can think again! Has it not occurred to you why nobody else is wearing ashes today?'

I looked around at my holy-innocent classmates. A familiar assortment of munchkins stared back at me. Their faces and bodies purposely distorted into grotesque, cross-eyed gargoyle-like monsters behind Old Tooie's back.

'Is it 'cos they 'aven't bin t' Mass, Miss?'

Muffled giggles escaped from the back row as she repeated my words back to me, imitating my childish voice.

'NO! It's – not – 'cos – thee – 'aven't – bin – t' – Mass – Miss!' Her voice now her own, she continued:

'It's because Ash Wednesday . . . is next week. OUT! And don't even dream of setting foot back into my classroom until you can spell 'benediction'.

As I walked past Joanie's desk, she looked up at the ceiling to avoid my glare. As usual she was wearing her butter-wouldn't-melt, holy-innocent look across her gob, which I was well used to, but which she always managed to get away with. If I hadn't understood what this little girl was like beneath that squeaky-clean, freckled-faced, blue-eyed façade, which was usually framed by two shiny waist-length plaits tied with pink ribbon, then I would have bought that holy-innocent act. But I knew it was all me eye, merely kidology. Inside, I knew Joanie was highly amused by this pantomime and most probably wetting herself laughing.

I walked home from school on me todd – face tripping me as I scraped the toes of my shoes along the ground and ran a rusty pipe along the railings of the old graveyard of St Stephen's disused chapel in Byrom Street. And while I walked home, I tried to remember what it was that Old Tooie wanted me to spell: *B . . . E . . . N . . .*

The second I walked through our door, me mam immediately wanted to know why I was home from school so early and before Betty, the lollipop lady, was on duty to see me safely across the road.

'I didn't know da colour of Farder Bunloaf's vestments, so I guessed, an' guessed wrong, and now Old Tooie won't let me back in 'er classroom 'til I can spell sum fella's name.'

'Jesus, Mary an' Joseph! Spell wha' fella's name?'

'Don't know . . . but, I think she said 'is first name wus Ben.'

With Joanie, I had to learn to duck and dive quickly to get myself out of trouble. She had a mind and a sense of humour that few could keep up with. She spoke at high speed, in a sort of rhythm, and you needed to get into that rhythm before you could understand what it was that she was on about. I understood her perfectly, and we could read each other almost telepathically. Beneath her zany humour was an intelligent, caring, sensitive person. Never once did Joanie appear remotely interested in learning anything at school, but when it came to an exam she'd sail through without a problem, while I'd still be staring at an empty page.

I remember one freezing winter's day. It had started to snow again. Ice had already covered the hills created by the bulldozer as it dug out the foundations for what was to be the Polytechnic College in Byrom Street, and which is today part of John Moore's University.

Joanie and I had spent hours building a sleigh out of an old wooden orange crate and we were having great fun sliding down the icy slopes of the waste ground, known as the 'olla. To keep our feet dry we would put plastic bags over a couple of pairs of thick woolly socks before putting on our wellies. Our hands got the same treatment, with plastic bags and then mittens. Woolly scarves and cardboard-like duffle coats bought from T.J. Hughes completed our outfits. The socks didn't match and neither did the mittens. We looked like two tramps, but we didn't care; the snow had stuck and left us a white wonderland to play in.

An old woman carrying a bundle of firewood interrupted our fun, when she slipped on the ice. We picked her up, put her firewood in our sleigh and escorted her home. We found she lived in a garret in Lacé Street with her nine cats. She had nothing, and we felt so sorry for her. Her old garret flat was freezing, so we both went home and smuggled some food and coal from our flats and returned with our stolen goodies. Old Biddy lit a fire and made us some tea and toast, and we sat listening to her life story for hours. We visited her each night throughout the winter months of 1965, until one night Biddy never answered her door, and Joanie, who hardly ever cried, sobbed her heart out.

As Joanie and I got older we did voluntary work after school at St Joseph's House, which was a home for the aged on Belmont Road adjacent to Newsham Hospital and run by the Little Sisters of the Poor. The old women who lived there reminded us of Old Biddy, and we would often sit with them at night and listen to their life stories for hours on end.

Everyone needs a friend they can regress with, and for me it's Joanie. We both share the same Halloween birthday. She knows nothing about this book, so I will send her a copy on our birthday and wait for the telephone to ring when she gets to this page.

7 The Letter

Throughout my childhood I remember John seemed to always have his head hidden beneath a towel and bent over a basin of Friar's Balsam to help his breathing. I hated the foul smell. John suffered with bronchiectasis, a legacy of his childhood pneumonia. Several times each year he'd need a course of Penbritin antibiotics. As the sixties came to an end, his health began to fail. His doctor advised him to move out of the city. Through his work as an engineer at Lucas, he was offered a flat in Runcorn's new town. This caused a big problem; Paddy was a painter and decorator and wanted to stay close to his work as he didn't drive, and it was like asking my mum to go to Outer Mongolia. She had no confidence and couldn't 'live amongst a gang of strangers!' This was how she referred to people who she didn't know, as if they were a pack of wolves waiting to pounce. John had no patience with her:

'Oh, for Christ's sake, Katie. You don't need a passport to cross the Runcorn bridge!'

So John bought an old caravan in Talacre, north Wales for weekend breaks and fresh air and he moved to a newly built flat in Runcorn, while I stayed with my mum and Paddy stayed with us. John came to visit us every few weeks, or we went to visit him. I missed him terribly, but relished having a bedroom of my own at last. Ironically, less than a year after John moved to Runcorn, we were forced to move ourselves. My mum and I moved to a lovely flat overlooking West Derby cemetery, and Paddy went to live in Fazackerley by his brothers.

It took a while for my mum to settle, but once she realised she wasn't living amongst a pack of wolves, she made new friends. She loved her new penthouse, as she called it, and filled the large balcony with potted plants, but complained that the flat was too quiet.

John didn't like Runcorn. There was often repairs on the Runcorn bridge, causing long delays, and his chest was no better. In 1972 he caught a flu virus, which turned into pneumonia. John had no telephone in those days and he was too weak to get himself to the front door for help. He lived on the third floor and his only neighbour was away on holiday.

If it wasn't for the postman hearing his cries for help, he was told, he would certainly have died. He had gone through the first and second stages of pneumonia alone. The pneumonia took its toll, leaving him weak, and a few years later he took the offer of early retirement from Lucas. With the bit of money advanced from his pension fund, he sold his caravan and bought a small bungalow in the Kimnel Bay area of Wales. It was a purpose-built holiday home, located within walking distance of the shore.

By this time I was working and had met my future husband Brian. One Christmas morning in the mid-1970s we drove over to Kimnel Bay and spent our entire Christmas holiday renovating this dilapidated bungalow, and by the following Easter it was habitable.

John knew nothing about property and his purchase turned out to be a disaster. It was built on an unadopted road, with no land drains, so when it rained the water had nowhere to go and poured into the foundations of the bungalow. Nothing stopped the damp from rising and penetrating. Eventually mould started to grow on his shoes in the wardrobe, and the smell of damp hit you as soon as you set foot through the front door.

The years went by and when I married Brian in 1980, John gave me away. Although his high blood pressure made him look healthy, we noticed his breathing was increasingly laboured and, after one of his many visits, my mum rang me in floods of tears. John had given her instructions in case anything happened to him. He had told her that he didn't want to be buried at Ford Catholic cemetery, where my nan had been buried; he wanted to be buried in West Derby cemetery. He had also told her that although his little bungalow had been a bad purchase, it had now trebled in value, and he had made a will and left it to me. This really upset my mum; she had never heard John talk in this way before.

My Uncle Tommy had died suddenly after a brain haemorrhage in 1976 at his home in London followed by his wife Maggie in 1982. And by this time Annie's health was failing fast and my lovely posh aunt, who had earned the nickname of Big Annie Oakley in her younger days, would later pass away suddenly in 1986. She was loveable and at the same time comical. Her death marked the end of an era for our small family. So even though they did nothing but bicker, my mum worried herself sick about her younger brother's health.

By 1982, Brian and I had both started our own businesses, although more out of force than choice. Having begun on a shoestring, we were both pathetically underfunded. But after a rather shaky beginning, juggling cash flow and propping up whichever business needed support at the time, we were now starting to become established, and earning a bit of money. We talked, and decided we could afford to take on another small mortgage and move John out of the hovel. It would be an investment for us, and the least we could do for John. We were a straight-talking family, so I told John that I wanted to return his gift now, while he was still alive to enjoy it. I told him to put his bungalow on the market and use the proceeds of the sale to supplement his pension. He soon found a small bungalow opposite Bodelwyddan Castle in Wales and he moved the following January.

It turned out that we had got him out of the old bungalow just in the nick of time, as only four weeks after he moved, his neighbour appeared on the six o'clock news being evacuated from his home by boat! The Irish Sea had breached the sea wall in what was one of the worst storms in over twenty years, flooding the whole of the bay area and destroying many homes. It was a lucky escape. John's health slowly improved and my mother was delighted. By the mid-1980s John was well enough to have some holidays abroad, and I often paid for them both to go to a friend's apartment in Marbella or to Majorca. Of course, being brother and sister they did nothing but bicker, and my mum refused to go on holiday with 'Mount Pleasant', as she referred to her moody younger brother, without taking her friend Martha along with them. So muggins here paid for Martha too.

It was lovely to see my mum getting onto a plane for the first time in her entire life. She enjoyed it so much, and was not in the least afraid of flying. But at the hotel she would not use the sun beds surrounding the pool as she considered that they were 'only fu da money-people'. My mum was intimidated by rich people – 'money-people', as she referred to anyone who appeared to have a bit of money. She was uncomfortable in their company and felt that she was beneath them, so she would never venture into any area where she felt she didn't belong. But when she returned home from their first trip to Marbella she looked tanned, healthy and rested from the first holiday of her entire life.

'You look like one of them money-people now, Mum.'

'Oh, go away yer little twerp.'

She always called me a little twerp whenever I teased her and pulled her leg. She had an alternative, off-the-wall sense of humour, always self-effacing, but she saw the funny side of everything, and whenever she laughed she couldn't stop. Sometimes she would offend people with her humour and I would be left to patch things up. She was before her time, and she seemed to drift from one adventure to the next and the next, as life went on around her.

But my mother also had a darker side to her nature, often suffering from bouts of severe depression, which grew noticeably worse from the mid-1980s, and she often thought about her own death. I put this down to the fact that she had survived cancer but lived in fear of it returning, and also that she now lived alone. She would never wallow in self-pity and soon snapped out of it and say. 'Yer can always find sumone worse off then yerself'. Then her mood would swing again and she'd find everything in her life hysterically funny.

I'll never forget the day when she hung out her washing on the line for the first time on the balcony of our new flat, which was on the thirteenth floor and overlooked West Derby cemetery. She was looking out of the window onto the main road using a pair of binoculars that John had given her, when she spotted one of the lampposts outside the cemetery gates had a white sheet draped over it that was flapping in the icy wind. After a couple of hours the sheet became frozen stiff, which slowed down its frantic billowing to slow motion and as night-time fell, the sheet looked like a ghost outside the cemetery gates. The effect was all the more macabre with the street light shining through it. My mum found this hysterical, especially when the Storrington Avenue fire brigade arrived with ladders to remove the sheet, which was now causing a traffic jam as inquisitive drivers slowed down as they drove past.

This entertained her for hours until she went out onto her balcony to bring in her washing and found only one pink bed sock left dangling all alone on her washing line.

'Jesus, Mary an' Joseph! Some little sod's pinched me washin' off me line!'

Then she remembered that we now lived on the thirteenth floor. It was unlikely that even Spiderman would be interested in scaling up to the thirteenth floor to pinch my mum's knickers, although they were so big that he could have used them as a parachute.

Totally bewildered, she scanned the area through the binoculars. Looking across to the Jewish section of the cemetery, she clocked bits of her washing strewn across the graves. Her stays were dangling from a tree, tinkling in the breeze like wind chimes, and draped across the wings of an angel in the Catholic section of the cemetery, hung her long, thermal vest. It was then that the penny dropped. That lamppost had been wearing her sheet!

* * *

It was the 19 January 1989. John had returned from Majorca and planned to go to my mum's for the weekend. He had called her several times that day, and when he got no reply he assumed that she was with me. But she wasn't with me and it was nine o'clock by then; she was never out that late. I told myself that she was probably talking to her neighbours. But when Brian and I arrived at her flat we found the door had been locked and bolted from the inside. My heart sank as reality kicked in. My worst nightmare was about to begin. By the time I got through to the emergency services, Brian had my mum's door kicked down.

When I ran down the hall I could see the bathroom and bedroom lights were all on, but she wasn't there. We kept calling her, but there was no reply. Brian checked my old bedroom while I ran into the living room. I found my mum lying on the couch in her pink, candlewick dressing gown. She looked so peaceful that, at first, I thought she was asleep. But when I took hold of her hand, she felt like a block of ice.

By the time the ambulance arrived her neighbours had gathered around her front door in tears. My mum was taken to what was then called Fazakerley Hospital and is now known as Aintree Hospital. Brian and I followed the ambulance in silence. Not even a tear.

The police talked to her neighbours. Mr Taylor reported that my mum had walked past him in the street at about four o'clock that same afternoon, and they had both wished each other a happy New Year. Later, the post-mortem revealed coronary thrombosis had been the cause of her death; my mum had battled with breast cancer a few years before and had lived with the fear of the cancer returning, but none was found. The post-mortem put the time of her death at about two o'clock that morning, which meant that she had been dead for approximately eighteen hours when we found her at ten o'clock that same night. This conflicted with Mr Taylor's information. It seemed Mr Taylor had been wrong. He disagreed. He remembered my mother had been carrying shopping, and he was sure it was today, because he was in Chester the day before, visiting his family. In her fridge were two fresh salmon fillets. She usually bought fish for John when he came to visit, and she liked to buy his fish fresh, on the same morning that she was expecting him. Given that the post-mortem suggested that she had died in the early hours of that morning, Mr Taylor's information made no sense. The police concluded that he must have been mistaken. My mum was just four weeks from her seventy-sixth birthday.

I think the worst thing about losing your mum in this way, or losing anyone who you are close to, is the – not knowing. Not knowing if she had suffered. Not knowing what was going through her mind. Not knowing if she was aware that she was going to die and if she was afraid. She had died as she had lived – alone, with nobody to hold her hand. Then came the heartbreaking job of sorting through her personal things, going back into her home, seeing her empty chair, her clothes, her little ornaments and her handwriting on notes to remind her of things she needed to do that day.

Buy fish for John

Need milk, butter and a Hovis

Pay phone bill

Arranging the funeral, choosing her casket, flowers and her gravestone, composing the words to inscribe on her stone; all these things are far from easy, and yet there is something comforting in doing them, something to clutch onto. It is the last thing that you can do for the person you have lost. But clearing out their home has the complete opposite effect. It feels disrespectful and invasive. It's like you are disposing of their life to make way for somebody else, before you can even accept that they have gone. While their personal things are at home, *they* are still at home, and this is where you want them to remain, forever.

I kept putting it off, until one day I got a letter from the council. They needed to re-let the flat. Disposing of her personal things such as her pieces of furniture and her clothes was heartbreaking. The Laura Ashley chintz curtains I'd bought for her only a few months before were still hanging on the huge balcony window, and for the first time I noticed that they had shrunk by about four inches. So, that's why she'd moved her couch – to hide them from me. Most probably she had washed them for Christmas. She always washed things ready to start a new year, whether they needed it or not. And no matter how many times I'd tell her off, she always washed things that needed to be dry-cleaned.

The same old brass ornaments that she'd used as her bank were still there, and they still contained copper and silver coins, albeit they were now decimal coins. Hidden inside an old teapot at the back of her china cabinet, I found a small bundle of £5 notes, tied together with lazzi bands. How familiar all this was to me. She had never stopped saving her pennies. Throughout my whole life my mum had always drummed into me,

'Neither a borrower or a lender be. Earn yer own money. An' if yer look after yer pennies, da pounds will look after thumselves.'

When I went into her bedroom I found everything was neat and tidy. She was always tidy, but this was different. Clothes were washed that had not been worn for donkey's years. Her sheets, towels and curtains all smelt freshly laundered. It was as if she was expecting this to happen and had spent time in preparing. When I opened the bottom drawer of her old-fashioned mahogany dressing table, tucked away carefully, I found my old teddy bear, which John had bought for me that day in the Co-op, now a lifetime ago. She had kept him all those years, wrapped in pink tissue paper, which was now faded with age. I picked him up to take him home with me, and as I unwrapped him from his blanket of tissue paper, a small, Basildon Bond envelope fell to the floor. The envelope was self-addressed and it contained a letter. It was this letter that led me down a path to uncover my hidden roots.

I sat on my mum's bed still clutching Ted and read the letter over and over again.

Flat 10a, Rose Bush Court,

35 - 41, Parkhill Road,

Hampstead

London

NW3

8th September 1987

I am writing in answer to your letter to the late Henry Freeman who was a resident in Flat 13.

I am sorry to have to inform you in this way, we had no response to the one address on his file card when he passed away in the Royal Free Hospital in May 1984.

I don't know if you are a relative or a friend – but would happily see you when you come to London. Please phone ------ ----- to make sure I am on duty.

Yours sincerely,

Janet Scott (Warden)

Above: Letter to my mum. Dated 8 September 1987.

What was this? Who was this Henry Freeman? Why did my mum write to a man in London? Throughout my entire life I had never known her to ever bother or even talk about men. My mother just worked all her life, read books and watched television. She never went out, apart from work or occasionally to the local church hall bingo with Joanie's mother. She didn't drink or flirt with men. This was totally out of character for her. Who *was* this man? Why had he never been mentioned? Was he the reason she had been so depressed lately?

I sat there thinking for a long time, my mind drifting off, then reading the letter again and again. This man . . . this Henry Freeman . . . somehow I knew, he just had to be my father.

She had told me that he had died in the war, but this man had not died until 1984. Why the lies?

I had concluded many years before that my father, whoever he was, must have been married with a family of his own and that my mother must have had an affair with him. I assumed this was why she had kept him such a closely guarded secret. After all, why else would she tell me that whopping, fabricated yarn about my father being killed in the war? I had believed that there was a grain of truth in that tale, I believed that he was dead, but I also told myself that there must have been more reason for all the secrecy and lies.

My mum wasn't the stereotypical wallflower. She could be quite strong-minded at times and had a clear sense of what *she* regarded as right and wrong. Although she lacked confidence in many ways, she was not lacking in brains. Leaving St Joseph's at fourteen, her lack of a good education was sometimes camouflaged by her rarely voiced, yet, surprisingly knowledgeable opinions on matters of local politics and world affairs. Always humbly given and laced with the usual self-effacing humour; mocking herself for knowing sod-all, as she would say. And yet her logical mind could simplify the most complicated problems with just a few, simple words. She was on first-name terms with all the members of parliament and world leaders. That is, she had nicknames for them all, which seemed to strip them of the power that they had inherited, been given or had taken. She read what she called decent papers and often had her head buried in John's books when he was out at work. She didn't approve of people who she would call home-breakers, so if she had made a mistake with my father in this way, I'm sure she would have backed away, humbly. She was not hard-faced and such a thing would have had a profound effect on her.

Even though the letter seemed to imply that he had no family, I was convinced that he must have been married and this had been the reason why some people had ostracised my mother. Attitudes have changed so much since the 1950s. Back then, to have an affair with a married man, especially if the man also had children, was a scandalous thing to do. Catholics who committed such a sin would burn in hell. Divorce was also out of the question. Old-fashioned sayings, like 'she was the talk of the parish' or 'the talk of the wash-house', are now comical to our ears, but their origins are deeply rooted in bigotry and suppression. But now I had a name, Henry Freeman, and an address, and although I was aware that I needed to be discreet, I just had to know more. By this time, Henry Freeman had already been dead for six years. Using the pretext of enquiring about a family friend, I rang Rose Bush Court. The warden explained that they kept their records for no more than three years, and as they accommodated elderly people, nobody living there today could remember him. I followed the telephone call up with a letter to the management office, but received a similar reply.

It would have been easy to ring John and tell him about the letter and ask him what he knew of my father. But I didn't. I never once asked John about my dad, not even when I was a child, and I can't really explain why. A lot of my actions or inactions were based on emotion, not logic or common sense. I was too close to John; it would have been far too upsetting. Besides, I didn't think he would know anything anyway. I think I was scared of finding out some sinister story, scared of hearing something bad. My mum was a good person and I didn't want to hear anything that would spoil my memories of her. I decided that I would ask John one day, but not yet; I wanted to find out about Henry Freeman myself first, and I wanted to do this discreetly. I wanted to be told by somebody, not too close, someone distant enough not to be emotionally involved, who could give me facts without opinion, truth without anything added or taken away. So I tried to find out who this Henry Freeman and his family were. I wrote to the Royal Free Hospital, but strict data protection prevented the hospital from giving me his details unless I could prove that I was his next of kin, which I could not. My birth certificate gave my father as nothing more than an ink blot.

The months passed so slowly after my mum died, and I kept thinking of the things she worried about. She always said her flat was lovely but lonely, and declared she would be found dead in it one day. She had fulfilled her own prophecy.

It was a nice neighbourhood at that time, and the flat was spacious and well designed, safe and warm with enclosed, well-maintained and heated public areas. In fact the flats were far nicer than many private apartments I had seen. But they were also lonely and quiet especially for elderly people living alone. Her flat was so close to West Derby cemetery that when asked for her address my mum would say that she lived *in* West Derby cemetery, and then she would give her flat number as *plot* number 79. That was . . . me mam.

To get her out of the flat I often bought her a book of theatre tickets for the Empire Theatre or the Liverpool Playhouse, and she would take her friend Martha to see a play, or perhaps Shirley Bassey or Ken Dodd. There wasn't much for women of my mum's age to do at night, and she was afraid of going out alone after dark. My mum didn't drink; but even if she had, she would never have walked into a pub on her own. So she really enjoyed those nights out. Equipped with a copy of the theatre's seating plan she soon took control and started to book her own theatre tickets – and of course, I would always pay.

I laughed to myself when I remembered catching my mum and her friend Martha giggling away like two school kids one day. I only caught the tale end of their conversation and heard Martha whispering to my mum:

'The size of it! It's a wonder 'e didn't poke someone's eye out!'

They both roared laughing, but they wouldn't tell me what they were giggling about. My mum, always quick-witted and inventive, quickly fudged it by telling me all about the comedy they had seen a few weeks earlier. Martha often stayed the weekend when they were going to the theatre and I was glad she had company.

The following night I picked up the *Liverpool Echo* and read about the commotion over the controversial new play at the Liverpool Playhouse. I thought to myself, *This must be what my mum and Martha were giggling about,* and I read on . . .

The play was the centre of much controversy because of the 'explicit sex scenes' it contained! They usually took sandwiches along to the theatre, and I had bought them front row seats! I imagined them both sitting quietly tucking into their chicken sandwiches, surrounded by bags of popcorn and Cornettos, both giggling away like two kids and Martha putting on her thick glasses to see every tiny detail. My head was full of memories like this, which made me laugh . . . and made me cry.

Above: My lovely mum. Circa 1930s.

Above: Mum. Circa 1970s.

Below: Mum with John at our wedding.

Below: My mum's key to the cleaner's cupboard at 39 Moorfields. A poignant reminder of her life.

Above: Mum (left) with my Aunt Annie. Mum kept her hat a surprise until our big day. It was a child's sunhat made of plastic. It cost just 35p from Woolies! It took off in the wind - never seen since.

Below: Annie and husband Bill. Circa 1930s.

Below: Tommy with wife Maggie. Circa 1960s.

Below: John at TA. Standing front, right side on end.

Below: John in Annie's garden. Circa 1940s.

Below: John and Tommy. Circa 1940s. Circa 1930s.

From top left: Me as a baby. At TJ's Grotto. At Southport and at Park Gate with our dog Lassie.

8 Mary – 'Yes. He Was, Love'

A few months after my mother's death, my cousin Mary, my Aunt Annie's eldest daughter, rang me to see if I was okay. I liked Mary. She was warm, compassionate and down-to-earth, but I had not seen her for many years until my mum's funeral. As we talked, I began to open up more, and I told her about the letter I had found at my mum's flat. She listened quietly, and for a long time Mary said nothing. I think she was bracing herself for my next question.

'Mary, was this Henry Freeman my father?' There was a long, heavy silence before I heard the words:

'Yes . . . yes, he was, love.'

Mary asked me to come and see her and she would tell me everything she knew, which she explained wasn't much, as my mum had always kept my father a closely guarded secret. She said she'd only found out herself from something she overheard her mum saying. We arranged to meet the following week in her local pub, but when it came to going, I chickened out.

It's hard to explain, but I guess I just didn't want to hear what I expected to hear about my mum in a pub. I thought the secrecy surrounding my father was so well protected that it must be something awful. So I didn't go, and I didn't ring Mary either.

We were once a close family, but we had drifted apart many years before. When I was growing up I often stayed at Mary's house. Mary's two children were about my age. Her daughter, who was also called Mary, so we called her *young* Mary, was just eighteen months younger than me, and her son George was my age, and we had some great times together when we were growing up.

As a child I loved going to their house. I felt like I was going to the countryside. The air felt so fresh and clean. The sun always seemed to be shining and people always looked healthy and tanned. Young Mary had beautiful skin and her brother George had blond hair.

He was good-looking, with big blue eyes, and he was artistic. We called him Georgie when we were kids, and he would sit for hours quietly sketching. From a young age he could understand shapes and angles, and how to work with shadow and light. He was self-taught and naturally gifted; he could sketch a person's face after only one glance. But George never got the chance to use this talent. He was killed instantly when his friend's car plunged over an eighty-foot drop when returning home from watching Everton play in the semi-finals in Rotterdam. He was thirty-one years old.

I have some great memories of those old days. Mary had a great sense of humour, and together with her husband they entertained the whole family at my Aunt Annie's house at Christmastime, when the night would be finished off with a song, with everyone gathered around my aunt's piano. Many homes had a piano in the parlour in those days. There was no room to swing a cat, yet it was shoved in behind the couch and everybody could sing. John sang 'Brother, Can You Spare a Dime?' as well as Bing himself, and then Mary would take her turn and then her youngest sister Ann's party piece was 'Scarlet Ribbons', while their sister Kathleen, who was born deaf, would dance to the piano's vibrations. When I was growing up, Kathleen taught me how to use a sewing machine and how to sign.

One summer when I was about seven or eight years old, Mary suggested that I stayed at their house for a couple of weeks during the school holidays to get some fresh air and sunshine, as I was such a poor eater and always looked so pale and sick because of anaemia. I was really excited and looked forward to it for months, counting the days to my holiday. Mum packed a small suitcase and we got the 12A to Huyton. But when we arrived at Mary's house we felt there was an uncomfortable atmosphere. My mum immediately sensed this and asked Mary if something was wrong. It was obvious that Mary was embarrassed. At first she said everything was fine, but then she confessed that she'd had a row with her husband; he had said I was welcome to stay, but he didn't want my mother in his house. I don't think I will ever forget the sadness in my mum's eyes that day. She picked up the suitcase, took my hand and walked out of Mary's house without a word. When we got to the bus stop my mum sat down on the bench and sobbed.

I was well aware that Mary's husband had no time for my mum, and I used to think about this a great deal when I was growing up, worrying about what it was that had turned him against her. I guess when the time came to find out, I got cold feet and told myself that I didn't need to know and didn't want to know. We drifted apart after this, and I really missed my visits to their house.

I was tolerated in our community and I made some great friends, but the atmosphere would change when my mum was with me. This always made me feel bad and so, even at a very young age, I preferred to go everywhere alone. As a child I could not put those feelings into words and did things from instinct, without knowing the reason why. Being always well guarded and defensive with people, mum often brought problems onto herself, especially when people delved into her business. She would say:

'Once they know all me business, they don't want t' know me.'

She had odd little sayings like: 'Never let ya left 'and know wha' ya right 'and's doin'.' Of course, I didn't have a clue what she meant by this when I was a child and sometimes there would be tension between us because she tended to dwell on those bad times which I just wanted to forget about and run away from.

My mum did have some good friends – lovely people, who were genuine and had a lot of time for her. The older she became, the more sensitive she became. As I grew older, I began to wonder if she had some sort of persecution complex, as she was often overly defensive and misunderstood people, and again, I would be left to smooth things over. I suppose she had been moulded by her circumstances.

She often talked about being melancholy. It was only as I grew older that I realised that my mum was clinically depressed. Then she would have good times when her sense of humour took over, and she became a different person.

As the years went by she hated the nights and would watch television until *The Epilogue* and then she would read newspapers or a book until the early hours. I think she was afraid to sleep at night. Often, she would go to sleep as it was breaking daylight and then she slept through until midday, when she felt safe.

She worked all her life, up until her early seventies. The only downside to her new flat was that the cemetery could be seen from her window and she watched the funerals. Again, she used her humour to mask her fear, 'I can feel da clip of da wings gettin' closer, but I've not seen me name listed in da deaths in da Echo, so I think I'm still alive.'

My mum always referred to herself as a coward, and when she found a lump in her breast it was over eighteen months before she told me and agreed to see our doctor. It was only sheer luck that the type of breast cancer that she had was slow-spreading; if only she had gone to our doctors sooner, she would not have needed a radical mastectomy. As usual she had buried her head in the sand and the lump was kept a closely guarded secret, just like my father.

But once she was admitted and got to know the other patients in her ward, the dark shadows disappeared from under her eyes and she looked like a huge weight had been lifted from her shoulders. Most of the women in the ward either had, or were about to have, a mastectomy and my mum made friends with Alice, who was a big, tall, well-spoken lady, who was quite sophisticated, with natural red hair and a larger-than-life personality. Alice was a godsend to my mother. With her surgery done and dusted, in her own words, she bounced back with a positive attitude about her recovery and this helped my mum. Alice had a presence about her when she walked into a room and a surprising sense of humour.

One day, Alice was wandering around the wards during visiting time. She stood at the entrance to my mum's ward with 'Arthur the drip' by her side, so called because she said that the drip reminded her of the drip that she was married to. One of the other patients informed Alice that Dr Santa had been looking for her earlier. Alice raised her head up high and, looking elegant in her long, green dressing gown, she then bellowed out her reply.

'Bah . . . That man gets on my friggin' tit.'

My mum was busy eating the box of Milk Tray that I had brought in for her, and without a moment's hesitation or even bothering to lift her eyes up from the chocolates, she chose her next soft centre and replied,

'Ha ha . . . you've only got da one now!'

The silence that followed was so abrupt that it was as if the sound had been turned off the telly.

'Oh for Christ's sake, muther!' I said under my breath as I looked around for a place to hide. I just wanted the ground to open up and swallow me. I glanced around the ward. The patients in the beds opposite were sat open-mouthed. The silence was broken by muffled giggles from an old lady who was tucked away in the corner bed. Then the ward erupted. Patients, doctors, nurses and visitors were in stitches. Even the patients who were waiting to have this dreaded operation could not help but laugh. The ice had been broken. Their fears were put into perspective. It was their way of dealing with the dreaded - 'Big C'. In my nan's day it was never mentioned by its name, but now they would face it head-on and they would laugh at it.

My mum lost a lot of blood when she had that first operation, but she pulled through and was soon back to work without needing further treatment, a part from Tamoxifen, which gave her a new lease of life. When people asked her how she was, she would tell them that she was now physically unbalanced too. Such was her humour.

It's only now that I have experienced life myself, that I can look back to those days with some measure of understanding, and I now realise how difficult life must have been for her. Gossip, bigotry and ridicule from small-minded people, who didn't understand and didn't want to understand, who seemed to take pleasure in condemning her and jumping to the wrong conclusion. She didn't have the confidence to stand up to this bigotry, although she tried her best to put on a front. It's only now that I realise just how deeply rooted her shame and loneliness must have been, and I wish with all my heart that I could turn the clock back.

For sixty years my mum never let her left hand know what her right hand was doing. Trusting nobody, she took her secret with her to her grave. I would soon find out why.

* * *

It was Christmas morning 1989, Brian left for the 2½-hour round-trip to Wales to collect John from Abergele Chest Hospital and pick up his dad along the way. John had been in hospital for three weeks and his consultant was allowing him out to spend Christmas Day with us, but we needed to return him to Abergele Hospital before midnight.

The turkey had about another hour or more to cook and I went up to our bedroom to change into something Christmassy, when the telephone rang. It was my cousin Mary.

'Merry Christmas! I've wanted to ring you so many times when you didn't show up at the pub. I really didn't know what to do for the best. I don't know if I'm doing the right thing ringing you. Are you okay? What happened to you? Why didn't you come to see me?'

I apologised and explained that I'd bottled it, and didn't want to be told about such personal stuff in a pub.

'Ah . . . I thought as much, but there's nothing sinister, you know, love, nothing bad to worry about. Would you rather I told you now . . . over the phone?'

At first I was a bit taken aback, but then thought to myself, *Well, this is probably much better and a lot less upsetting.* 'Okay,' I said slowly.

I sat down on the edge of our bed and braced myself for a long story about my father. Expecting to hear about the wife and half-dozen kids he probably had. I was frozen, waiting for whatever Mary was about to tell me.

There was total silence, and then, I heard Mary say quickly: 'He was a Jew.'

Then more silence, before she added,

'Your father's name was Henry Freeman, and he was Jewish. So, I suppose that means that you're also half-Jewish!'

I looked over at my reflection in the dressing table mirror, and I swear to God, my nose seemed to grow before my eyes! That old saying, 'as plain as the nose on your face', sprang to mind.

'Hello . . . Hello . . . are you still there?'

'Yes. . . yes, I'm here, Mary. I'm just picking myself up off the floor! I'm half-Jewish? My father was . . . Jewish! Are you sure?'

My whole life was now flashing before me. It felt weird, like I didn't know myself, like I was being introduced to *me* for the first time. Suddenly everything in my life began fitting into place, and I really didn't know whether to laugh or cry. I think I was just so relieved. I thought to myself: *Was this all it was? Was this the BIG secret?*

'Is that all, Mary? I was expecting something awful. I was waiting for you to tell me about some terrible scandal. Are you absolutely certain that there's nothing more to this than just . . . religion?

'Oh no, love. I don't think he was ever married. Your mum would never talk about him to anybody, but I know she was going out with him from when she was not long left school, and there was no other man in her entire life other than Henry Freeman. Your mum met him secretly for nearly twenty-five years. You know, life is different today, but it was so hard back in those days. Some people had very peculiar ideas. It's hard to understand now. Thank God times have changed.'

As far as I was aware, my family didn't know any Jewish people, so this was the furthest thing from my mind. I was often asked if I was Italian or Jewish as I was so dark, and stuck out like a sore thumb in a family of auburns, redheads and strawberry blonds. I would just laugh. Then sometimes I would stop, and I would think to myself: *Italian. Hmm, I wonder if . . .*

I would not have been at all surprised to be told that my father was Italian, as my mum's friends the Volante family were Italian and we lived in Little Italy, for Christ's sake! Surrounded by Italian families! I had to admit, this was my mum's biggest red herring of all.

We talked for ages about my mum and the old days, and Mary pulled my leg about my father's family and who they might have been, and her daughter, young Mary, my second cousin, chipped in with:

'Perhaps you're related to Freeman's catalogue. Or Freeman Hardy & Willis shoes!'

I started to relax and settled back against my pillow. I asked Mary if she knew what my father had done for a living.

'I'm not a hundred per cent sure about his work. I know that he lived somewhere around the south end of Liverpool and *I think* he had a scrap metal business around that area. I remember your mum would get dressed up, and she looked beautiful. I'd scream to go with her. I was always with her when I was little. She would run away from me, throw her coat and bag over the wall, then she would jump over the wall so that I couldn't follow her. She never talked to anyone about him and I'm afraid that's all I know about him, love.'

We talked and talked, and then after Mary's call, I lay on our bed thinking. My father dealt in scrap metal. Comical images of *Steptoe and Son* came into my head.

Tears of laughter were now streaming down my cheeks at the thoughts of my father sitting on a horse-drawn cart shouting, 'any ol' iron!' Then my mind began to drift and I began to think about stuff that I hadn't thought about since I was at school. Stuff that I had dismissed many years ago, thinking it was only a dream.

When I was very young, before John came home to live with us, we had a terrible feud with another family. One of my earliest memories was standing in the street in the rain watching my mum being beaten up by three women who were sisters. And my nan, who had just been told that she had cancer, was fighting with a woman who was just as old as my nan was. I remember my nan's long silver hair was pulled down from its hairpins and her face was covered in blood. It was the hatred in the faces of these women that often crept back into my dreams, and crowds of people were standing around watching from the landings and shouting for the fight to be stopped.

The argument had started earlier that day after I'd had a fight with the daughter of one of these three sisters, who was a year or two older than me. She had organised her mates to take it in turns to punch me, and they had knocked my tooth out. I don't know how old I was, but I know it was long before I had started school, as my mum changed the school that she had arranged for me to go to, because of the trouble with this family. I dreamt about this for a long time afterwards, and eventually I began to think it had only been a dream, because it was never spoken about. I now remembered what they had been chanting at me: 'Judy, Judy, Judy.'

Of course, the name Judy, was, and still is, a Liverpool nickname for a girl, in much the same way as Australian men call women Sheila. So I probably didn't recognise the name as anything more than that. Besides, at that young age I would not have related the name to Jews, because I would not have understood. It was more likely that I thought that the name Judy had something to do with Punch and Judy!

Now, everything about that fight made sense to me. That horrible day had not been a dream and I now realised that what those kids had been chanting at me all those years ago had been . . . Jewdy.

I had put that day out of my mind, but now I could see it clearly. I remember my nan had clumps of hair missing and neighbours were trying to coax my mother to go to hospital. I remember feeling so scared that I felt sick and I couldn't stop shivering. My nan sobbed:

'May God stiffen thum. Wha'll it be like when she starts school? Dem feckin' little baskets . . . may God fugive thum.'

My mother was in our bedroom with some of our neighbours and they wouldn't let me in to see her, but I could hear her crying, and this made me cry all the more. Then Mrs Volante picked me up and took me into her flat. She washed me in the big white sink and put her granddaughter's pyjamas on me and gave me a cup of warm milk and a junior aspirin, which soon put me to sleep. I was woken early the next morning by shouting and screaming. It was my Aunty Annie's thunderous voice bellowing from the landing just outside of Mrs Volante's bedroom window and I could hear my mum saying, 'Oh Annie, let it be now.'

My Aunty Annie was formidable. Not taking a blind bit of notice, she marched down to sort this family out. I vaguely recollect the roar of my aunt's voice echoing throughout the flats. She was like a lion, and her bouncy, red curls seemed to move independently, like each individual curl had a mind and a temper of its own and they were preparing themselves for battle, like the snakes on Medusa's head. What she wasn't going to do to those three sisters didn't bear thinking about, and I could hear some of our neighbours muttering to each other, 'Oh Christ, Annie's kicked off!'

There was going to be a fight. Not wanting to miss the revenge of Medusa, I climbed up onto the headboard of Mrs Volante's bed and peeped through the gap in her net curtains. I can remember feeling the tension in the atmosphere as neighbours gathered on all four landings of the surrounding blocks of tenement flats to watch. Each positioning themselves to get a good view. A few seconds later, a red blur went flying past the window like a bat out of hell. The sheer presence of Big Annie Oakley had sent the three sisters fleeing indoors, and they wouldn't come out. I remember my stomach churned. This was when my aunt was at her most dangerous, when she couldn't get her hands on the person she wanted to deck. I couldn't see much but heard the thuds of my aunt's fist beating against their front door. Spine-chilling screams were followed by a deathly silence. One of the three ugly sisters, as my aunt called them, had been captured – alive!

The silence was broken when a group of lads began to chant. 'Fight! Fight! Fight!' After what sounded like rumbles of thunder, my aunt was back. I dived under the blanket before she could see me at the window. The bedroom door was nearly taken off its hinges as she crashed through it. Without a word, she swept me up into a blanket and the next thing I can remember was being unceremoniously plonked next to her on the 12A to Huyton.

Mrs Volante's granddaughter's jim-jams were too big for me and kept falling down so I clung onto the blanket all the way to Huyton, while my livid aunt bent the bus conductor's ear. To get away from her, he let her off with her fare and then moved along the bus jangling his metal ticket machine saying, 'fares, please'. He escaped to the upper deck and didn't come down again until the bus stopped at Page Moss. When he next passed my aunt she kicked off with the story again from exactly where she had left off, apparently totally oblivious to the fact that the bus conductor had been missing for the past twenty minutes. There seemed to be no escape for the poor man, so he sat himself down at the end of the bus and began filling in paperwork, but when I peeped through the handlebar of the bench seat, I could see he was only doodling, pretending to be busy.

I loved going to Huyton. It was wintertime and I remember there would often be mist drifting low in the fields. I spent the rest of the journey looking out of the window. As we approached our stop, my Aunty Annie calmed herself down, put on her lippy, powdered her nose, adopted her airs and graces, and Big Annie Oakley was once again transformed into Mrs Hennessy, as if she had been sucked through a wormhole into another world and quickly returned to being my lovely sophisticated posh aunt who I had always loved and admired. But I now knew that if anyone hurt her family, they would be laid out!

I had no idea why this family hated us. But I was aware that it was *I* who was the cause of this hatred. So after that day, whenever trouble came my way I would say I'd fallen over, and I kept my mouth shut. I always thought that it was because I had no dad. But now it all made sense to me. It wasn't because I had *no* dad; it was because I had a *Jewish* dad.

My family were not churchgoers, and I was neither encouraged or discouraged from going to Mass. And yet a crucifix hung on the wall above our beds, apart from John's, and my mum and nan never uttered a sentence without the mention of His holy name in some form or other. The usual typical Catholic phrases:

'If God spares us . . . '

'We're only mere mortals . . . '

'May God fugive yer', and not forgetting the classic, 'Jesus, Mary an' Joseph!'

They had no time for people who they referred to as 'religious fanatics' and 'do-gooders' – people of any denomination, including Catholic, who they thought used their faith as a condescending tool to purposely belittle others deemed less holy than themselves, who considered themselves closer to God the almighty and therefore much more important. So my family never, ever went to Mass. Instead, my nan preferred an empty church, like after she had scrubbed the steps of St Joseph's. My mum and nan quietly believed in God, but they never displayed their faith or followed the herd – or should I say flock. To them, religion was not competitive and nor was anything else in their lives. They did things at their own pace, for their own reasons, without bothering to look at what others were doing. They were simple, uncomplicated people, with no two sides to them, and what you saw was what you got. And of course, John was a heathen.

As I lay there, all these thoughts were spinning around in my head. It was obvious to me that some people must have known about my father, or at least suspected. It would have been difficult for my parents to have met each other secretly for over twenty-five years without being spotted by somebody, somewhere.

Strangely, I began to feel better. For some peculiar reason, I understood why some people had hated us. It was no longer personal against me, or against my mum. It had been racial or anti-Semitic, and it was a part of that era, part of those 1950s days of intolerance, ignorance and bigotry, and somehow it didn't feel as bad.

When I first read the name Henry Freeman in the letter, it never even entered my head that Freeman was a Jewish name. I knew lots of people with Jewish-sounding names who were not Jewish, so it was the furthest thing from my mind.

I was half-Jewish, and I had been told on Christmas Day, of all days, ho ho ho . . . the story of my life! My mother would have seen the irony and thought this hysterically funny. This was so typical of her humour. All my life I had thought that my mum was hiding a dark, sordid secret and all the time she was only trying to protect me from what she was going through. She was single, forty, Catholic, with not a penny in her pocket, and she'd had a child to a Jewish man. She had ticked all the boxes for excommunication by people who appointed themselves judge and jury. No wonder she kept her mouth shut.

It would have been difficult for her to bring me up if she had admitted openly that I was half-Jewish. I began to realise why my mum was so guarded and defensive. Thank God for the Marie and Angie Volantes of this world and the people who had enough compassion to make her life a little easier.

The feud fizzled out soon after John came home. John was the diplomat of the family, using his words in a different way to his big sister. He was not tough, his chest condition saw to that. So John learnt the art of diplomacy. He had the ability to calmly defuse a situation and he was so well liked that people listened to him. The more I thought about John, the more convinced I became that he knew nothing about my father being Jewish. Although, just like me, John had no time for religion, if he had known, he would have taken the time to learn about Jewish culture.

We were not a family who showed our feelings; we didn't hug or kiss, there were no displays of affection between us, and so it was strangely heart-warming to see John so openly upset at my mother's funeral. They would always bicker. I suppose all brothers and sisters do. Our family conversations must have sounded as if we were arguing each time we spoke to each other, but John had obviously cared for her deeply, more deeply than I had ever realised.

Many times I had thought of writing to John and telling him in a letter about my dad, but I never got around to telling him, and I can't explain why. I suppose I thought that, if John knew and wanted to tell me, he would do so in his own good time. Besides, there was plenty of time. I would wait for the right moment. I admit I'm not good at talking about emotional stuff. I find writing much easier than talking. Like my mum, I buried my head in the sand and that right moment never ever came. Over the following twenty years, there were many times when I deeply regretted not talking to John.

I was still lost in thought, trying to untangle old memories from reoccurring dreams and putting two and two together when the smell of burnt turkey brought me back to my senses and I thought, *Christ . . . the potatoes!*

I could hear Brian driving onto our path with John and his father Frank, and I ran around the house like a headless chicken. They loved their Christmas dinner, and I hadn't even peeled a potato! I flew down the stairs, opened the front door, wished them a Merry Christmas and ushered them into the front living room, explaining I was running a bit late. After plying them with drinks, I left them gabbing about football and putting the world to rights. I flew back to the kitchen, opened the oven door, and wished I could turn the clock back an hour!

After lifting the pathetic, cremated remains of our Christmas turkey out of the oven, I began peeling potatoes like a mad woman. Brian walked into the kitchen, and of course, he immediately clocked the shrivelled black turkey.

'Why isn't anything ready? Jesus Christ, what's happened to the turkey? It's black!'

'Just shut up and help me peel these potatoes, quick. The turkey is meant to look black. It's a Norfolk *black* turkey.'

I salvaged some turkey from the middle of the bird and we finally sat down to eat. John and Frank were good company and it was so funny to listen to them both reminiscing. They always had a new story to tell about the old days and most stories began with,

'Did I ever tell yer about the time . . . '

My father-in-law Frank had a great sense of humour, and pulled John's leg about the oxygen tank he'd brought with him, calling it his companion and decorating it with a paper hat and party streamers. After a couple of more drinks, they both turned into Les Patterson, so I made some coffee. John looked at me as I handed him a cappuccino.

'You're very quiet tonight, Jess, is everything okay?'

'Oh, I'm fine, just everything went wrong with the turkey.'

They were concerned about the long journey back to Abergele, and John had to be careful what he drank, so shortly after ten o'clock they called it a night and Brian parcelled Frank and John, along with his oxygen companion, back into his car, each of them carrying handfuls of Christmas presents. I stood at the door with our spaniel at my side and waved them off. The road was covered in sheets of black ice and I went back into the kitchen and began loading the dishwasher, with our old spaniel never missing an opportunity to lick any trace of food off the plates before I shut the door. Just before Brian arrived home, I made a pot of tea to take up to bed, which was something we always did on Christmas night. A tray of tea and some goodies for a picnic in bed, and then we would open our pressies.

I lay in bed with lots of memories going around in my head, thinking about my mother and the wasted life she'd had. She could be so stubborn at times and I didn't understand her. Throughout my adult life I had asked myself . . . why all the secrecy? What was she hiding? Now, I had my answers, and I felt guilty for every single time I had lost my patience with her. I regretted every argument I had ever had with her. If only I had been more understanding. Why had I not seen this coming? My mum had simply fallen in love with a Jew, she had done nothing wrong. She had done *nothing* wrong. I didn't understand . . . I just didn't understand.

When I heard Brian's car pull onto our drive, I poured him a cup of tea. Christ almighty, did I have a surprise for him!

'God, I hate that journey. There's always lunatics on the road at Christmastime. I thought John looked a lot better, though – he reckons they'll let him out next week.'

He hung his trousers up and then kept disappearing into the bathroom. While he was doing this, I was quietly rehearsing to myself how I was going to tell my Catholic, ex-altar boy husband my news. Not that I thought for one minute that he would be the least bit bothered; if anything, he'd find it all hysterical. He had always got on with my mum and had understood her moods more than I ever did. After he crawled into bed, complaining non-stop that he was getting far too old to be chauffeuring people around until all hours in the morning, I passed him his cup of tea. By this time he was beginning to sound like Victor Meldrew, so I handed him his Christmas present and shoved a chocolate biscuit in his gob. Marks and Spencer's chocolate chip cookies were guaranteed to shut him up. It was like giving a child a dummy.

'You've been very quiet today. Is something wrong?'

I let him ramble on, and eventually he settled back against his pillow, still munching away at his biccy, he took a sip of his tea, while I took a deep breath:

'Well, it's a long story, but . . . how do you feel about getting circumcised?'

The tea came spurting out of his mouth, pebble-dashing us both. Roars of laughter followed and, when I finally finished telling him the story, he just looked at me and simply said,

'*Shalom.*'

9 Remember Me, Jess

Over the following years, I tried many times to discreetly find out more about my Jewish father, Henry Freeman, but nothing seemed to be known about him. I didn't dedicate my life to looking for him. I must admit that my attempts were half-hearted and I gave up too easily, as I worried in case Mary was wrong about him not being married and I might upset any family he perhaps had. Plus Brian and I were now working every hour God sent and had been for many years. But I often read the letter from the warden of Rose Bush Court and remembered my cousin's words. I even thought of hiring a private detective but our lives got so busy and complicated, and it's true – life happens while you're busy making other plans.

We had more than our fair share of problems over the years, enough to fill another book, so Henry Freeman went onto the back burner, though I always promised myself that I would look into him one day. He was my little secret and I told only a few friends about him.

A few more years went by and John went into Abergele Chest Hospital, as usual, to have two weeks of physiotherapy to drain his lungs. He had already booked a holiday to Majorca, and had even exchanged some money for his trip. Although this postural drainage was routine, and he seemed fine when we visited him every Monday night, by this time, he had been in hospital for five weeks. He was bored and worried that he might need to cancel his holiday, but said that he felt better since his antibiotics were now given intravenously.

On our next visit, we found he had been moved to another ward. He told us he didn't know why. Although it didn't occur to me at the time, I later realised that this was untrue. John didn't bury his head in the sand like my mum, so he would have asked questions and found out why he was being moved. But he appeared fine, so no alarm bells rang and we sat watching the Everton game together. When visiting was over, I asked John if there was anything he needed me to bring in for him when we visited the following week. He usually had a list, but this time he needed nothing. As we stood up and walked past his bed, I felt his eyes following me and when we reached the end of the ward and turned to wave to him, I caught him looking at me with such a strange sadness in his eyes. It was really disturbing. I felt as if he thought he would never see me again. I said nothing and dismissed the thought, but as we were driving home this began to play on my mind, and I got a strange sudden urge to turn back. It was the look in his eyes that I could not get out of my head. One minute he was debating the match with Brian, and then his mood changed. I now know he had been told there was nothing more that could be done. I can only guess that maybe he put it out of his mind while we were with him, and then reality kicked in when we stood up to leave.

The telephone call came in the early hours of the morning. I was already wide awake. I think subconsciously I was expecting it. The nurse gently told me that John had taken a turn for the worse and they didn't expect him to live through the night. I asked her to tell John that we were on our way. She tried to stop me, explaining that he had now slipped into a coma and was close to death, and there was nothing that I, or anyone else could do for him. She advised me to try and get some sleep and to travel over in the morning. When I insisted, she fell silent. Then, she quietly informed me that John had already passed away. It was at that point that I realised that John had died before she had picked up the telephone.

She was trying her best to balance compassion with professionalism, but the breaks in her voice were letting her down. It was clear that she was upset. She explained that John was one of their regulars, who they had all known for many, many years. That was so true. John had been in and out of Abergele Chest Hospital for over fifteen years and all the nurses and doctors were on first-name terms with him. It was the 10 February 1993. John had just turned seventy-three a few weeks earlier.

I will never forget the way he looked at me that night. Not a word was spoken, and yet that look said, *Remember me, Jess*... and, I always will.

The hospital asked my permission to do a post-mortem as they suspected John had contracted MRSA, and after years and years of use, the antibiotics no longer had any effect. Their suspicions were confirmed. I buried John at West Derby cemetery beside my mum, as he had wished.

It was many months before I dragged myself over to Wales to sort through John's personal things. It seemed so very wrong to even contemplate selling his home, even though we had bought the bungalow for him. In our eyes, it was John's home, and if his home was still there, then, in my heart and in my mind's eye I could see John still there tending his little garden. Death comes to us all, but it is so hard to accept.

I had been through it only four years before when my mum died, and I knew how it felt. It was a feeling I did not want to experience again. John was the father I never knew and I was his Jess. Eventually, I was forced into action when I opened a letter from the hospital asking me to collect his car from their car park. John's old Austin Allegro looked so forlorn, waiting for an owner who would never return. It was seeing his car that made me realise that John had gone, and I sobbed for the first time as I drove it back to his bungalow.

I organised the Red Cross to collect and auction off his furniture. There was nothing of any great value. But the one thing I could not bring myself to part with was his record collection of over 1200, 78 rpm records, and his old record player with the 78 rpm setting. The records were mostly His Master's Voice label, and some of the Bing Crosby and Satchmo records were quite rare, with many still having their brown paper sleeves, marked with the handwritten prices of 1/6d, and 2/-.

I could hear my nan ... *da state of tha' feckin' gobshite an' 'is posh music.*

I brought home an old shoebox which contained his personal papers along with old photographs and trinkets. One rainy afternoon, I made myself a pot of coffee and began looking through the things that were in the box. John was interested in photography, and most of his photographs were old transparencies, the sort viewed through a slide projector or magic lantern. Many were of scenery – a Spanish carnival or the Welsh Eisteddfod.

John kept a lot of things out of sentiment and looking through all his stuff was like stepping back into my childhood. I came across a pair of expandable armbands, the sort that were once worn to hold up men's shirtsleeves. I remembered buying them in Woolworth's for him for Father's Day when I was about twelve years old. He nearly choked drinking his cup of tea when I presented him with these armbands and said to him:

'I got yer these bands fu Father's Day, 'cos I don't 'ave a dad, but yer're like me dad. So, I go' yer these.'

Everything that I had ever bought him, usually from pocket money he'd given me for washing his old car, was carefully looked after as if it was cherished. I found a tiny box of cufflinks, and remembered saving up my pennies and carefully choosing each pair for him.

I opened an old brown leather wallet, which was empty apart from a tiny calendar, the sort that was often stuck to the bottom of a large landscape picture. The year was 1946. On the front of the tiny calendar was a picture of a red rose and inside on the February page, I found two photographs with the dates 14th, 21st and 28th all being underlined in pencil. The 14th being, of course, Valentine's Day.

One photograph was a sepia print of a young woman. She wasn't particularly stylish or any great beauty, but she was attractive, and she looked interesting and sophisticated in her clerical, brown pinstriped tailored suit. At a guess, she looked to be perhaps in her early twenties and the photograph was taken about the mid-1940s.

I wondered who she could be, as she had obviously meant a lot to John, yet there had been no mention of her in our family. The second photograph took my breath away.

The second photograph was a black and white photograph of a young girl. She was between twelve and maybe fourteen years of age, and she was the absolute image of John! She had John's eyes, his nose and thick, straight hair that could have been red or perhaps strawberry blonde. I sat there quietly, staring at the two photographs. It was like the day I found the letter with my teddy bear when I was going through my mum's personal effects. That letter had given me a name, Henry Freeman, and his last address, but no photograph. This time, I had two photographs, but no names.

Who were these people?

Did John once have a family?

If so, what had happened to them?

Had they split up?

Or had they been killed in some tragic accident?

I had nobody to ask. I was certain my cousin Mary would not have a clue about these people. To John's nephews and nieces, John was a confirmed bachelor, and my cousin Ann; my Auntie Annie's youngest daughter, would always pull John's leg whenever she saw him. She would wind him up by pulling his leg about something, and then she would stop, look at him straight in the eye and say to him:

'When are yer gettin' marrrrrried?'

I have found no record of marriage for John anywhere in the UK, yet the young girl in this photograph just had to be John's daughter, and I wondered if her name was . . . Jess.

I've been torn over whether or not to include John's mystery women in this book. Would I be tearing a person's life apart? Or fulfilling another person's lifelong dream? I decided that if the reader of this book discovers herself or her mother in one of these two photographs, then they can at least decide for themselves to either do nothing, or to contact me for further details. I know what I would do . . .

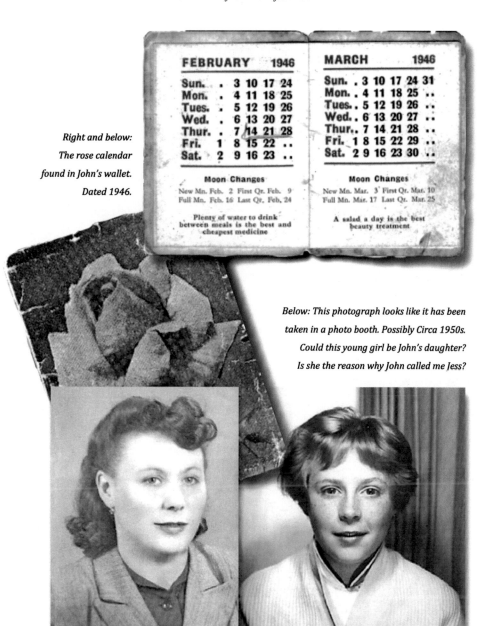

Right and below:
The rose calendar
found in John's wallet.
Dated 1946.

FEBRUARY			1946	
Sun.	.	3	10 17 24	
Mon.	.	4	11 18 25	
Tues.	.	5	12 19 26	
Wed.	.	6	13 20 27	
Thur.	.	7	14 21 28	
Fri.	1	8	15 22 ..	
Sat.	2	9	16 23 ..	

Moon Changes

New Mn. Feb. 2 First Qr. Feb. 9
Full Mn. Feb. 16 Last Qr. Feb. 24

Plenty of water to drink
between meals is the best and
cheapest medicine

MARCH			1946	
Sun.	.	3	10 17 24 31	
Mon.	.	4	11 18 25 ..	
Tues.	.	5	12 19 26 ..	
Wed.	.	6	13 20 27 ..	
Thur.	.	7	14 21 28 ..	
Fri.	1	8	15 22 29 ..	
Sat.	2	9	16 23 30 ..	

Moon Changes

New Mn. Mar. 3 First Qr. Mar. 10
Full Mn. Mar. 17 Last Qr. Mar. 25

A salad a day is the best
beauty treatment

Below: This photograph looks like it has been
taken in a photo booth. Possibly Circa 1950s.
Could this young girl be John's daughter?
Is she the reason why John called me Jess?

Left: John's mystery woman. Circa 1940s.
Who was she? Was she the love of his life?

Right and below:
John at work as an engineer at
Lucas factory Edge Lane,
Liverpool. Circa 1950-60s

Right:
My lovely
Uncle John.
Circa: 1970s.

10 Hard Times

The years went by, our businesses grew, and along the way we had bought a bit of property. We had started off with nothing, but by the 1990s we were well established and we were starting to get some money behind us. We had taken a massive risk, and thankfully it was starting to pay off. Brian's mother Nell had died back in 1982, only a few months before I had started my retail business, and just a few weeks after her sixtieth birthday. So now, only my father-in-law remained, and we were very close to Frank.

Suddenly, the life we had built for ourselves began to fall apart when Frank was diagnosed with a form of Alzheimer's disease caused by a series of undetected mini strokes, and we couldn't bring ourselves to put him into an EMI (Elderly, Mentally Infirm) nursing home. Frank had always been so astute, having a quick mind and razor-sharp wit. He needed only a few minutes to get the measure of a person and it was just heartbreaking to see him disintegrate from the strong person that he once was, to a mere shadow of his former self.

Although we didn't know it at that time, caring for Frank would take up the next five years of our lives, and Brian ran himself into the ground trying to keep his promise to his father to keep him out of a nursing home. Brian could not bring himself to step back from his father's care, consequently, Frank was given only one hour's help each day from social services leaving Brian on the frontline in the care of his father. I was merely back-up troops, washing Frank's clothes and his bedding, and cooking him easy-to-swallow meals each day, while I tried to keep both businesses going under some very difficult circumstances. It wasn't long before our minds went to mush. But bad times have to be put behind you and forgotten about, otherwise you don't get over them. They stay and fester if you dwell on them; something my mother used to do. So Brian and I only ever reminisce about the good times and the memories we have of Frank are heart-warming and some quite comical, and that would be what Frank would have wanted.

After Frank died a few days before Christmas 2000, Brian and I were at a very low point in our lives. We were both physically, mentally and emotionally drained with problems flying at us from all different direction. So we rolled our sleeves up and got back to work immediately and, unless experienced first-hand, nobody knew what we'd been through.

I had more than a few complicated problems to sort out at my business. The details of which could fill another book. We also had more than our fair share of personal problems over the years; in fact, we had that many problems that they were just not worth worrying about. We both tend to worry more when we have one problem, and can cope far better when we have problems racing at us. But this all took time to sort out and my mother was right when she often said:

'Yer life speeds up as yer get older.'

It was about October 2007 when my thoughts shifted again onto the mysterious, elusive Henry Freeman. Brian's dad Frank was the last of our close family. Perhaps it was a desire to reach out to people who had passed on that gave me a strange sudden urge to find my roots and to touch base with people from my childhood. It was quite a weird feeling, and difficult to understand unless you have an ink blot, but not knowing your roots is unsettling. Plus, everyone connected to me seemed to have some deep mystery surrounding them. John was a mystery. My mum was a mystery. Now, this Henry Freeman. Besides learning that he was my dad, I was soon to realise that he was also the daddy of all mysteries.

I got interested in family history after finding that so much information had become available online, and so I wondered if it was possible to find out more about Henry Freeman, discreetly and anonymously, and without having to travel down to London. I wrote to Mary in January 2008, asking for her help to do our maternal Welsby family tree, something that John had always been interested in doing, and I explained that I was also going to try again to trace Henry Freeman, because the hospital would give no information about him.

Mary had retired to Colwyn Bay in Wales many years before, and I had not heard from her since John had died in February 1993, apart from a Christmas card. Mary replied with a nice letter and agreed to start making notes of all she could remember about our family, but explained again that she had told me everything she knew about my father, and that she only wished that she knew more. I wrote back and asked if I could come to see her one Sunday when the weather improved and after I had done some research, and I asked if she would make my favourite Sunday roast. I was always underweight being a picky eater, but I would eat anything Mary cooked.

More importantly, I wanted to sit down and talk to Mary about John and to show her the two photographs I'd found in John's wallet. Since John's death in 1993, I had told nobody. I felt it was wrong to reveal his personal life. Like my mum, John was a very private person. But over twenty-years had now passed. I wondered if that young girl in the photograph was still alive. Did she long to know who her father was, just like I did? But I knew Mary thought the world of her Uncle John, all his nieces and nephews did, so I knew she would be upset if she knew nothing about this. So I didn't want to break this news to her over the telephone.

I had a terrible problem with my eyes, which shelved my plans of travelling to Wales to visit Mary. The following April 2008, I opened a letter from Mary's daughter and read the sad news that her mum had died suddenly. Mary's IBS symptoms had been misdiagnosed.

Mary's death had happened so quickly, and her daughter was completely devastated. Her passing saddened me deeply. She was a genuine person, the sort of friend you would want to confide in when you had problems, as she was always a good listener and a realist who was so down to earth, and I know that she thought the world of my mum.

I had let far too much time go by and it was now too late. I had not seen Mary's daughter, young Mary, for over twenty years, but after her mum's death we began writing to each other regularly and reminiscing about the old days and, although I didn't know it then, those letters became a precursor to this book.

Mary's sudden death was a massive wake-up call for me. It made me stop and think; life is not a dress rehearsal. We only get this one take, this one chance at life and it was far too short. I needed to find out more about my father and his family, and where my roots lay, and whether Mary's information had been accurate about him not being married, and I didn't want to put it off any longer.

A few months later Brian and I met up with some friends who we had not seen for many years. We were having great fun reminiscing and filling each other in on the past twenty-odd years of our lives when the conversation gradually drifted on to our various businesses and property and then on to the internet. Our friends began talking about the general advice that can be found on internet forums and self-help-groups that have sprung up online over the last few years. I didn't have much trust or confidence in the internet back then. Although I'd had a computer for many years I only used it for buying online, letters, invoices and emails. I was aware of forums, but had always shied away from them, imagining them to be similar to chat rooms where bored people discussed mundane topics, so I was intrigued and wanted to know more. One of our friends explained further:

'Well, on almost every subject under the sun, you will find a forum or self-help group on the internet, which you can join for free, and using a made-up username so you don't need to disclose your identity online, you can then ask for whatever advice you might need, safely and privately. They have improved a lot these last few years.'

This information stuck in my mind. I had previously joined findmypast.com a few months earlier to search the website's death indexes for Henry Freeman. I was hoping his death certificate might give me information about his family, but I could not find his death. Of course, I was a complete novice to family research and it takes a while to get the hang of. So I started researching my maternal Welsby family, as I imagined that they would be easier, given their old Anglo-Saxon name, and I thought, perhaps if I practiced on the Welsbys first, that would give me the research experience I needed to find information about my father. I managed to trace back four generations of my Welsby ancestors easily enough, and on the way I had gathered a wealth of information about my maternal family, the details of which have helped me to write the first half of this book. But the credit for tracing my Welsby ancestors is not all mine. I had a stroke of luck . . .

I had left a list of names I was researching on the Liverpool and South West Lancs Genealogy website in the hope of finding another researcher who was also tracing the same Welsby family. It was not long before I got a message via this website from Susan Brugnoli; an experienced researcher who had been tracing her Welsby ancestors for over twenty-five years and Susan had lots of information, as she had traced the family back to the year 1573! She had documents to verify all her research and details of the source of her information. My maternal Welsby family was Susan's grandmother's family, and her grandmother was one of four siblings who had been raised in the Cottage Homes Orphanage in Fazackerley, and so her grandmother never knew her parents. It was this that instigated Susan's research and she became addicted. Susan was delighted to learn about my branch and so we pooled all our information and found our trees joined in the early 1800s with two Welsby brothers.

Finding another researcher who has a link to your tree, like Susan found me, is what makes genealogy completely enthralling; as it can save years of research for both parties. It's like finding someone who's doing the same jigsaw as you are doing yourself, and who has the missing pieces of a puzzle that you have perhaps lost or knew nothing about. I learnt that it's in the smaller website forums that a lot of in-depth research takes place, where like-minded researchers are often found who you can pool your research with and ask for advice if you hit a brick wall and get stuck.

There are lots of genealogy websites, and even people who are unfamiliar with family history research, as I was myself at this time, will no doubt have seen the adverts for ancestry.com, findmypast.com and genesreunited.com. These are the best known websites but there are also many others. On some websites you can search records free of charge, while others charge to view their records. For England and Wales you can search through the GRO (General Register Office) of birth, marriage and death indexes from 1837–2005 and UK census records from 1841–1911, plus a multitude of other records and websites that can also be searched from the comfort and privacy of your own home, without the need to go trekking around the entire country to each town's records office.

All these websites each have their own little idiosyncrasies, so they do take a bit of getting used to. Scotlandspeople.com, as the name implies, is a website to search for Scottish ancestors, but the records that are available for Ireland leave a lot to be desired. Tell a seasoned genealogist that your ancestors were Irish and you will be sure to hear a rather sharp intake of breath. For this reason I gave my nan's Irish roots a wide berth.

Despite the success with my mum's family tree, I could still find no record of death or birth for Henry Freeman and no scrap metal business in his name. Of course, I was still a novice to family research and I knew nothing about Jewish culture, other than being told it was extremely difficult to research Jewish ancestors and many Jews don't even attempt it.

It was the 14 February 2009, we were planning a quiet night in and I had a pot roast in the oven. Brian rang to tell me he was stuck in traffic, so I knew I had a few hours to kill. I thought about the problems I was having trying to find details about this mysterious Henry Freeman, and I wondered if there was a family tree self-help group or forum, which was less high profile than the forums attached to the main genealogy websites. I also felt a bit guilty, as my mother was such a private person and I felt uncomfortable telling her personal story to complete strangers, even though I did not need to reveal her name. As for Henry Freeman, I knew that he had lived in Liverpool, at least from when my mother was the age of fifteen; that he *possibly* had a scrap metal business around the south end of Liverpool's inner-city; and that he had lived at no. 13 Rose Bush Court in Hampstead when he died in May 1984 at the Royal Free Hospital. But there were far too many things that I didn't know for me to go around blabbing to people willy-nilly that he was my father.

Brian and I were now living in an area of south Liverpool where many Jewish people lived, and I wondered if any of my father's relatives were still living in Liverpool. That's *if* he had any relatives. And if he did, I wondered if I knew any of them, or if they knew about me!

I had Jewish suppliers, Jewish customers *and* competition in business. I had Jewish friends and neighbours. I was surrounded by them! I began looking at all Jewish people tentatively, wondering if I was related to them in some way. A member of my father's family could be one of our neighbours, a customer or supplier at my business. Christ, they could even be my competitors or among our friends! Or if it turned out that Mary was wrong and he had been married, I could have spoken to a half-sister or brother and not had a clue who they were!

So researching my father's Freeman family incognito solved a massive problem for me, and I could now do this online without even needing to leave our home. I also felt that, if I was lucky enough to find any of my father's relatives and they knew nothing whatsoever of my existence, then it wouldn't be fair for them to find out about me via the Jewish grapevine. I'd thought this through and decided that, if I did find that my father had been married and had a family of his own, then I would keep my distance. I saw no point in upsetting others.

I was also concerned about what kind of reception I was going to receive from any of my father's relatives. I worried that maybe my father's family knew about me, but didn't want anything to do with me. After all, I only knew ten percent of my mother's side of my parents' story. So I was opening the door and entering the unknown. I needed to be careful. I could be taking the lid off a lovely box of chocolates . . . or a huge can of worms!

But I was dying to know more about my father, what he looked like, where he came from, did he just do-a-runner, what kind of person he really was, and of course, the obvious, did he love my mum? In fact, I was desperate for any details. Did he smoke? Did he drink? The tiniest bit of information was so important to me and I was excited by the possibilities of what I might find. For the first time, I felt I could finally make progress and it was no longer prohibitively expensive or impossible to find more information about my mysterious and elusive father – Henry Freeman.

*Left to **Right**:*
*My father-in-law Frank with **John**.*
*Christmas Day **1990**.*
*The day I was told that my father **was***
Henry Freeman.

11 Hospital Records

I began exploring the smaller website forums for family history, of which there are many, and eventually I stumbled upon a small website called familytreeforum.com, which was fairly new at that time. After reading a few of the threads I decided to join this free website and explain the catch-22 situation I found myself in when trying to obtain information about my father from the Royal Free Hospital. What I didn't know then, was that the decision to join this small website would take me on a journey of discovery into my father's life that I could never have imagined.

I suppose you could say that this chapter marks a turning point in my research. It shows how, with help from a bunch of amateur researchers, I uncovered information about my father and his roots which has left me wondering if there is some instinct or memory locked away, hidden within the depths of our DNA. Because in finding my father's family, I have found thought provoking roots that have literally made the hairs on the back of my neck stand on end.

To this day, I don't have a clue who many of these amateur genealogists are, they are just members of a website using usernames, just like myself. But I do know that they are scattered around the four corners of this globe, from the UK to Australia, Canada, America, Israel, Italy and also from a boat last reported to be anchored off the coast of Martinique.

Although I had previously joined many of the bigger websites, a few of which I have already mentioned, I liked the look of FTF, as it's called, because there were no adverts and emails asking for money. There were no records to search; this website was purely a free forum, a self-help-group where you could ask or give advice and gain experience from watching how other researchers uncover their information. If you were lucky, you could also link up to a researcher who, could be researching the same family you were researching, much the same way as Susan found me and we shared our information on our Welsby trees.

The members seemed friendly towards each other, as if they had known each other for a long time, at least online. I clicked onto the home page and then to the research forums where I found the following message:

There will always come a point in your family history research when you hit the dreaded 'brick wall'. In other words, you are completely and utterly stuck. This is when the Family Tree Forum membership can come to your aid.

My brick wall was the size of China's, and up to now, nobody had been able to help me to knock it down by finding either Henry Freeman's death listing or to get around the problem of acquiring any information about him from the Royal Free Hospital, unless I could produce documental evidence that proved I was his daughter, which I could not. I began reading other researcher's threads and noticed the amount of time and effort members were giving to help each other with their research. I came across one thread that I found fascinating, and much more complicated than the problems I was facing. The lady who had started this thread had been researching for many years, and her family was shrouded in secrecy with complicated issues relating to the Second World War, which involved the Official Secrets Act and sensitive Government documents, which were closed. Some members suggested that she should approach an investigative journalist who could perhaps access the information that she needed from these documents, or to hire a private detective as she was hitting brick walls in every direction and getting nowhere with her research. I had also considered the services of a private detective many times myself, but there's no way of estimating the cost of such an undertaking. So this member was in the same boat that I was in.

If, as I was myself at that time, you are unfamiliar with website forums, I will explain; a thread is simply the name given to a topic you want to discuss. You start a thread, give it a title and then other members can post messages, which display the times and dates posted, and they can share their experience with you. Or another member might read your thread to find answers to their own questions. It's a bit like leaving a message on a message board, but you never reveal your true identity, personal details or mention a living person by name.

So I decided to dive in and introduce myself using the username Wallaby, which was one of the nicknames John gave me when I was growing up. I started a thread under the title 'Hospital Records', as this was my brick wall. Some of the wording of my first post will now be familiar to you as I have used it elsewhere in this book:

14 Feb 2009 at 17.11pm.

Hi Everyone,

I have just registered today. I'm very new to the whole area of family tree research, so I will be posting some very green questions! Although, from what I've read in the forum while I was waiting in the queue to be 'fully installed' I can see that there are plenty of experts amongst the members of this website. I'm from Liverpool and in my mid-50s. I've been married for twenty-nine years, but we have no children. Apart from a 2nd cousin on my mum's side, I have no close family left that I know of.

My father has been a complete mystery throughout my life, as my mother never married him, or anyone else. She had me at the age of forty, which must have been a difficult thing to go through in the 1950s with her being from a small Catholic family with no money. I later discovered that the reason for all the secrecy was that my father was Jewish.

My mum was a very quiet person and never bothered with men. I've been told that there was never another man in her life other than my dad, who she had kept a secret from when she was only about fifteen years old. The embarrassment and shame I felt as a child for being illegitimate, has now been replaced with pride, for a woman who struggled all her life to bring up her love child. It was after my mum died in 1989, that I first uncovered the details of my father. I have his name and his last address. He died in the Royal Free Hospital in May 1984. But even with this information, I can't find his death listing.

Seemingly, in 1987, my mum wrote a letter enquiring about him to the warden at the apartments where he lived in London and she enclosed an s.a.e. The warden's reply gave my mum the news of his death. It was a sad ending to a sad story.

I have found lots of information on my mum's family but trying to uncover anything about my father is where I'm coming up against brick walls, even though I have his name and his address.

The Royal Free Hospital declined to give me any details of his hospital records, because of data protection. The only information that I have of his life here in Liverpool during the Second Word War was that he had some sort of scrap metal business, maybe located around the south end of Liverpool's inner-city, but, I don't know the name of the business, or even if it was his business, or a family business. I'm not sure where to go from here and there lies my first cry for help! I look forward to any pointers from anyone who reads this post.

Thank you for reading this.

Wallaby

It was so unlike me to pour my heart out in this way, but remaining incognito and hiding behind a username gave me some Dutch courage. I had hoped for some advice, maybe in a few days or weeks, and I was just about to log out to prepare our meal when replies began to appear on my thread from other members, with lots of advice about applying for hospital records, regulations of the Data Protection Act and messages of welcome.

Some of the members asked for my father's name so that they could help trace him, and at first I was hesitant about giving his details because although these members seemed genuinely helpful, I still worried about disclosing my father's information. Up to this point, I had given only the gist of my parents' story without naming names. But I needed help, and what attracted me to FTF was the fact that it was small, in terms of membership numbers, and not well known. So I felt that I wasn't shouting my parents' business from the rooftops.

Some of the members began researching and coming back with an assortment of Henry Freemans who had died within the London area around the time Henry Freeman had died, but just as I had found myself, none of the Henry Freemans that they found matched a May 1984 death. At first, the replies suggesting Henry Freeman candidates and advice were being posted slowly from a few members who were actively searching, and I was replying to each of them easily enough, but then as more members logged on and read my thread the replies were being posted so fast that I could hardly keep up with them. Shortly after six o'clock, I had more than a couple of dozen replies with lots of good advice from members who were thinking outside the box. However, absolutely nothing had been found for Henry Freeman. Some members were not holding out much hope about finding him without more details from the hospital, and they also explained how difficult Jewish research could be. It appeared my father could remain as much a mystery to me in death as he had been in life.

Then, completely out of the blue, the following message was posted from a UK member who, up to that point, had not posted before.

Hi Wallaby and welcome to FTF,

*I can't be 100% sure, but I know that the Royal Free Hospital comes under Camden Register Office and I found this one: **Harry** Freeman. Age at death: 76 years. His death was registered in May 1984. Page 2092. Volume 14. Birth Date: 17 Nov 1907.*

I have lots of 'Henrys' in my tree that appear as 'Harry' on the censuses, so this could possibly be him.

Joan of Archives

Harry? Henry could be Harry? My heart sank and I felt physically sick. If this was a film or perhaps a television series then this would be an appropriate time to stop and take a commercial break or to maybe continue next week, as this next part of my parents' story has been the most difficult for me to explain, because when I read this information that Joan of Archives had found, I realised that I had made the biggest mistake of my life and I have nobody to blame apart from my own blinkered stupidity.

My mind went back to a mysterious telephone call to my business many years before. I'm not certain of the exact date of the call, but I had opened other branches of my business and the *Liverpool Echo* had done an editorial piece on it around about April 1984. My friend Linda took the call, which was from a woman who sounded elderly and who had a London accent. She asked to speak to me personally and refused to give Linda any further details, but she had asked for me by my name. I spoke to this lady, who sounded confused, and she told me that it had been disclosed to her that a friend of herself and her husband had a daughter. She referred to their friend only as 'Harry' and she explained that they had been shown a cutting from a Liverpool newspaper about their friend's daughter's business. She added that this had really shocked them, because they never knew their friend to have any family whatsoever. I could hear a man's voice in the background, who I assumed was the lady's husband, reading aloud from the newspaper cutting, and he was reading the editorial that the *Liverpool Echo* had written about *my* business!

I can usually handle anything that life throws at me, but this was completely out of the blue and it really unnerved me. I explained that they must be mistaken as my father had died when I was a baby, which is what I had been told and, at that time, had always believed. I asked her if she could give me any further details about their friend, his full name, address and telephone number, but my questions seemed to cause her to back away, as if she felt that she had said too much. I heard a man's voice whispering something that I couldn't quite catch and she ended the call quickly, saying something about checking their information. This was before you could dial 1471 to retrieve a caller's number, and I remember getting off the telephone shaking like a leaf.

The next day I went to see my mum who had not long had her second mastectomy, and she was still quite poorly at the time, so without making a big song and dance about the telephone call, I diplomatically quizzed her, nonchalantly fudging it by explaining that a girl I knew mentioned her Uncle Harry was asking how she was.

''arry who?' she asked, looking puzzled, as she poured me a cup of tea.

I explained that I didn't know his surname but I thought he might live somewhere in or around the London area. My mum didn't bat an eyelid and managed to convince me that she didn't know anyone called Harry.

Mark, a friend of ours who was adopted, told me he once had a woman who rang him quite regularly claiming to be his mum when his business first started to take off:

'You need to be very careful because you tend to get all kinds of cranks coming out the woodwork when your business starts to become successful. Your name was in the paper, so people can easily act on that. If they did not leave their name and number, then forget it. If this was genuine, it would be a letter you would receive, not a telephone call. Wait and see if they ring back.'

Well, the London couple never did ring back, so eventually I let it drop and forgot all about it. To now be told such news, over twenty-five years later was utterly soul destroying. I just wanted to close the lid of my laptop and think it all through, undisturbed.

I felt like I'd received some really bad news in a very public place and so I hesitated in answering Joan of Archives' message, and replied only to the members who were joining the thread for the first time, skirting around the main issue. I didn't know how to respond to this information that Joan of Archives had found. I was lost for words. It was so complicated, and I found it difficult to explain myself. I also felt like a complete dope. So for a while I said nothing other than to thank Joan for her help and to acknowledge that it was quite possible that the death she had found for *Harry* Freeman could be *Henry* Freeman.

By this time, messages from many more FTF members were being posted on my 'Hospital Records' thread, and in the midst of it all, a debate began on the location of the Royal Free Hospital, and alongside this debate, many messages were posted giving useful suggestions and helpful advice. In fact, I was overwhelmed with the amount of members offering help. I had hoped for some advice on how to get information from the Royal Free, but I didn't expect *this* amount of help and interest. Then, when the following message was posted I knew that I needed to tell the members about the telephone call.

The Royal Free Hospital is in Hampstead – don't know what registration district that comes under, it could be Camden. Odd though, because I thought, when I read your first post, that I remembered the Royal Free being on Holloway Road, N19 when I lived there in the 1960s. That hospital is now called the Whittington and the Whittington came up when I Googled for the Royal Free Hospital.

I hope I don't sound too negative here, but one or two things are bothering me about your information. Your mother wrote to Henry Freeman in the 1980s. This suggests that she knew where he was and had had some contact with him over the years, unless that was his last known address as far as she was concerned. If she was in contact with him, and he was your father, then why did you never meet him? Do you remember meeting any men as a child? If he never married, then why did he not marry your mother? They could have married in a civil ceremony, which would have been a lot better for you and for your mother than your illegitimacy at that time, even though it would not have satisfied either of their religions. Did your mother never speak of your father to you?

Sorry to ask so many questions, but this isn't sitting right for me at the moment.
OC

Well, I have many unanswered questions myself OC, and nobody to ask. So I can't answer or explain my mother's actions, or those of my father, but I will get to the bottom of it all. No, she never talked to me about him, but I do believe that they had some contact. Perhaps it was that he stopped writing to her and maybe that's why she eventually contacted the warden at his apartment. I don't know. I can only guess. My mum was a good person. It will all fit into place one day. For whatever reason she kept this so secret it will be okay with me, whatever I uncover. I have a feeling he might have kept an eye on me from a distance, because . . .
Wallaby

I went on to explain every detail about the telephone call. I felt embarrassed, as it was now blatantly obvious that this telephone call had been genuine all along. I was angry with the London couple for not giving me more details, but even more angry with myself for getting into such a state that day and failing to persuade them into giving me more details about their friend, Harry. But they had seemed as cautious with me as I was with them, which I had put down to them not being completely sure of their information. Besides, I had always believed what I had been told – that my father had died – and I assumed that he was also married, and that was why my mum had told me that ridiculous, made up story of him being killed in the war. But why had I not associated that telephone call to Henry Freeman when I found the letter? Shock? Grief? A million other problems all taking place at the same time? Or just plain stupidity? It was all crystal clear to me now, and yet I had not put two-and-two together when I found the letter, and neither did the few people close to me who knew.

By eight o'clock I'd had over fifty replies, and all the time I could think of nothing else other than that telephone call from the elderly couple with the London accent. The more I tried to pinpoint the timing of that call, the more horrified I became. The *Liverpool Echo* that featured my business was published around the third week in April 1984. It could have been sometime after that appeared that the couple had rung and . . . I had chased them away!

By the time Brian arrived home from work I was in bits. It had now sunk in that this couple might have been trying to establish if I was their friend's daughter, because their friend, Harry, was dying, or perhaps he had already died and maybe they were trying to find his next of kin.

If only they had given me more information about their friend, his full name instead of just, Harry! Perhaps I could have gone to see him if I had been given his address. I could have taken my mother to see him. I could have met my father before he passed away. I had dismissed that telephone call as just a mistake or a crank caller, and now I discover that Henry and Harry were both one and the same person, and now it was too late. Henry/Harry Freeman is long dead, and my mum too, and I can't turn the clock back.

The good thing about communicating through a computer screen is that you remain invisible. The people I was communicating with couldn't see how upset I was that night, and the members of FTF only knew me as Wallaby. So they carried on with their many questions, including the inevitable:

Was it possible Harry could have been married?
Kit

All my life I assumed that the secrecy surrounding my birth was that my father had been married. Until, after my mum died in 1989, my mum's niece, Mary, who was very close to my mum, told me of my mum's story. She told me my father's name was Henry Freeman and he was never married, as far as she knew, and that he was Jewish and my mum had no other man in her life other than him. Of course, I have no documental evidence that this is true other than the letter and knowing my cousin's sincerity and she has now died herself. Now, my only living relative that I know of is my cousin's daughter, who knows very little about all this. I am aware that some of this information may not be accurate, so I will be careful. I've no wish to cause any upset to any relatives that might exist and I am prepared for some . . . surprises!
Wallaby

To me, it felt like we were discussing somebody else's problem, not mine, as the members analysed my mother's dilemma, offering the various scenarios of why she and my father had not married. Some of the members were Jewish or had Jewish relatives, and they explained all the obstacles that I was bound to come up against and shared their anecdotes of the many brick walls they had experienced.

It could be that neither would convert to the other's religion so they couldn't marry, or that Henry/Harry's family would not have wanted him to marry-out to a gentile. I should imagine there could be loads of obstacles ahead of researching his side; if he was interred at a Jewish cemetery his headstone could well be in Hebrew so may need translating. He may also have been born with a different surname and it could have been anglicised to fit in with British life, especially if he had German origins, for instance. I must say, if I were in your shoes, I would definitely think it is worth while finding out if he was the man my mother fell in love with. Good luck in your search.

Joan of Archives

I had many messages of good luck and advice, far too many to select and place within the pages of this book. In fact, it has proved very difficult to sift through and choose the most relevant messages from my 'Hospital Records' thread to make this story easier for you, the person holding this book, to follow what, from then on, became the most complicated search for even the most experienced of professional researchers. But that night, when I replied to the messages on my thread, the only thing that was on my mind was that telephone call over twenty-five years before, coupled with the fact that I had blown my only chance of ever meeting my father. I agonised and beat myself up over this more than anything else, and I looked up the name Harry on the internet and read that the name was a short version of Harold, which I was aware of. But then when I read on, it also said that the name Harry, could also be another name for Henry. I was devastated.

While all these messages were being posted on my 'Hospital Records' thread, some members were still twittering on about the exact location of the Royal Free Hospital. It was quite bizarre. I felt like I was sitting among a group of complete strangers and listening to different conversations taking place around me all at the same time. After twenty years, I might have finally found my father, so it didn't matter to me if the Royal Free Hospital was in the middle of Timbuktu!

Before I got the chance to make any comment on the hospital's location, Peppie, a member of the forum who would later put a lot of time into my research, explained the confusion with the hospital's location, and then the following message was posted:

Thank you Peppie, you have made a doddering old fool very happy! Apologies to Wallaby for turning her thread into the maunderings of a senile old woman.
OC

Senile old woman, me eye! Please don't be misguided by the above post. This member, OC, whose full username is actually Olde Crone Holden, became so involved with my search that I eventually appointed her the project manager of my quest. Without the help of OC and many other members of this small website, I would still be looking for *Henry* Freeman, and never in a million years would I have found my late father.

It turned out that this 'doddering old fool', as she calls herself, had a mind like a filing cabinet, and I would later discover the reason why OC had analysed and probed into my story in her earlier post in such depth. OC had a plan . . .

12 An Unmarked Grave

I don't think I slept a wink that night with all the information floating around in my head. The next morning I logged on to the forum before I left for work and found dozens of messages had been left on my thread overnight from people who lived on the other side of the world. I tried to speed read as many as I could before dashing off to work. One message stopped me in my tracks and I got the shock of my life when I read . . .

Hi Wallaby and welcome to the forum,

There are many different Jewish cemeteries in and around London and which one is used depends on whether the family are e.g. Orthodox, Sephardic or Ashkenazi Jews and whether they have other burials in the cemetery. My grandfather was buried in Golders Green cemetery, although he lived in Essex.

However, I might have found Harry Freeman's burial. (Well, it's a Harry Freeman who was buried in May 1984) If you enter, Bushey–Harry Freeman–1984 in the search fields of the following link, you'll find it.

theus.org.uk/support services/find your family/burial records

If you contact them, they may be able to give you more details to establish if he's the right Harry. Good Luck.

Night Owl

I couldn't believe it. With the help of the members of FTF, within just twenty-four hours, not only had I been given a possible listing of Henry/Harry Freeman's death, but I might also have been given the location of his grave!

I clicked onto the link and followed the instructions that Night Owl had given me, and when this photograph came up, my stomach did cartwheels.

Grave Search

Cemetery:	Bushey
First name(s):	Harry
Last name:	Freeman
Year of Burial:	1984

SEARCH

First name(s)	Last name	Date of burial	Section	Row	Plot
HARRY	FREEMAN	28/05/1984	X29	11	389

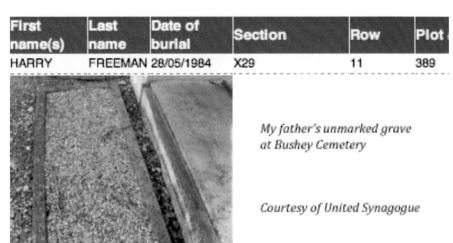

My father's unmarked grave at Bushey Cemetery

Courtesy of United Synagogue

Months went by before I received confirmation that this actually is my father's grave. United Synagogue confirmed that they had buried Harry Freeman ten days after his death on the 28 May 1984, after they had tried in vain to trace relatives. It is customary for Jewish people to be buried within one or two days of their death, before the next sun goes down, so they had indeed tried to find a relative.

I wrote to Rabbi Meir Salasnik at Bushey Synagogue in Hertfordshire and he was very helpful. He explained that the date Harry Freeman was buried was actually May bank holiday Monday, and that he had made enquiries and found that my father did not attend any local synagogue, which seemed to suggest that Harry did not practice his religion. Records are kept of seat rentals or purchases at synagogues, so this information can be useful to family history researchers. It's the Jewish equivalent of passing the plate around the congregation for a donation. I found my father's stoneless grave so sad. To me, it was like a pauper's grave.

Meanwhile, I waited impatiently for Harry Freeman's death certificate. It took two weeks, but it felt like two months. I passed the time by searching for a birth listing for him, based on the date of birth given on his death listing that Joan of Archives had found, which was the 17 November 1907.

I was extremely lucky that birth dates were now given on death listings, as this was not always the case for earlier deaths. Of course, at the time, I didn't know if my father was born in Liverpool or if he was an immigrant to this country. Or maybe he was born in London, and perhaps he had family there at one time and maybe that's why he was living in London when he died.

I searched over and over again, but couldn't find a birth listing for either Henry or Harry Freeman in Liverpool or anywhere else in the UK, for the last quarter of the year 1907. I checked again and again until one night, I noticed one possibility:

I've been searching findmypast.com for Harry Freeman's birth while waiting for his death certificate to arrive. I can't find any birth listing for a Harry or Henry Freeman in Liverpool or London, or anywhere in the UK. I'm using the date of birth of the 17 November 1907 as Joan of Archives has found on his death listing. The only possibility I have found is this one; Harry Freedman, whose birth was registered in the last quarter of 1907 in Liverpool.

I'm wondering if maybe his name was anglicised as Joan of Archives suggested in her earlier post? It's a long shot, but if it's the same Harry, I have also found a Harry Freedman on the 1911 census, aged three years old and he lived not far from the south end of Liverpool, which is where I was told my father had lived. But, his age is a year out. If this is the right person, then his father's name was Louis Freedman and the census states that Louis Freedman was a German National and there are many siblings, some with very Jewish sounding names. The census doesn't mention if his father is widowed or divorced and yet, there is no mother listed on the census with the family.

This could be a wild goose chase, but it's better than twiddling my thumbs while I'm waiting for his death certificate to arrive.
Wallaby

The following morning his death certificate arrived in the mail and I held my breath as I opened the envelope. I don't think my feet touched the floor when I flew to my laptop to post the following message:

The death certificate has arrived and IT'S HIM! Harry Freeman: Address: 13 Rose Bush Court, Parkhill Road, Hampstead, London. Occupation: It just says, Retired. So no leads there.

He died at the Royal Free Hospital, as we know, on the 18 May 1984. Date and Place of birth: 17 November 1907. Unfortunately, his place of birth is left blank. Name of Informant: S------ W-------------. Qualification: Occupier. Cause of Death: Deep Vein Thrombosis. Pneumonia. Date of Registration: 25 May 1984.

Oh, I can't believe this! I just want to say THANK YOU to everyone for your help.
Wallaby

My search had changed from what many of the members of FTF considered to be a complicated investigation that could take years, into finding my father's death listing, his grave, and possibly his birth and his family on the 1911 census and we had completely bypassed the Royal Free Hospital's records. The members were delighted, and more and more of them were leaving messages on my thread and taking an interest in my research now that we had something to get our teeth into and we knew what we were working with.

I tried to put this information together in my head. His death certificate mentioned he had pneumonia, which causes delusions, so perhaps the hospital or the elderly couple who had contacted me were trying to establish if he was lucid or just rambling. Or perhaps he'd had dementia for a long time and they could not make any sense of his sudden claim of having a daughter.

Perhaps he had already died, and letters were found among his personal things that my mother might have written to him. Even if my mum had put her address on the letters, which I very much doubt, as she never usually bothered putting her address on a note when she was writing to a close friend who already knew where she lived, and even if she did give her address, her handwriting was so shaky that it would be illegible to anyone who was unfamiliar with her scrawl.

It was around this time that my mother had her second mastectomy, so I can see why she had let so much time go by before writing to the warden at the apartments. Perhaps the only lead the London couple had to go on was the cutting from the editorial in the *Liverpool Echo*. Maybe my mother had sent him this cutting and she had received no reply, perhaps because he had already passed away by then. Or perhaps he was so ill by that time that he was unable to reply to my mother's letters, and maybe that's why my mum wrote to the warden at the apartments. Perhaps . . . Perhaps . . . Perhaps . . . this was all guesswork.

Have you fully gone through all your mother's things? Just checking there are no boxes in the attic or something that you are planning to go through one day. If your mother had such a long-standing and secret relationship, I would have thought she would have kept some memento from your father. Although of course maybe it is something so innocent you haven't realised.

Kit

*Yes Kit, I've gone through everything. My mum didn't have many belongings and I can't see anything else that would give me a clue. Apart from a few things that she kept all her life, such as the imitation pearl earrings she's wearing in her photograph, which I've used as my Avatar image on my thread. Although she never wore them, she kept them all her life and I've always felt that I should keep them too. So Kit, I think **I** am my mum's only memento of my father, and those last few words of your sentence above, are so true of me when I was growing up. Although, I would change the word 'innocent' to . . . stupid!*

Now, everything in my entire life fits into place. Sometimes when you are too close to something, you just can't see it.

I'm not sure where I go with my research from here. I now have his death certificate, which gives his last address so I know I have the right person. But, I can't see a birth listing for him anywhere in the UK. The only close match is for this Harry Freedman in Liverpool who I've mentioned in my earlier post and he is also listed on the 1911 census. Although, his age is stated as three years old on that census, which puts his birth year at 1908 not 1907. Although he was born in the last quarter of 1907, so maybe this is him.

You wouldn't believe it, the copy of his death certificate was printed on 19 February. That's my mum's birthday! It's almost like it's their way of confirming everything and letting me know I'm on the right track.

Wallaby

The members thought it was worthwhile ordering the birth certificate of this Harry Freedman, who I had found born in Liverpool, even though the information on the 1911 census didn't match his age, they thought that he could still be the same Harry. They also thought that the person who registered Harry Freeman's death was most probably hospital staff. This was confirmed a few months later when I wrote to a lady at the Friends of the Royal Free Hospital, who was a contact of Peppie's.

While we waited for Harry Freedman's birth certificate to arrive, the members of FTF sent me details of the pogroms that took place in what was then Imperial Russia. Pogroms, or the fear of pogroms, caused many Jews to flee their homes during the 1800s and early 1900s. So I embarked on reading everything I could lay my hands on about the turbulent history of eastern Europe, the political upheaval during this period and the effect it had on the Jews. Then, the final outcome – the Holocaust.

I educated myself about the various political and socioeconomic reasons behind why these people left their homes and often their families behind. What a chance they took, often travelling in the squalor of steerage. Many of them were illiterate back in those days, with little money and often no job to come to. It was a difficult decision for anyone to make, even today. And yet, these people left in their millions to come to live in the overcrowded cities of London's East End, Leeds, Manchester, Glasgow, Wales, Dublin and the slums of inner-city Liverpool, a mere stone's throw from Little Italy where my nan Annie raised her family.

The main ports of departure were Hamburg, Hanover and Bremen in Germany, Antwerp in Belgium, Le Havre, Cherbourg and Marseilles in France or the Italian ports of Palermo and Messina. They travelled to these ports by boat, train or overland on foot. Up until the 1870s immigrants made the journey on sail ships, which carried cargo such as rolls of cloth and spices. Immigrants were human cargo, filling any space that remained and maximising profits for shipping companies who advertised the fares in the major European cities. Although steam ships were introduced from the mid-1800s, conditions for steerage passengers didn't improve a great deal and so many immigrants continued to travel on sail ships, maybe they were a cheaper option than the new steamers.

The main ports of arrival in England were Liverpool and Southampton along with Hull and Grimsby. In Ireland, Queenstown was the major port, along with docks at Dublin, Belfast, Limerick and Galway. Many immigrants continued on to countries such as America, Canada and South Africa.

Some immigrants went to family or friends who had previously paved the way. Those who had no family to go to were helped in their resettlement by the organisation known as, *Landsmanschaft,* which was a network of social support, run by Jews for Jewish immigrants. This organisation helped immigrants financially and practically, such as finding a place to live close to other Jews who had come from the same *shtetl* back home, so they were at least close to their own kind. *Landsmanschaft* also helped immigrants to find work and whatever help they needed until they were able to stand on their own two feet. Travel information was translated into Yiddish, Hebrew and Russian and it was distributed throughout the *shtetls*. Jewish emigration was generally well organised, but I've also read plenty of horror stories of immigrants who fell victim to bogus ticket agents and never reached their chosen destination. Some were sold a ticket at Hamburg, or whatever port they had departed from, to take them to America or wherever their intended destination was, only to find that the ticket took them no further than ports such as Liverpool. With no money and little choice, many stayed in Liverpool and tried to earn the rest of their passage, but then changed their plans, or had their plans changed for them and settled for what they had – Liverpool.

Liverpool's Jewish Quarter, as it was known, stretched around the streets branching from Brownlow Hill, where many artisans, kosher shops and businesses traded their wares. Tailors, cabinetmakers, watchmakers, hawkers and woodcarvers were the main trades, each of them working every hour God sent.

Strangely, this was not my first introduction to the persecution of Jews. Not that it was ever a part of the Catholic school curriculum in the 1950s; the only thing I remember being taught about Jews in school was that they didn't believe that Christ was the Messiah and were still waiting for him, and were therefore, according to Old Tooie, bound to roam the earth as nomads until the end of time. There was also a vague hint of the Jews having something to do with Christ's crucifixion, which was never quite clear to our childish minds and served to do nothing more than to confuse the life out of us, given that Jesus was himself a Jew. It didn't make sense because it was never explained in full. So I would come home from school and tell me mam and she would tell me not to listen to such feckin' rubbish and I would go into John's bedroom and read the books that *did* make sense to me.

But there was nobody to knit all this together, nobody to explain the information that was being fed to us; was it opinion, fiction, fact or just feckin' rubbish? In any other subject, if A didn't line up with B, we knew what questions to ask and the reply would be explained; we didn't get: 'Have you no faith, child?!' Of course, as kids, we didn't know enough to know what questions *to* ask. And besides, we didn't have the words. So we didn't ask questions and eventually I stopped listening.

My education about the plight of the Jewish people was brought to me courtesy of the BBC, from watching what I shouldn't have been watching. Why would this very adult subject interest me? As an adult, I often wondered why I had been so interested in Jews being exterminated by Nazis, at an age when my mates were more interested in *Doctor Who* and who was being exterminated by Daleks!

I remember when my nan, who was supposed to be minding me, would sneak out, leaving me home alone. She would tell me that she was only going to see Mrs Volante, but instead she would sneak off to the Morning Star and I would be left with our dog Lassie and an open fire, and to watch all kinds of stuff on the telly. I often watched programmes about the Second World War and even though it terrified me watching Jews or anybody who opposed the Nazis being persecuted in concentration camps, I still forced myself to watch it. I didn't associate the piles of dead bodies with real people. I was too young to understand why they were so thin and stiff. To me they looked more like dummies from a shop window. Although it was a strange programme for me to be interested in at that age, for some reason I was drawn to watch it. Something in me wanted to understand why this was happening. What had these people done to deserve this? Why was this allowed to happen?

When my mum came home from work, there would be blue murder when my nan arrived home drunk. If that happened today I would probably be taken into care. But my mum could never be mad at my nan for long; she understood her hard life and problems.

Harry Freedman's birth certificate seemed to take ages to arrive. I was a bit sceptical that the name Freeman had been originally Freedman, but I had my fingers crossed because the family I had found on the Liverpool 1911 census was fascinating. They were living at no. 49 Pleasant Street and there were eight elder siblings listed along with Harry on the census. Surely these siblings would have some descendants who might have kept a photograph and would perhaps give me more information about Henry/Harry Freeman/Freedman.

The 1911 census stated that Louis Freedman, who was the head of this large family, was forty-three years of age, and he was a German national. *German?* I remembered what Joan of Archives had explained about German Jewish immigrants anglicising their names. The census stated that Louis was married and gave his occupation as 'Hawker, own account', which meant that he had worked for himself. I wondered if he had ever knocked at our door! My image of a hawker was what we used to call the door-knockers.

Although Louis had stated that he was married, not widowed or divorced, no wife was mentioned on the census. Many of the children had Jewish-sounding names. The eldest son, Gedaliah, was listed as being aged twenty, single, and working as a woodcarver, and he had been born in Leeds. Next was another son, Hyman, who was eighteen, also single, and he was a sewing machinist in tailoring and was born in Liverpool.

I wondered if Hyman had ever made a suit for my Uncle John, or perhaps the one and only tailored suit that my mother possessed and had kept all her life, and which I just loved.

It looked like it was from the 1940s in style. The jacket was short and pinched into the waist and the pencil skirt was calf length with a split in the back. I borrowed it one day when I was going to work at Biba on Kensington High Street in the early 1970s and her eyes filled up when I walked out of our bedroom wearing it. 'May I borrow this suit, mam?' The designers at Biba loved it. It was the early days of my working life and I loved everything about design, from clothes to architecture, and my Aunt Maggie's flair for buying vintage clothes from flea markets and turning them back-to-front, inside-out or upside-down had rubbed off on me.

Other children on the 1911 census included a daughter, Nellie, who was sixteen, and another son, fourteen-year-old Samuel, an errand boy, again in tailoring. Nellie and Samuel were both born in Liverpool.

Then came a bolt of lightning, which seemed to leap out at me from the census page: another son, Abraham, was listed as being thirteen years old and he was born in . . . RUSSIA!

My eyes remained glued onto the word Russia before I could bring myself to move down the list to the next child, who was twelve-year-old Elias, followed by Isaac, aged ten, both of them also born in Liverpool. A gap of five years followed Isaac before another son, five-year-old Terrence, was born in Liverpool, and at the very bottom of the list was Harry Freedman, who was the youngest of this large family, at only three years of age.

Germany, Russia, Leeds, Liverpool . . . was it possible that this could be my father's family? I was keeping my fingers crossed that it was, as I was fascinated about Abraham being born in Russia, the country that I'd always been drawn to as a child. Louis Freedman, the father of this large family, certainly had his hands full, given that there was no wife listed on the census. So who and where was Louis' wife?

When Harry Freedman's birth certificate arrived, I admit, I opened it half-heartedly. I understood what Joan of Archives had explained about names changing, but I didn't expect Harry Freedman to have the same date of birth as Harry Freeman's death certificate had given, because I thought that would be too many name changes. I had been really lucky up to now, but I was bracing myself for some disappointment.

The registrar's elaborate handwriting was difficult to read on the birth certificate, so I scanned it into my laptop and zoomed onto his date of birth. You could have knocked me down with a feather when the date matched with the date of birth on his death certificate. The address was the same address as the Freedman family I had found on the 1911 census, or at least it was the same street, Pleasant Street, which was not far from Brownlow Hill, although it was a different house number – 34, not 49 – which it was on the 1911 census.

His birth certificate gave his father as Louis Freedman, and the census gave Louis Freedman as the head of the household. So it was definitely the same family!

I now had my father's death certificate and I knew where he had been buried. I also had his birth certificate and I had found his family on the 1911 Liverpool census. I had found the beginning and the end of my father's life. The only thing I needed to do now was to fill in the middle bit, and find what my father had done in those seventy-six years of his life. Not exactly a walk in the park, but at least I was on the right track. With the collective help from members of FTF, I had at last found Henry Freeman and Harry Freedman. I had finally found the daddy of all mysteries . . . my father.

13 My Bubba Rebecca

The birth certificate for Harry Freedman has arrived this morning and his date of birth is the same date that's on his death certificate, the 17 November 1907! It gives his father's name as Louis Freedman and he has registered the birth signing with a cross.

It says: Father: 'This is the mark (X) of Louis Freedman' Address: 34 Pleasant Street, Liverpool: Name of Mother: Rebecca Freedman. Late Cohen and formerly Cohen.

It's him, and it looks like Louis Freedman and Rebecca Cohen were my grandparents!
Wallaby

The members were absolutely thrilled, and those who were logged on searched for more information. Margaretmarch, who was another great help to my research, advised me to downloaded the original image of the census for Louis Freedman. Margaret explained the original image gave more details than the household image, which I had downloaded from findmypast.co.uk, but the cost of the original image was thirty credits, at that time, as opposed to the household image, which costs ten credits, unless you have a subscription, which at that time I didn't. Thinking I was about to embark on a journey that was going to cost me an arm and a leg, I had bought credits in a feeble effort to control my budget. I later learnt that I was being pennywise, pound foolish, as my mum would say, and I now have a subscription so I don't need to be watching the meter.

So my father's birth certificate gave his mother's name as Rebecca Cohen, and it was listed as 'Late Cohen and formerly Cohen'. It appeared Rebecca had been married before she married Louis Freedman, to a man whose surname was the same surname as her own. The name, Rebecca Cohen, must be one of the most common names in Jewish families. Tracing her was not going to be easy, but I was delighted to at least finally know the names of my Jewish grandfather and my grandmother – in Yiddish terms, my zayde and my bubba.

The house number was different from the 1911 census, but families often moved within the same street in those days, if maybe a better house became available, which had more bedrooms or perhaps a bathroom. But where was Harry's mother, Rebecca? Why had she not been listed with the rest of the family on the 1911 census? Unlike previous censuses, the 1911 had a new section of questions to be completed by married women, such as:

How many completed years the marriage had lasted?

How many children were born alive to the present marriage?

How many children were still living?

How many children had died?

Louis had no need to complete this part, but he did – or rather his son Samuel did, as it was Samuel's signature on the census. It stated that Louis had been married for seven years, which meant that Rebecca must have been Louis' second wife, and so some children listed on the census were obviously from a previous marriage, most probably the five year gap between Isaac's birth in 1900 and Terrence's birth in 1905 indicated the break between the two marriages. Louis' census also showed that there were three children from his second marriage to Rebecca, with two children still living – indicating that another child had been born, and had died.

Rebecca's whereabouts remained a mystery for a long time. But eventually it was Maudarby, or Moggie as she is known on FTF, and who was a godsend to my research, found Rebecca listed on the 1911 census in some sort of institution. However, Rebecca's surname was listed as *Friedman*, not Freedman *or* Freeman. This wouldn't be the last time my father's family's surname was found spelt in this way.

Could this be Louis' wife in 1911? Rebecca Friedman born 1874, in Russia, age thirty-six years, in an institution in Liverpool. Her year of marriage was 1905.
Moggie

The institution turned out to be the old Liverpool Royal Infirmary, Pembroke Place, where Rebecca was a patient. Confusion then followed when Margaretmarch noticed that Rebecca's census didn't quite tally with the information that Louis had given on his census. According to Rebecca, she had been married to Louis for *six* years, not seven, and she had *five* children, not three, with three children still living and *two* children who had died. Louis had stated that only *one* child had died. But what made the hairs on the back of my neck stand on end was the next section. Place of birth: RUSSIA. My grandmother Rebecca was also from Russia. I had Russian roots!

Alas, my excitement at discovering my Russian *babushka* was short-lived, as was my grandmother, because we found that Rebecca had died just two weeks after the 1911 census had been taken, from cancer of the oesophagus. She died at home: no. 49 Pleasant Street. Her husband Louis was by her side. Rebecca was only thirty-six years of age.

We could only conclude from the 1911 census for Rebecca, particularly bearing in mind that she was then only two weeks from her death, that she had misunderstood, and so she had listed *all* her children from *both* marriages. Russian-born Abraham Freedman, who was listed as 'son to head,' on the 1911 census, was probably Rebecca's son from her first marriage, therefore Louis' stepson. So he had been born with the name, Abraham Cohen. Also, his birth was too close to the birth of Elias, so he could not have been a child of Louis' from his first marriage. This explained how Abraham had been born in Russia.

It helped my research immensely when Arnold Lewis kindly sent a list of burials for variations of the name Freeman who had been interred at Rice Lane and Broadgreen Jewish cemeteries. Arnold, who is a Liverpool Jewish community archivist has undertaken the huge task of photographing and documenting all the headstones in Liverpool's Jewish cemeteries. It was from Arnold's cemetery list that I found that Rebecca had been buried at Rice Lane.

I asked permission to visit Rice Lane's closed cemetery in the hope of finding a stone on her grave with some inscription that would give me a lead, but sadly I found only the indentation of graves in the ground. Of course, only the well-to-do could afford a gravestone back in those days. It was becoming obvious that my father's family were just as poor and as hardworking as my mum's family had been, with just as many problems. We would later find that my grandfather Louis had actually been widowed twice up to now, and it appeared from the census that he had also buried at least one child, and was now left with eight children, plus his stepson Abraham, to raise. It must have been a very difficult time for him. Whether Irish, Italian or Jewish, it appears we were sailing together on the same boat.

My father's family were beginning to unfold before my eyes and I was dying to know more. The members of FTF were fantastic and I now realised why OC had questioned my mother's story in such depth that night when I first joined the forum on 14 February 2009. She obviously wanted to be certain that I had my facts right before she and the other members put so much time into my research. Of course I didn't immediately give the entire details of my mum's story on my first post because I still felt that I needed to be cautious. Besides, I didn't expect this amount of help from the members. What I was hoping for was some advice so that I could toddle off and try the Royal Free Hospital again. I didn't expect the amount of help and support that eventually grew into a small army of members over the following months. A small army that helped me to bypass the Royal Free Hospital and find my father's family without their records.

I opened an online account with the General Register Office, gro.gov.uk. It's the direct source and cheapest way of ordering certificates. Family research can cost an arm and a leg if you're not careful, and many people believe it to be beyond their budget, as I did myself. The television series *Who Do You Think You Are* is fascinating to watch. However, the subject is always a celebrity, of course, and money seems to be no object when it comes to obtaining certificates. If it's found that the celebrity has a John Smith in his or her tree and there are three potential candidates for the birth of that person, they think nothing of ordering all three certificates to find which John Smith is the right one for them, and the certificates arrive the next day. Obviously, this is necessary for the programme, but the expense of next-day delivery on top of website subscriptions mounts up, so you and I need to find a cheaper, if not a free way.

Many local libraries hold family history courses and their computers give free access to ancestry and findmypast, but joining a free genealogy forum gives you the opportunity of working alongside experienced and novice researchers, and the experience is invaluable. The results can be remarkable, without having to spend the family's fortune to find them.

Margaret in Burton was another brilliant researcher who put a lot of time into my search, and it wasn't long before she found the birth listings in the GRO index for most of Louis' children. She had included all the necessary reference numbers, and over time I applied for all of the birth certificates for my father's siblings as and when I needed them.

The next part of the search had us tearing our hair out. Depending on whether Louis or Rebecca had given the correct number of children who had been born and had died on the 1911 census, then there were either one or two more children to find, who had died. Although OC didn't think it was worth pursuing, given that these children would have no descendants. Nevertheless, I wanted to know more. All this information helped me to get a handle on my father and his family. To learn of all their struggles helped me to paint a picture in my mind of how my father's family had lived their lives.

To give Louis credit, he was consistent with the spelling of his surname when he registered the births of his children. All the children born before Harry had the surname Friedman, although Harry was registered as Freedman, but perhaps that was just a mistake. So we looked for the births of children with the name of Friedman or Freedman who had been born between 1905 – which was the year Louis gave as being married to Rebecca – and the early part of 1911, and who had died within that same time frame. Most likely the births, and also the deaths of these children, had been registered in Liverpool. In order to narrow down the research we needed Terrence's date of birth to see if it was feasible to slot the birth of another child in, between Terrence and my father Harry. Terrence's birth certificate gave the date of the 25 October 1905 and he had been registered as Teri. We knew Harry was born on the 17 November 1907. So that only left us a small window in late 1906, and from 1908 to Rebecca's death in April 1911, to search. There was no clear result for either spelling of the surname, until Breckland Jane, another member of FTF who lived in Tasmania, posted the following message:

Could this be a child who died?
1907 Qtr 4. Jacob Freedman. Age 0, Liverpool. Vol. 8b. Page 99. I can't find a matching birth.
Breckland Jane

In the records for Broadgreen cemetery I had found a Jacob Freedman who had died in the Liverpool Workhouse Infirmary and had been buried on the 8 December 1907, but his age was given as seven *years* old. I ordered Jacob Freedman's death certificate, age 0, which meant that the little fellow had not reached his first birthday. I wanted to see who his father was and to confirm his age, as I was curious to see if he was perhaps my father's twin brother. But Jacob's death certificate gave his age as seven *months* old, not seven years, and he had died on the 7 December 1907. The cause of death was tuberculosis and meningitis and his father was Louis Freedman of 34 Pleasant Street. So the Jacob who had been buried in Broadgreen cemetery on the 8 December 1907 had to be the same Jacob as he was buried the day after he had died, in accordance with the Jewish religion. Given Harry's date of birth of the 17 November 1907, it didn't make sense for Jacob to have died at seven months old, as the two pregnancies would have overlapped. Yet he was not Harry's twin and we could find no birth recorded for Jacob. One of the archivist at the Liverpool Register Office advised me to always trust the information given on death certificates.

We considered the possibility of my father being born premature, but it was thought to be unlikely in the early 1900s for a baby to have survived at only five or six months into the pregnancy. So, this mystery was shelved for more than twelve months and little baby Jacob was like a piece of a jigsaw puzzle that had fallen down the back of the sofa.

Workhouse records were closed for one hundred years after the last patient was discharged, but I was able to check the workhouse discharge records on microfiche at the Liverpool Records Office. I found that baby Jacob had been discharged, dead. The number seven was placed in a box under the heading 'age'. Unfortunately, it didn't state whether he was seven years or seven months old, so I was none the wiser. I searched admission records, which were still in original book form, but all original records had moved to a temporary home while the Liverpool Central Library's Grade II-listed building on William Brown Street and home to the Liverpool Records Office, underwent a £50 million restoration.

The admission records often gave more details than the discharge records, and I also found creed records. So I made an appointment to view these records at their temporary home. Looking at a cross section of all these records helped me to conclude that baby Jacob was seven *years* old, not seven months, so it was actually his death certificate that gave the wrong information. This meant that Jacob Freedman must have been born around 1900, before Rebecca and Louis married. Abraham was listed on the 1911 census as Louis' son, yet Abraham could only have been Rebecca's son and therefore Louis' stepson. So we concluded that Jacob must have been Louis' stepson too, and like Abraham, also born in Russia even though his death certificate stated that Louis was his father. So death records can be wrong.

We know nothing about Rebecca's first husband, other than his surname was Cohen. Although adoption was not legal until 1926 in the UK, Abraham and Jacob were both Cohens who had been given the name Freedman when Rebecca married my grandfather Louis.

Old records are fraught with human errors such as Jacob's wrong age. Often the information was wrongly transcribed. With no photocopying machines back then, all copies were laboriously handwritten, leaving plenty of opportunities for mistakes. I was happy in the knowledge that I knew all about baby Jacob; he had been my grandmother's son and my father's half-brother, and little Jacob's brief life had now been acknowledged over one hundred years after he had died. I then left the little fellow to rest in peace.

Based on the numbers Rebecca gave in the census, we knew that there was possibly one more deceased child of Rebecca's to find, to either my grandfather Louis or to Rebecca's first husband. I found him quite by accident, when I was looking for Rebecca and Abraham.

I looked at the admission, discharge and creed records for the old Liverpool Royal Infirmary where Rebecca was listed as a patient on the 1911 census, in the hope that the records would reveal a little more information about my grandmother. I was grasping at straws, trying to find anything that would open a door into my Russian grandmother's past. I also looked at the Workhouse Infirmary records again, in the hope that her son Abraham may have been treated there at sometime in his life. Unexpectedly, it was my grandmother Rebecca who I found in the Workhouse Infirmary's admission records. The records revealed that she was admitted on the 19 December 1910, then discharged on the 4 January 1911. Rebecca's admission number was 2438. I spotted a handwritten note alongside her record. The note was not much more than a faint watermark and impossible to decipher, so I took a photograph of the page and also any other pages listing variations of the name Friedman and Cohen in the hope of finding Abraham, and once home I enhanced all the photographs. The note on Rebecca's record read, 'allowed out without child'. What child?

I began enhancing and enlarging the other pages I had photographed and carefully studied every Friedman, Freedman and Freeman on every photograph hoping to find any information about this unknown child. On the last photograph I found the admission record of a baby named Bertie Friedman. He was admitted on 26 December 1910. One week after Rebecca was admitted. There was a side note on his record which gave me goose bumps. The note read, 'Mother 2438'. This was the admission number for my grandmother Rebecca. This was the child Rebecca was allowed to go home without.

The information which was given in his discharge notes read, 'Died 28 January 1911'. I had found the missing child who had died. He had only been included within the numbers of children who had been born and who had died in the 1911 census. Now he had a name – Bertie Friedman. Now he was real.

I found his birth listed as Bernard Friedman. Bertie had been born on 13 May 1910. He was the son of Rebecca and Louis Friedman, so he had been my father's full brother. The information on Rebecca's discharge notes helped me to understand the overall picture of what had happened, providing a detailed timeline of heartbreaking events.

After being discharged on the 4 January, Rebecca was readmitted two weeks later. Workhouse Infirmary records state that she had surgery to relieve an obstruction in her throat. On the 27th of the same month, Rebecca was then transferred from the Workhouse Infirmary to the Liverpool Royal Infirmary, where she was then listed on the 1911 census. The following day, little Bertie passed away at the Workhouse. He was just nine months old.

Bertie's death certificate gave the cause of his death as, otitis media (middle ear infection) and pneumonia. The poor little fellow didn't stand a chance.

Rebecca was not discharged until the 6 April 1911. Just ten days later, she was dead. We now know from her death certificate that the obstruction in her throat was cancer of the oesophagus. Louis had lost his baby son and his wife in only a few short months.

Perhaps Rebecca was not confused when she gave the details of *all* her children from both her marriages for the 1911 census. Maybe she knew *exactly* what she was doing. Perhaps recording all her children was important to Rebecca. Maybe she was well aware that she would not be listed on the next census and wanted all her children to be recorded in some way, and remembered. If Rebecca had not done this, I would never have known about Bertie or her other son, Jacob.

My thoughts drifted to the children my Catholic grandparents Will and Annie Welsby buried. Mary, James and William-John, the two baby boys who had never been spoken of. Perhaps people were afraid of being judged and blamed by some people in the community. Ashamed of the filthy living conditions that they had to live in. I remember my nan would often shrink my clothes because she would boil them in the gas boiler in the back-kitchen and my mother bleached everything in sight, including her false teeth. No Steradent for her! Or perhaps they just could not bring themselves to talk because the hurt was too deep.

By this time, more and more members were following my 'Hospital Records' thread and it had broken all records on FTF with the amount of hits it was accumulating. I was overwhelmed with the many private messages of support through the FTF website and the messages posted on my thread. I even received help from a neighbour of an FTF member. Christine in Herts put a lot of time into my search and her neighbour, Danielle, called into Bushey cemetery to see if there was a plaque on my father's grave, which perhaps could not be seen on the United Synagogue website's photograph, but sadly, there was none.

I sometimes went to London on business, and promised myself that I would visit his grave one day, but for now I was concentrating on finding descendants of my father's family.

I was absolutely overwhelmed with the response to my parents' story, and I knew that my mother would have been too. In fact, I knew she would have been just gobsmacked. I wondered if she could see what was happening and I kept saying to her:

Mam . . . are you watching this?

14 Politics, Peasants and Pogroms

The 1891 Leeds census gave my grandfather's name as *Lewis* Friedman, not the usual *Louis*. His first wife's name was Rachael and their eldest son Gedaliah, who was born in January 1891, was listed on the census as Daniel. They lived at no. 37 Back Byron Street, which was in the Leyland district of Leeds, where many Jewish immigrants settled. The census gave Louis' occupation as 'licensed Hawker, own-account', which meant that Louis had worked for himself even in his younger life. This also confirmed that my grandmother Rebecca, was Louis' second wife, although we searched in vain to find a record of their marriage.

I learnt that, because of lack of money, many Jewish couples resorted to the *Stille Chuppah*, for second marriages, which translated literally means 'silent canopy'. A marriage under religious auspices without civil sanction. Living together out of wedlock was deeply frowned upon within the Jewish faith, as it was in Catholicism. So it looked like my Jewish grandparents had most likely opted for the *Stille Chuppah*, which unfortunately gave me no opportunity to find any further information about my Russian-born grandmother Rebecca, whose place of birth I was looking forward to learning more about.

So I researched the address of no. 37 Back Byron Street and the Jewish immigrants of the Leylands and took a tour of this area on the leodis.net website, where I found many photographs of the clusters of impoverished terraced houses that lined the cobbled streets. This district was home to nearly 8,000 Jews by the end of the 1800s, and it was one of the poorest areas of the city, with most of the streets having an accompanying back street. Access to Back Byron Street was gained through a narrow alleyway from Byron Street itself; the deprivation well-hidden from view, reminding me of the Victorian court dwellings of Comus Street where my nan Annie Welsby raised my mum and her siblings.

The Jews' Temporary Shelter, which opened in London in 1885, was often the first port of call for immigrants, many then carried on their journey to join family in America.

Information about this temporary shelter is available at the movinghere.org.uk website. Immigrants would seek out *landsleit,* meaning people from the same town or village, in order to be near people who shared the same background in their homeland. With thanks to the Leeds historian Murray Freedman, whose work can be read on the jtrails.org.uk website, I learnt that most of the Jews who settled in Leeds came from the Russian-controlled areas of north-east Poland and the Kovno *gubernia*. Kovno is today the Lithuanian city known as Kaunas and a *gubernia*, or province, was an administrative division in the Russian Empire. These immigrants would have all been classed as Russian nationals unless they naturalised.

The Polish synagogue in Byron Street was referred to as the *Pailisher Shul* in the Lithuanian (Litvak) dialect, which was prevalent among the Jewish immigrants of Leeds. It was here in the Leylands that the Jews found their feet. Many being attracted by the clothing industry were prepared to work every hour God sent to earn a pittance in the notorious sweatshops. No matter how bad the working conditions were in the factories of Leeds or the discrimination they encountered while there, it was better than what they had left behind. In that respect, they were at least safe from Russian persecution and pogroms, and from what eventually spiralled into the stuff of nightmares under Nazi occupation.

There were many success stories from the Jewish immigrants who settled in Leeds. The tailor Moshe Osinsky, aka Montague Burton who founded the *Burton* menswear shops and also Michael Marks who, after humble beginnings as a hawker, then a market trader, grew the business into the most famous of all our high street brands - *Marks & Spencer PLC.* These were just two of the Jewish immigrants who first settled in Leeds and worked their way out of poverty.

Shtetl life was depicted in the musical *Fiddler on the Roof.* Of course, history tells us that the reality was a life of terrible hardship, discrimination and religious persecution and far more sombre than Topol entertainingly portrayed. Nevertheless, the musical gives a fascinating snapshot into the lives of Jews living under Imperialist Russian rule.

Identifying the *shtetls* where my grandparents were from was not going to be easy, and frankly, I thought I didn't stand a cat in hell's chance of finding where, why and when they left their homeland; it was difficult enough trying to track them down here in England! I did not find them listed in the records of the Jews' Temporary Shelter, so to pinpoint exactly where their homeland was, I would need proof of the *shtetls* from which they came. Louis persistently stated that he was from Germany on the censuses, which had me puzzled. I felt at home with my Russian roots but could not see myself being from German descent.

However, in more general terms, I learnt that the Jewish immigrants who settled in Leeds left their homeland in the former Russian Empire for a number of different reasons, from socioeconomic to far more dark and sinister.

I read everything I could find about the history and treatment of Jews in Imperial Russia, and was amazed to find that Old Tooie wasn't too far wrong. Jews were hated for a number of reasons, most of which seemed to stem from ignorance, but smouldering beneath the surface of those reasons was religious fanaticism. What was it that Old Tooie had said? Something about Jews being bound to roam the earth as nomads until the end of time? I found it difficult to comprehend that much of their earlier persecution stemmed from Christ's crucifixion, nearly two thousand years before and that these fanatics were so-called Christians! I read that it wasn't until the 1960s when Pope Paul VI declared *Nostra Aetate*. Meaning, 'in our time'. Finally, the Roman Catholic Church accepted that it was wrong to pin the blame on to all Jews. But anti-Semitism went further than religious fanaticism in Russia. Hatred of Jews seemed to be ingrained into the very fabric of Russian society, which, albeit unproven, some still believe was fuelled by political conniving. Using Jews as a political tool to divert hatred felt by Russian workers and peasants away from the Russian government, towards the Jews. What my nan called, 'takin' da granny off it.' To shift attention and blame.

I read various books, so as not to be influenced by any one author's interpretation of historical events. The BBC had given me a glimpse of Jewish persecution and extermination when my nan sneaked out to the pub, but I knew little of the earlier problems Jews endured. I read that it was Catherine the Great who created the Pale of Settlement back in 1791 to contain the Jews who came with the Russian Empress's newly acquired territories of Poland and Lithuania. It became the world's largest ghetto, eventually stretching from the Baltic Sea up in the north, down to the Black Sea in the south – the areas of what are today known as Poland, Belarus, Moldova, Ukraine and Lithuania. By the end of the 1800s, over five million Jews lived in the poverty-stricken area, representing over forty percent of the world's Jewish population. Jews called it *der hame*. It would remain their home for over one hundred years.

Jews were discriminated against even within the Pale causing a worldwide outcry. The Jewish religious tradition *tzedakah,* meaning righteousness and signifying charity, was developed into a sophisticated social welfare system and the Jews took care of each other.

The previous Polish and Lithuanian Commonwealth already had laws in place, known as disabilities, which Russia kept up. These laws placed limitations and restrictions on Jews and were first introduced back in the dark, middle ages when these Medieval laws required all Jews to identify themselves in public by wearing a Jewish hat and yellow badge; the badge of shame. That old adage of forgive and forget seems to have been forgotten. Chilling images were coming into my head of a certain mad man who ordered Jews to wear a similar cloth badge, which bore the yellow star of David.

I also read other researchers' messages posted on the various Jewish family history websites, telling their fascinating stories that had been passed down the generations of how their great-great-grandfathers had fled Russia during the mid-1800s to avoid conscription. Tsar Nicholas I, who ruled Russia from 1825–1855, extended conscription to include Jewish boys from the tender age of twelve years, under the *cantonist* system. For Russian citizens, conscription was from eighteen, not twelve. The young boys were sent far away from their homes to military schools where they were given a good education. Service in the Russian army or navy began at the age of eighteen. Back in the early 1800s, that service would then last for twenty-five years. The term was reduced in various stages, and by the mid-1800s it was down to twelve years. Young Jewish boys were treated brutally by Russian soldiers. Kosher food was unavailable and, while cut off from their families in a far away school, pressure was put on the youngsters to convert to the state religion of Orthodox Christianity.

The Russian Empire was hostile to Jews along with other perceived non-conformists. If the draft quotas could not be filled, bounty-hunters kidnapped boys as young as eight to make up the numbers. For many it was a death sentence, and most never returned home.

People needed to duck and dive just to survive back then, and I read stories of many desperate kids cutting off fingers, parents registering several son's births under the same given name to cause confusion, or they registered the birth of a son a few years after he was born, in a desperate attempt to buy time to get their sons out of Russia to safety, so the boys would at least be a little older and therefore more able to fend for themselves.

These kids risked everything. I imagine they grew up fast. Many were still children often travelling alone on foot overland through the forests with false or no identity papers, and only a few roubles in their pocket to bribe a corrupt border guard. Those who had no money for their passage stowed away on the North Sea crossing, which took between one and five days, depending on which port they embarked. Many had no food and only the clothes that they stood up in. They were alive with fleas and suffered from diseases such as typhus, cholera and dysentery. When looking at the Leeds censuses I found many teenage boys listed as a lodger. Typically, their occupations were apprentice cabinetmakers, tailor's journeymen and errand boys or machinists working in the notorious sweatshops of Leeds.

How alone they must have felt living in the industrial slums. They had escaped their Russian persecutors and they were more than used to hard work and poverty, although I imagine city poverty being far worse than country poverty, as city poverty was bereft of fresh air and sunshine, and chickens and geese were probably replaced with 'roaches and rats.

The future began to look rosy for Russia and for its Jews under the reign of the more liberal minded Tsar Alexander II, who became ruler after his father's death in 1855, to 1881. Russia had been left in a mess after being defeated in the Crimean War and corruption was widespread. From the account I've read of Tsar Alexander II, he seemed to be methodical and business-minded. He managed to steer his Empire out of trouble with the welcomed introduction of fundamental reforms, such as the Peasant Reform Manifesto of 1861, which abolished serfdom and granted serfs the full rights that free citizens had enjoyed. He also allowed Jews, who he considered useful, to settle outside the area of the Pale of Settlement, and when work opportunities came along Jews grasped them, causing a great deal of unrest. Russian businesses saw Jews as competition. The authorities thought the Jews a destructive influence who had gained too much control. Consequently, Jews were resented and pogroms swept through the Empire. Many thought Alexander II's government turned a blind eye.

While Alexander was busy reforming, his brutal secret police were exiling thousands of Russian dissidents to Siberia and many Russians grew skeptical of Alexander's objectives, thinking that, although his tactics were different, his aim was just the same as his father's. So life was not so rosy after all, and Russian revolutionaries could see no end to the hated autocratic system and wanted a democracy. Besides, although some useful Jews had been allowed to settle outside the Pale, former areas of Poland and Lithuanian had been excluded from the majority of Alexander II's more liberal policies. Lithuania had been under martial law since 1863, and continued to do so for forty years, with native languages of Lithuanian, Ukrainian and Belarusian being banned from books.

March 1881 seemed to be the turning point for Russia's Jews, after a third attempt at assassinating Tsar Alexander II was successful. The assassins were members of the left-wing revolutionary group People's Will. One of the members was a pregnant Jewish girl named Gesya Gelfman. I read that her involvement was to provide a safe house. However, this was reason enough for the police to blame *all* Russia's Jews for conspiring to murder the Tsar. Consequently, life for rebel groups, and especially for Jews, rapidly went from bad to worse. The aftermath was swift and bloody and chilling accounts of the most bloodiest pogroms are recorded during this incredibly volatile period of the Russian Empire's history.

Alexander's son and heir, Alexander III, brought peace and order to his country, albeit at a price. He was a huge figure of a man, who, unlike his father, ruled the Russian Empire with an iron fist from 1881–1894. He had seen his father die and was on constant guard for fear that he too could succumb to the same fate. Wasting no time in bringing his father's assassins to justice, Alexander set to work on reversing many of his father's liberal reforms. Refusing advisors, the determined new Tsar knew exactly what he wanted for his Russia: One language. One nationality. One religion.

Meanwhile, pogroms escalated, amounting to over two hundred in this period alone. Alexander III launched an investigation into the cause of the attacks. His government came to the conclusion that, because of Jewish clannishness, Jewish people were seen by their competitors, to exploit business opportunities and that caused hostility towards the Jews. So these anti-Jewish riots, which are estimated to have caused the deaths of somewhere between 70,000 and 250,000 Jews, including the elderly, woman and children were seen to be the fault of Jews themselves. Concentrated within the Pale, the Jews were outnumbered, weak and easy targets.

In May 1882, new laws were introduced, known as May laws. Supposedly temporary, these new laws lasted for over thirty years further restricting Jew's civil rights and causing them hardship. Jews were once again forbidden to settle outside the Pale of Settlement. Any lease of property or land to Jews outside the area of the Pale was cancelled. Jews were forbidden to trade on Sundays and Christian holidays. Restrictions were placed on their occupations, which is why many Jews traded as watchmakers, cabinetmakers, tailors, and hawkers. It was not because Jews were incapable of further achievement, it was because of restrictions in work and education, and the police brutally enforced all these regulations.

In addition to the May Laws, new taxes were imposed on Jews with strange names such as the so-called Candle Tax, which was placed on Sabbath candles. Also, a Box Tax was placed on every pound of kosher meat purchased. Consequently, Jews could no longer afford to practice their kosher dietary rules. Ironically, over a hundred years later, it's these Box and Candle Taxes that provide a good source of records for us researchers to trace Jewish family roots. Paper trails come in all shapes and guises.

Although his reign was fairly short, this man of iron had at least restored peace to his country. His son and heir, Nicholas II's government carried on from where his father left off, encouraging further hostility towards Jews in the hope that one third of Jews would die-off, a third would convert to Orthodox Christianity and the rest would leave Russia.

According to history, the government got at least one third of its wish. I learnt that between 1881 and 1914 over two million Jews fled Russia.

History is open to interpretation if not witnessed first-hand and Imperial Russia was not alone in its discrimination against Jews. But stories can be easily distorted and diffused over time, especially when witnesses have long gone. I was not there, and I'm certainly no historian. I can only rely on what's already been written about these historical events and incorporate a snapshot of my findings in to the story of my Jewish grandparents in an effort to try and make some sense of the events that moulded their lives and caused them to leave their homes and often their families behind.

Above: Map of the Pale of Settlement

15 Louis – the Granddaddy of all Mysteries

On the 1901 census, we found Louis and his first wife Rachael living at no. 3 Segrave Street in Liverpool and their eldest son was listed as Darl, not Gedaliah, as he had been named on the 1911 Liverpool census, or Daniel, as he had been listed on the 1891 Leeds census. These were just three first names of many more we would later find Louis' eldest son using.

Their second son, Hyman, was born in Liverpool on the 24 March 1893, the year that saw the birth of the Liverpool Overhead Railway, the world's first electric elevated railway, which served the dock road until 1956 and was known locally as the Docker's Umbrella. Hyman's birth certificate gave their address as no. 43 Gt Orford Street. So the family had moved from Gt Orford Street to Segrave Street by 1901, and they had moved from Leeds to Liverpool sometime after the 1891 census in April, but before Hyman's birth in March 1893. We found that Louis' first wife Rachael had died on the 26 February 1904 of cardiac failure after suffering with emphysema for the previous five years. She had died at their Segrave Street home, with Louis by her side. This was my grandfather's first loss, and he was left to bring up six children from the age of four to thirteen years. So it's understandable that Louis married my grandmother Rebecca within twelve months of Rachael's death, given that Rebecca was also widowed and had been left with two boys to raise.

We had no idea when Louis first arrived in the UK, as many incoming passenger records had not survived, so our only hope was to spot him on a passenger list *if* he left from Hamburg, as records of some Hamburg departures have survived. At this point in the search, we didn't know if my grandfather Louis had come here alone or with family, but Louis does not seem to appear in the 1881 England and Wales census. Although none of the censuses revealed any obvious relatives, apart from his immediate family that is, on closer inspection the 1901 Liverpool census held a very interesting piece of information that we had not spotted earlier.

Under the column heading 'Where Born', Louis stated, 'Born Germany', as he had done on the previous census, but this time with the barely perceptible abbreviated note 'nat. British subj', which we took to mean that he had naturalised since the previous census. It was not much more than a faint watermark that was only legible after some computer enhancement. On the following 1911 census, Louis was a German national again, with no mention of being a British subject. Naturalisation records contain a wealth of information about an individual, including the date and place of birth, parents' names and date of arrival.

Annswaby, who is one of the few professional researchers on FTF, kindly offered to look up Louis' naturalisation records on her next visit to the National Archives at Kew, where the records are kept. But unfortunately, even with all Annswaby's experience, she could find no records for Louis. This was a massive blow for me because without being 'natted', as we called it, Louis could not vote, and therefore he would not appear in the electoral rolls, which I planned to search at the Liverpool Record Office.

So I had a big problem. No naturalisation records. No record of Louis arriving in the UK and no sign of any other family for Louis, apart from his two wives and the children we had found. Louis stated that he was from Germany, so if he did not naturalise, he would be classed as an enemy alien and interned during the war years. But I found no record of Louis in the records available of enemy alien internees. Louis was a mystery, the granddaddy of all mysteries. Like father, like son.

It was from then on that OC began organising her troops. Not allowing the little problem of a lack of records to defeat her, she became completely enthralled with my search:

I can think of a lot of avenues to follow. Trace Harry's siblings forward and try to find living descendants who you could approach for a photo of Harry. Jewish people love big weddings and photos and he may appear in one of them. Leave a note on Harry's grave and find the synagogue near to where Louis lived in 1911 and approach them for any information about the family. Judging by the names of the children, Louis practiced his religion.
OC

I'll try to piece his family together, but there are so many of them, I hardly know where to begin! I don't know whether to go backwards to research my roots or forwards to find living descendants. But, I must admit, I'm absolutely fascinated by Louis' German origins and

especially my grandmother Rebecca's Russian roots. But yes, you are right OC, a photo would be my ultimate goal.
Wallaby

Wallaby, what we have done in the past on FTF is to put the information on a Tribal Pages tree – this is completely private and free! But if you give any of us an editor's password, we can each work on a bit and fill in the tree as we go along.

    I do still think that finding a living descendant of your father's family to approach for a photo – you don't need to say exactly why – is the way to go at the moment. I have a feeling that once you see him, you will know him.
OC

I know what you mean with the photo OC, and I agree. So I'll weigh up the descendants when, and IF, I find any. I'll see how approachable they are. I would love to see what he looked like, to see if I look like him. But I feel like I would be asking far too much of everyone to have you all putting time into my family tree with this 'Tribal Pages'. I would feel I would be asking far more than just advice from you all. I don't want you, OC, or anyone else who have given me so much help, becoming fed-up with me and my family tree!
Wallaby

Wallaby, we've done Tribal Pages trees for other people and I for one would be very happy to help with yours, I don't consider it a waste of time, nor an imposition either. The offer is there if you change your mind.
OC

But what if the living relatives know about me OC? I mean, I might be the only person who doesn't know about me! For all I know, the whole of bloody Liverpool might know about me and could also be related to me! Especially if my grandfather Louis' virility was hereditary! I'll tread carefully until I find out more. But to see a photo of Harry would be just perfect. Although, I doubt I'll be so lucky.

    If everyone who has helped doesn't mind the idea of the Tribal Pages tree as you called it . . . then how do I do this? Are you sure this is not going to look cheeky OC?
Wallaby

Hmmm . . . I see, cat amongst the pigeons here.

Well, in the meantime, I've found two possible marriages for Harry, which I will send you in a private message. One is in 1926, the other in 1947. Of course, neither of them may be him, but frankly I think it would be amazing if a good Jewish man were never married! If it was an arranged marriage then that might explain why he went to London and why he never married your mum.

For the T.P. tree, go to tribalpages.com and follow the instructions. It's very easy.

OC

I immediately ordered the two marriage certificates and held my breath while I waited for them to arrive. That mystery telephone call to my business from Harry's friends gave me the impression that my cousin Mary was correct in thinking that my father was not married, and given that the United Synagogue failed to trace any family, but we needed to be certain. Meanwhile, I searched on.

To trace Harry's siblings forward was easier said than done, as once you get past the 1911 census it gets harder to find people if they did not naturalise – that is, until they die. But we were having no luck in finding Louis' death in the GRO listings or any records of his family after their Pleasant Street address in 1911. My only option was to search the electoral rolls willy-nilly, combing every electoral ward in the south end of the inner-city in the hope of finding Louis' eldest sons, Gedaliah aka Daniel or Darl, and also Hyman, once they came of age to vote, which, being born here in the UK they were of course entitled to do. We were convinced that the family had emigrated to America or somewhere, perhaps after Rebecca's death in April 1911, but we could find neither hide nor hair of them, and we wondered if perhaps something awful had happened to Louis and his younger children had been put into care. So ideas and suggestions poured in . . .

I think it's just worth considering if you're looking for Louis' death or his sons' marriages or deaths or their movements after 1911. Europe was in turmoil in those times, which was the reason your ancestors were here, culminating in a bloodbath between 1914–1918. Then the Russian revolution in 1918.

They were nomads really. They came here for peace and again found themselves in a country at war, a world war involving the whole of Europe by 1914.

Maggie_4_7

Maggie was right, and because of the treatment Jews had been subjected to, they were afraid of authorities and their records. The majority of them wanted nothing more than to live peacefully with their neighbours, to get on with their lives and practise their religion in the same way as other religious groups were allowed to do.

Perhaps some of the Freedman family emigrated to America. I've looked on findmypast.com and between 1911–1914 there were 131 Friedmans and fifty-four Freedmans who left Liverpool for America. Including two Louis Friedmans who were born in 1865 and another in 1868, who left in 1914 for New York.
Moggie

I was in London today looking at probates for my own research, so while there I looked for Harry Freeman too. There are no wills/administrations for anyone of that name and address 1984-89. I also checked under the name Henry.
Jill on the A272

Thanks for thinking of me Jill. I didn't expect him to have made a will. I would be very surprised if he had any money. The grave at Bushey Cemetery has no stone; I would have thought if he had money, surely he would have had a gravestone. Besides, I started this search thinking he had no money so I'm not bothered about that. My mum never had any money and the bit I have, I've made myself. But, thanks again for thinking of me Jill.
Wallaby

The other thing I've thought about Louis. He gave his occupation as a Hawker on the 1911 census. Many people deliberately played down what they had and Jewish immigrants would be particularly sensitive to playing it down as they may have already lost everything in their home country and didn't want to have that happen again. "Hawker" covers a multitude of things – Mr Marks was a hawker before he started Marks and Spencer!

I have also wondered if 'scrap metal dealer' covered up what Harry was really doing, which was possibly trading in precious metals, gold and silver, etc. No one with half a brain goes around bragging about being a gold dealer, the fewer people who know about that, the better. This would make much more sense than scrap metal as in steel and tin.
OC

I was a bit over sensitive when probate was mentioned and wanted to assure the members that money was not the reason that I was searching for my father. I was neither interested in his money, nor was I entitled to it. Besides, I never considered Harry to have had money, because rich people intimidated my mum and she would shy away from wealth, so I couldn't imagine my mum to have had a relationship with a wealthy man; a gold dealer, as OC had suggested. Besides, he was buried in a pauper's grave, so surely he can't have had any money.

I later realised that I'd missed the point completely. The members explained that the reason that probates are researched is nothing to do with the deceased's estate, it's because of the possible information that the records could give about beneficiaries, such as names and addresses. I obviously still had a lot to learn at this stage, and a lot of humble pie to eat.

We ran the search like a well-organised office, as members organised themselves into teams and trawled through the various indexes, splitting the dates so as not to duplicate each other's work. They then gave me the GRO details of anything that they found. There was such a staggering amount of information to sift through and analyse, but we had OC . . . our filing cabinet.

I had started out 'as green as feckin' shamrock', as my nan Annie Welsby would say, but I was learning fast. Any information we found would be added to my Tribal Pages tree and many members of FTF requested a password and helped with my research.

Elaine in Spain, who is a moderator of FTF's website, advised me to move my thread to the Adoption/Reunion forum, which has since been renamed Sensitive Research, as this area of FTF could only be seen by the members and not by visitors to the website, nor could it be picked up by Google. If I wanted to remain incognito until I found more details about my father, it was wise to keep the thread as private as possible as I was still waiting to receive the two certificates for the two marriages that OC had found. If I was lucky enough to find descendants of my father's siblings, and they knew nothing about me whatsoever, then I didn't think it was very appropriate or fair for them to stumble across my thread via Google. Of course, there was always the risk that somebody connected to my father or his family was a member of FTF! But if that was the case, I could do nothing and would have to take that chance. At the end of the day, my search for my father was open and honest, or at least it would be when I 'came out', so to speak, and apart from the odd bit of leg-pulling, we conducted the research into my father's Freeman family with the greatest of respect, which every family deserves.

Meanwhile, I was on pins waiting for the marriage certificates for the two possible marriages for my father for 1926 and 1947. I had put a check on the order stipulating that the groom's father's name had to be Louis, to avoid receiving any wrong records and about two weeks later I got an email from the GRO informing me that the groom's father was not Louis for the 1926 marriage. That was one down and one to go. Although I didn't know it at the time, the 1947 marriage certificate got caught up in a GRO technical hitch, which caused a delay. Not knowing the reason for this delay, I thought to myself, *if that groom's father was not Louis either, then surely the GRO would have sent me a second email to inform me of this.*

So I convinced myself that the 1947 marriage just had to be my father. He must have been married after all. I was on a real downer and I felt so sad for my mum. I wondered if I had any half-brothers or sisters. I had always suspected that my father was married and it looked like my suspicions had been correct all along. How should I handle things now? Carefully, was the answer. I was rehearsing in my head how I was going to break the news to the members of FTF that I wanted to back away. Of course, being an only child, I was dying to to know if I had any half-siblings, but I had no intention whatsoever of approaching them. I seen no sense in turning another person's life upside down just to satisfy my own curiosity.

It took a further two weeks before the 1947 marriage certificate finally arrived and when I opened the envelope – wrong Harry! This Harry Freedman's father's name had been Myer, not Louis! The GRO apologised for the long delay and for their error in sending the wrong certificate and refunded my payment. The money didn't bother me in the slightest; the torment and suspense I could have done without.

No other marriages were ever found for either Harry, Harold or Henry Freeman, Freedman or Friedman. The information that my cousin Mary had told me before she died appeared to be correct; just like my mum, my father never married.

Although Harry stayed single, it was evident that he had a large family of siblings, so:

Why had my father died alone?

Why was it thought that he had no family?

Why had he been buried by the United Synagogue in a stoneless grave?

16 Brick Walls and Red Herrings

So this was how the team was formed. Just a bunch of faceless, nameless family history buffs making use of free websites for our virtual office to conduct a search for my mystery daddy. I had joined tribalpages.com and given some FTF members an editor's password as and when they offered their help with the research. I placed myself at the bottom of the pecking order and gave myself the job title of Gofer. Any research at the Liverpool Records Office or other legwork to be done, like trekking through Jewish cemeteries looking for gravestones, writing letters and emails, or ordering BMD certificates would be my department, and I kept a log of everything in my laptop. When I did take a short break to watch some television, I watched the programme *Who Do You Think You Are*. I just couldn't let go!

Brian took the username of Columbo and turned himself into a private detective, making discreet enquiries in whatever direction the clues sent us – although he insisted that I assured all the members of FTF that he looked more like Steve McQueen than Peter Falk. In his dreams! My other half has always been delusional about his looks.

I gave OC the title of Project Manager and she had a great team of experts around her with an array of experience including people with legal backgrounds, medics, civil servants, teachers and even an opera singer, and no doubt everything in-between. I didn't have a clue about the real identities of the members of FTF, nor they of mine. I could only guess their backgrounds by whatever knowledge they displayed over the following months.

A lot of members were retired, and were very experienced in family history research. They were from all over the UK, as well as Italy, Spain and afloat on a boat off the coast of Martinique, which had me intrigued. While we slept, the night shift took over, with members who lived in the southern hemisphere – such as Australia, New Zealand and even Tasmania. We had the search for Harry covered 24/7! It felt like the whole wide world was desperately seeking Harry!

Many were happy to put their subscriptions to various websites to good use, and in return I would often receive private messages via the FTF website to do some research at the Liverpool Records Office for another member who lived in another part of the world and who perhaps had family roots in Liverpool. I had been told that genealogy can become very addictive, and I quickly began to realise why. By this time, I was well and truly hooked.

If I ever see my mother again, Christ . . . I will be in big trouble! She was so private, but now, as she would often say to me, 'Yer little twerp. Da whole wide world knows all me friggin' business!'

By now, we were starting to show signs of battle fatigue. We were convinced that Louis had a reason to come to Liverpool from Leeds. Maybe he, or his first wife Rachael, had family here. But who were they? OC had her eye on a cabinetmaker named Harris Freedman as a possible candidate for Louis' brother, so all our attention shifted onto Harris Freedman. OC built a tree for him on tribalpages.com and Margaretmarch rounded up all the Liverpool Freedman families she could find living in the area at that time, while I set up camp at the Liverpool Records Office and searched Kelly's street directories and the electoral rolls:

I've done a bit of checking and find that there are three families and two individuals. One family is of course our Louis and Rachael or Rebecca and their children. The next is Harris Freedman, his wife Minnie and their seven children, who OC thinks might be Louis' brother. It looks like Harris didn't arrive until after 1891 as I can't find them on the 1891 census. The 1901 census shows their first two children were born in Russia. The next five children were all born in Liverpool and I have found that Harris Freedman applied for naturalisation in 1892. His father's name was Isaac Freedman. That means, if Harris' father's name was Isaac, and he and Louis were brothers, then Isaac Freedman was your great grandfather!

Harris was living at Islington in 1901 and he was a German-born cabinetmaker, maybe Louis' eldest son Gedaliah, worked for him. There is also another family headed by Abraham Freedman who could be connected in some way. I'll do some more digging.
Margaretmarch

There were a number of things that pointed to Harris Freedman being Louis' brother, one of which was the fact that OC was seldom wrong. Two: he was about the right age. Three: he was born in Germany. Four: he was a cabinetmaker, which had us wondering if that could possibly be the reason why Gedaliah chose his craft of woodcarving, rather than tailoring, which his younger brothers Hyman and Samuel had chosen. We wondered if perhaps Margaretmarch was right and Gedaliah had worked for Harris Freedman. So when we found the details of Louis' marriage to Rachael née Simon in Leeds in January 1890, camouflaged under the spelling of Louis *Friedman*, I ordered their marriage certificate. All of us were quite certain that Louis' father's name would also be Isaac. But when I opened the envelope, the news was not good. Their marriage certificate gave Louis' father's name as . . . Tobias! Everybody was gutted, especially OC:

Throws self on sword! I am so sorry everyone. I feel very guilty because it was I who was so convinced that Harris and Louis were brothers. I apologise most sincerely for causing everyone to waste their time.
OC

Ahhh, please don't commit Harry-Carry OC. I would still be looking for Henry Freeman, and not Harry Freedman without your help and the help of the members of FTF.
Wallaby

Dries eyes and blows nose. I have now amended the tree and unhooked Harris and Louis, but I cannot bring myself to delete Harris and family!
We need a brainstorming session of sensible and not so sensible suggestions, to trace back Harry Freeman's life before Rose Bush Court?
OC

I think that was the only time OC ever wandered onto the wrong track. It was a bitter blow, and lots of posts along with private messages flew around the FTF website regarding this huge disappointment over Harris Freedman not being Louis' brother. I could sense some of the members were feeling deflated because of all the time and effort that we had all put into finding details about Harris Freedman who was a German-born cabinetmaker in Islington, Liverpool.

So when Moggie posted this following message I had to respond and give everyone a group hug. When a website thread takes off like my 'Hospital Records' thread took off, the excitement can be electric, but so can the tension too, as even researchers can sometimes disagree about which road to take:

I know that a lot of members think that we have gone all around the houses only to find ourselves back where we started, by looking through naturalisation records, passenger lists, checking various addresses from certificates in the census and creating a tree for Harris Freedman, who now turns out not to be related to Louis. But we just could have found a vital bit of information.

The time you spent in the Liverpool Records Office certainly wasn't wasted Wallaby, because although most of the entries that you found do relate to Harris Freedman's family there are several entries that don't and they are worth following up in other directories or the electoral rolls.

Moggie

These members were unpaid researchers. They were either complete amateurs, seasoned researchers or semi-professionals, who were all kindly helping out, each of them giving their time, experience and know-how to help me find my father's family, and I could not have found them without their help. So I could not believe they were feeling this way. To reassure them just how much I appreciated their help I posted the following message:

Moggie, OC, Everyone . . . please listen to me!

I don't feel like any time has been wasted by gathering the information on Harris Freedman's family. I have said this many times before – I would never have gotten this far without your help. If it were not for the help of the many members of FTF I would still be looking for Henry Freeman!

How could any of us have known that Louis and Harris would not in the end be brothers? There was so many things that tied them together! I felt awful having to announce that Louis' father was this . . . Tobias Freedman! I mean, where the hell did he come from!

I even contemplated telling you all a fib, because I just didn't have the heart to announce this bad news!

So when I read Moggie's post I just wanted to give each and everyone of you a virtual group hug (((:-o)))

OC, Moggie, Margaret, Tilly Mint and everyone! I promise you all, that when I go back to the Liverpool Records Office, I won't leave without some good leads. Don't worry everyone. We'll be back on track by the end of this week. As Scarlet said . . . tomorrow is another day.

Wallaby

It wasn't long before back on track was exactly where we were, when Margaretmarch found one of the most important breakthroughs of the research. Well, at least we thought it was important at the time . . . but you know what thought did!

I have just found a record of a Louis Friedman age twenty-three, birth year 1866, arriving in the UK at Hull, via Liverpool on 2nd Nov 1889, just in time to marry Rachael in March 1890! The list says he's from . . . Lomza
Margaretmarch

Margaret's exciting find had everybody frantically Googling nineteenth-century European maps in search of Lomza. We searched parts of eastern Europe that I'd never even heard of. I contacted Saul Marks of BrothersWish.com Genealogy Services and Saul kindly allowed me to pick his brains and explained Lomza in more detail:

Be careful. Lomza is a city in modern-day North East Poland but it's also the name of a gubernia (province) of the Polish part of the former Russian empire. If someone said they came from Lomza, they could mean the city or just somewhere else in Lomza gubernia.
Saul Marks

The passenger list also gave his occupation as *händler*, which was German for dealer and a dealer could be described as a hawker, which fitted Louis' occupation given on the censuses of 'licensed Hawker-own account'. He appeared to have been travelling alone, as there were no other passengers of the same name. So we felt confident that this was my grandfather, Louis. But we needed solid proof. We knew that my grandfather must have had some reason to settle in Leeds and then to move to Liverpool, but we could find no proof to connect with any other family of the name Friedman or any variation of that name, in Leeds or Liverpool.

After weeks of research we found no evidence that my grandfather Louis was also this Louis from Lomza. So I decided to follow the person who was listed after this Louis Friedman, on the passenger list of the *Kaffrina*, which was the ship that he had sailed on. He was twenty-year-old Ethan Gramecki. The passenger list stated that Ethan was also from Lomza, and I thought that maybe they could have been either friends travelling together, or perhaps cousins. Of course, this was pure speculation. Ethan Gramecki could quite easily have been just the guy behind him in the queue, and had absolutely nothing whatsoever to do with this Louis from Lomza. But they were the only two people who were listed on the *Kaffrina's* passenger list who came from the same place. So I decided to follow a wild hunch. I followed Ethan Gramecki.

I searched for Ethan in Liverpool, Leeds and Hull in the hope of finding a connection to his travelling companion, Louis Friedman. The name Ethan Gramecki was less common than my grandfather's name, so there would be less of them to untangle. Perhaps if I found a marriage for Ethan, Louis might pop up as his wedding witness. I found no trace of Ethan anywhere in the UK.

It was at this point in the research that Christine in Herts introduced a Jewish e-friend to FTF. Her username was Naomiatt, and she had many contacts in family history. Naomiatt and her friend Watson introduced me to the many Jewish family history websites, such as jewishgen.org and british-jewry.org.uk, and I posted messages on these websites in the hope of finding another researcher who might be tracing the same Freedman family. I thought that maybe a descendant of the same family who had perhaps stayed behind in their homeland of Germany, or wherever they were from, might also be researching his or her family tree. I got helpful replies, but alas, no positive leads.

Meanwhile, I was still stalking Louis Friedman and Ethan Gramecki from Lomza and getting nowhere, until Naomiatt recruited help from Barbara Zimmer who lived in the USA. Barbara eventually found Ethan. He popped up in the Ellis Island records, of all places. After first arriving at Hull, Ethan must have made his way through to Liverpool, most probably by train, and he then carried on to New York. He arrived on the *Egypt* ship on the 23 November 1889. Then, the bombshell dropped – Louis Friedman from Lomza was with him!

We searched incoming passenger lists from America on the ancestry.com website in case he had returned from New York, or perhaps had been refused entry. Although incoming passenger lists from Europe are scant, there are some records for America. But nothing was found for Louis from Lomza returning to the UK. So it was now very doubtful that he was my grandfather, which meant that for me, it was back to the drawing board. To say that we were all disheartened at wasting time on another wild goose chase, would be an understatement. Especially me, as I had to rewrite many sections of this book and I could have cried. I also didn't have a clue where to turn to next to confirm my grandfather Louis' country of origin.

Of course, in only a few short months, we were discovering what would usually take one lone researcher about twenty years to find, but by this time I had helpful members of FTF and other e-friends from all over the world working around the clock. I was so lucky.

We were never told my grandma came from India; it's only recently that I've found out her wealthy family disowned her for marrying a commoner – my granddad. Her family knew nothing about us until I started my search two years ago. I've recently made contact with my great aunt's daughter. Her mum was also disowned, but she stuck it out in India. Don't give up; there could be family out there who don't know you exist . . . so never give up.

Tilly Mint

I never gave up and neither did Tilly Mint or the other members of FTF. How could I give up when I had this amount of support? We also had many laughs along the way, like the day Margaret in Burton found a census where a woman whose relationship to the head of the family was recorded as being his concubine! Nothing to do with our Freeman family, I hasten to add. There were also sad findings too. Like the tragic deaths that Moggie found of a young mother and her one-week-old unnamed triplets. How on earth did people pick themselves up from a tragedy like this? It's when you see stuff like this recorded on a document that it makes it all the more real and brings it home to you how lucky we are to live in today's world, rather than in our grandparents' time. This was just genealogy doodling, as we were all fed up to the teeth with red herrings. Then, we got lucky . . .

We had worked out rough dates for when each of Louis' sons would have come of age, and could then have married. Also, unlike their father Louis, they would have been eligible to vote, being British citizens – all apart from Louis' Russian-born stepson Abraham Freedman, that is. For his older sons – Gedaliah, Hyman, Samuel and Elias – their dates came slap-bang in the middle of the First World War, when, for security reasons, no electoral registers were compiled, and they could have been away fighting in the war and may even have died for their country. There was still so much that we didn't know at this point.

Our breakthrough came when Tilly Mint found First World War service records for Samuel, under the name Freeman – not Freedman or Friedman. His age fitted in with him being Louis' son Samuel, who was born in Liverpool in 1896. His address was given as no. 48 Moon Street, Liverpool when he enlisted in 1915. Samuel's father was given as his next of kin, but named simply as Mr Freeman of the same address. With no first name mentioned, this didn't prove he was my grandfather Louis. Plus, now that the family's name had come full circle, evolving into Freeman, the name my search began with, we were aware that there were many Freemans floating about Liverpool that could get tangled up with *our* Freemans, with many having the first name of Samuel.

Until we found further proof to confirm we had the correct Samuel, these service records didn't help us much at this time, but they told a sad story of him having part of his middle finger amputated, after being injured while fighting in France. If this was my father's brother, this must have been a devastating blow for Samuel, who had been a tailor by trade before he enlisted. However, although I didn't know it at that time, I would be able to put this information to good use later in my research.

Meanwhile, the address on Samuel's service records of no. 48 Moon Street started ringing bells for us as we had seen this address before, somewhere.

While OC had spent days preparing a timeline, I opened a thread specifically for all the proven information we had and called it 'Hospital Records Facts and Reference Thread'. We made a separate post for each family member so that we could see at a glance what facts we knew about each person, and to make it easier to identify anything else we found later. This included all the details from certificates, censuses, births, marriages and death listings and cemetery lists. It's vital to separate proven facts from unproven information. When we rechecked the 'Facts and Reference' thread, we noticed a burial for a Mrs Rosie Freeman on the list of burials that Arnold Lewis had kindly sent me for Rice Lane cemetery. Her age was sixty-two and she had died in April 1934. Rosie's address was given as no. 48 Moon Street!

At this point, we didn't have a clue who Rosie Freeman was, although we hoped she would be a sister-in-law of Louis', leading us to a brother. But when I opened Rosie's death certificate, Rosie turned out to be wife number three for my grandfather Louis!

This breakthrough also confirmed that the service record that Tilly Mint had found for Samuel Freeman, was definitely *our* Samuel. We had suspected that Louis had married again after my grandmother Rebecca had died in 1911, as Louis would only have been in his mid-forties with a large family to raise. But we could find no trace of any other marriages after his first marriage to Rachael née Simon in Leeds in 1890. So we concluded that Louis' third marriage to Rosie was also a *Stille Chuppah* ceremony.

Rosie's death was registered by her daughter Betsy, who we found was born in 1908 in Manchester to Rosie's first husband. We then traced Rosie on the 1911 census and she was then living in Liverpool with her daughter Betsy and she was listed on the census as a widow. I have excluded details of Louis' third wife for reasons that will become clear later.

We then found the birth of yet another daughter for Louis and Rosie. Eva was born in 1914. So my father now had another half-sister who was seven years his junior, and also a stepsister, Betsy, who was only one year younger than my father Harry.

To recap, my grandfather Louis had now fathered no fewer than ten children in all: Gedaliah, Hyman, Nellie, Samuel, Elias and Isaac, a total of six to his first wife Rachael. Then he had Teri, my father Harry and Bertie, the baby who died in January 1911, a total of three children to my grandmother Rebecca. Plus, two stepsons; Rebecca's sons, Abraham and little Jacob who had died in 1907, and now he had another daughter, Eva to his third wife Rosie. Plus another stepchild, being Rosie's daughter Betsy, bringing the total to a baker's dozen. How the hell did my grandfather cope!

Surely, out of thirteen children, it was possible that there could be some descendants still living in Liverpool who would perhaps know some information about my father that had been passed down from their parents?

Addresses are just as important as people in family history, and no. 48 Moon Street became an important anchor address from then on, connecting many other people together. At last we were on a roll!

By this time, Louis had married three Russian women. What could this be telling us? He had always stated that he was from Germany. He had not naturalised, and yet he was not found on the enemy alien register, nor had he been found interned in any alien camps. I had a gut feeling that my grandfather Louis could have also been from Russia, regardless of his Germanic claim. Louis' German roots just didn't sit comfortably with me, so I was wishing I would find that he had been from Russia too.

I couldn't wait to tell Brian's Uncle Thomas about my Russian grandmother. Thomas often visited Russia throughout the 1980s in connection with his work before he retired, and he sometimes brought books on Russian architecture home for me from his trips to Moscow and Odessa, because he knew of my fascination with the country. I still have stacks of books on eastern European architecture, including a book about the onion cathedral, St Basil's, which is on my bucket list of things to see before I die. I've collected old violins since I married Brian in 1980, three of which are Russian, and they hang on the walls of our home. I also have a collection of Russian dolls and all kinds of odd-looking Russian bric-a-brac.

One of my favourite possessions was a Russian-style maxi coat made by Biba, which I wore and wore until it was worn out. This was the beginning of the 1970s, the early days of my working life, and I loved everything about design, from architecture to fashion, and I remember this coat down to the finest detail. The fabric was heavy, black wool, and it was designed to pinch tight into the waist. The skirt of the coat was cut on a circle and it had a Nehru collar. Looking very Gothic for the time, it buttoned from the neck down to the waist with giant frog buttons made of black braid. I used to wear it with brown, knee-high suede boots, also made by Biba. It was that one fashion piece, which was so representative of the early 70s. It's a woman thing; I don't expect you men to understand. But how uncanny to now find I have Russian roots after surrounding myself with Russian curios.

I joked with the members of FTF about finding a lead that could one day take us to Russia, and we took great delight in the thought of a bunch of us meeting up and flying off to do some real live field research in Russia, whose records I learnt are meticulously kept.

I was absolutely enthralled with this Russian discovery and I was just as interested in tracing Rebecca's bloodline back to her home in Russia as I was in researching my father's family forward, to find a descendant who could tell me about my father Harry and give me a photograph of him. The thought of introducing myself to a living descendant of my father's family was a bit scary, to say the least. What if they were not nice people or uninterested and chased me away!

The entire process was a learning curve for me and I found that the borders of eastern European countries were very fluid and extremely volatile throughout history, and especially during the 1800s and 1900s. Often entire regions could belong to Poland, Russia, Lithuania, Prussia or the Ukraine, depending on whatever date in history that you happened to be looking at the map!

There's an old joke about a Jewish tailor who woke up one freezing morning to find that his entire village was no longer under Russian Imperial rule. Overnight the political borders had changed, yet again, while he and his family were asleep and it had become a Polish village.

'We must thank the Almighty!' He declared to his wife.

'Why?' She snapped back at him sarcastically.

'Because I just couldn't stand anymore of those freezing cold Russian winters!'

17 Driven *Meshugeh*

Family history, by its very nature, is quite intrusive to say the least. Records for people's births, marriages and deaths are public records in the UK, so anyone can order them, but to a person who knows nothing about genealogy it can seem rather odd and prying to obtain them. No harm can come to the dead; nevertheless, a massive measure of respect, sensitivity and tact is needed to research a person's roots and I had given a lot of consideration to this from the beginning of my research. I just thought about how I would feel if someone delved into my mother's family, and I tried to give others the respect I would have wanted them to give to my family. I was also conscience of being a *shiksa*, a non-Jewish girl, or in my case, woman, probing into a Jewish family, my father's family, who might be completely oblivious to my existence. Although my father was also my family, to descendants of his many siblings, I was a complete stranger. Fear was beginning to creep in, the closer I got.

The biggest problem with tracing Jewish roots is the name changes, and by now, we were drowning in complicated name changes with too many aka's. The team had now grown to well over twenty core FTF researchers, with about thirty more chipping in with ideas and snippets of helpful information. Plus there were e-friends I had made via other websites who were scattered all over the world. Without the support of all of these people I think at least six of us might have lost the plot, not to mention any names, and could quite easily have ended up in a padded cell. Me being one! In Yiddish it's known as driven *meshugeh*.

Regarding the names changing. My grandfather was Alfred (Alf) and that's how I knew him until the day he died in 1978. He grew up in the East End of London during the early part of the 20th Century when there was a fair bit of anti-Semitism going on. It wasn't until after he died that I found out his real name was Abraham. That might be what happened with Harry's family.

Granddad married-out and my grandmother, who was his second wife, was not allowed to bring up his children from his first marriage, because my grandmother was not Jewish. The children stayed with my granddad's first wife after he remarried.

None of the Jewish side of my family was particularly religious, but I know of other people who were cast-out by their family for marrying-out. They were treated as if they had died and the family actually sat shiva for them. That could be a reason why your parents didn't marry.

Night Owl

I may never know, Night Owl. But there are such sad stories. Religion, of any kind, is to blame for so much heartache in this world. Or at least people's use or excuse of religion, to carry out their actions. Perhaps this is why Harry ended up alone and was thought to have had no family when he died. But if he was cast-out, then why didn't he marry my mother? Some of these questions may never be answered.

Wallaby

Talking about name changes, I'm reading a book at the moment about a Holocaust survivor. Her name is Ellie Friedman – I nearly fell out of bed! Absolutely not our family, but she says some interesting things.

Quote: 'My name is Ellie, but my Jewish name is Leah. When we returned to our Czech-Slovak village after the war, there were only 36 Jews left out of 772. At synagogue it was decided that our new family name would be Friedman. Soon, our neighbours forgot our old names. All the Jewish survivors used this same surname, as a way of denoting that they were now one family. My brother went to America, his name was Davidson, patronymic of his grandfather. My mother and I went to Israel where I became Lee Sforsanova.' Unquote.

Her Aryan great grandmother's family name was Sfors.

Hmmm . . . I think we have our work cut out here!

OC

OC was right, we certainly did have our work cut out for us, because as far as Jewish name-changing goes, OC had only uncovered the tip of the iceberg. I learnt that up until the early 1800s, Jews did not have a family surname that was passed down the generations. Jewish people had personal first names given on their birth certificate, a nickname or everyday name, known as a *kinnui*, and also a religious or Hebrew name, the *shem hakodesh*, which then also had its Yiddish interpretation. Jewish people were then identified by their father's name. For example: Rebecca daughter of Isaac or Samuel son of David. In Hebrew this would be; Rebekah bat-Yitschak or Shmuel ben-Dovid. So a person was known as son or daughter of; Bat or Ben of their father, and the name was only one-generational. At least this was the case for Ashkenazi Jews, which is what my father's family were.

The introduction of Jewish family surnames was brought about by legislation at various times in the different countries of eastern Europe from about the 1780s through to the early 1800s. Jews were instructed to choose a name by the authorities of their country and they chose their surnames via a variety of methods. Some Jews added the suffix of vitch onto their father's name, as in Solomonvitch or Abramvitch patronymic of their father, then later 'vitch' was anglicised to son. The surname of Levy comes from the biblical tribe of Levi, descendants of Levites, priests who had distinctive duties in the temple. The surname Cohen and its many variations means 'righteous priest'. But, this is where it gets really complicated, because many people have Jewish *sounding* names such as Cohen, Abram or Freeman who are not Jewish and don't have Jewish roots, which can be very misleading.

Some Jewish families took their name from their occupations, so Samuel the shoe maker became Samuel Schuster. Other Jewish families just took names they simply liked the sound of, such as rose blossom which then became Rosenblum. Some adopted the name of the place they were from; like a family from Warsaw might choose the name of Warsawski. It was no different from the way my maternal family name of Welsby was chosen, because they happened to live by the well. At some point in our history – none of us had a name!

But the complexities of name-changing didn't stop there. I'm only halfway through the iceberg that OC found the tip of. When many Jewish people fled their homelands they either changed their names by choice, or by necessity. Many passports or identity papers were forged, especially in the build up to the First and Second World Wars, and if Joe Bloggs could not obtain a passport with his name on it, he took whatever was available and became Samuel Cohen or whatever name was on the passport that he could obtain. Often names were wrongly transcribed simply because of human error. I found countless naturalisation records giving a person's name with a side note, for example: Isaac Goldstein formerly Samuel Rosenblatt, or Samuel Rosenberg aka Syd Rose. Often names were simply plucked out of thin air, with no obvious link to anything. Many people were refugees; I imagine there was no time to worry about such trivia as they were too busy looking over their shoulders.

For researchers trying to find their roots, all these name changes makes Jewish genealogy a nightmare to trace, to say the least, and many people don't even attempt it. But it's all these difficulties that have brought researchers together and has created a faceless, nameless online community of family history buffs using online usernames, and the free support that has become available within these online communities of DIY researchers makes genealogy such a sociable and interesting hobby. You also get to communicate with some fascinating people, and make life-long friends with people from all over the world. Admittedly, you do encounter some oddballs now and again, but hey . . . it's not utopia!

The other hurdle for non-Jews tracing Jewish roots is learning the many different traditions for the various communities, each of them having their own individual culture whose customs vary. Non-Jews like me and many of the members of FTF needed to be aware of these rules and also be aware of the fact that they are sometimes broken. As with every other religion and culture, Jews are not all observant of every single rule.

The main subdivisions are: Ashkenazi, who are descendants of Jews originating from earlier Eastern Europe and the Mediterranean region, before settling in Northern Europe; and Sephardi, descendants of Jews from middle eastern countries who settled in Spain and Portugal. Sephardic Jews along with Muslims were driven from Spain during the Inquisition. Like other religions, Catholicism included, Jews come in various shapes, sizes and colours including black, yellow, and fair-skinned, blue-eyed blondes. Not all Jewish people are dark-skinned with brown-eyes and raven-black hair. It is their core beliefs which unites them all, just like religion united the Italian and Irish Catholic immigrants who settled in Little Italy. Yet, within those Jewish core beliefs there are many variations and different customs, just as in Christianity. I had such a lot to learn.

Meanwhile, we had endless debates about why my parents never married. It seemed like such a waste of two people's lives. They had kept in touch with each other for all those years and yet neither of them had married each other, nor anyone else. OC's theory was . . .

Perhaps your mum realised with your approach that Harry was never going to marry her and she ended the relationship? Religion has a lot to answer for in my opinion, but so do interfering relatives sometimes. Or, have you ever considered it was perhaps your mother who refused to marry your father? When Jewish people married out, they lost their family. But when Catholic's married out, they faced eternal damnation! Well, they did then.

OC

My mind is open as far as what their reasons for not marrying were, OC. When my cousin Mary told me, 'Henry Freeman was a Jew' she said it as if that was the reason and it was all the explanation that was needed. But I do think there was more to it than that. I think she was afraid of the reaction from the community more than anything. She had some good friends and by and large they were good people. But, some were intolerant of anyone different in those days and we had some bad times.

Maybe she would have needed to leave her home and my nan would then have been left alone. Or maybe Harry simply didn't love my mum enough to marry her. Or perhaps she worried that the marriage would not have lasted and she would then be a Catholic divorcee, with a half-Jewish child. Yet they kept in touch with each other all those years. So, I don't know. Wallaby

We expected to have a problem with the surname change from Friedman to Freedman to Freeman. Although Freeman wasn't up there in the top ten of the most common surnames, it wasn't too far down the list. I wished Louis had insisted on traditional Hebrew names for his daughters, although he may have done, but they were not found. But the Jewish first names chosen for his sons should hopefully make them stand out in the crowd, or so we thought.

We had high hopes of easily finding a marriage for Hyman, but the names Samuel, Elias and Isaac were not exclusively Jewish names. We thought Teri might give us a problem too, but as for Gedaliah, well, he seemed to have changed his name as often as he changed his socks.

We found a few possible marriages for Samuel, and I ordered the marriage certificate for one in particular, who we had a hunch about for a while – only to find that he was not *our* Samuel but a widower remarrying after his first wife had died in childbirth. You need plenty of Kleenex handy when delving into the past as you will find many sad stories. I could fill ten books with sad stories we found and people we traced only to find that they were not connected to my father's family after all. The red herrings I've selected to include in this book will I hope go some way to show how complicated the research was into my Jewish family, and I had a team of helpers working 24/7. If not for all their help it would have taken me a lifetime to find my father's family.

The research into my roots became a learning curve for all the members who helped in my research, whether experienced or novice researchers. It helped me, and at the same time it was good experience for anyone taking part:

Margaret in Burton was a great help to me and she sent me information about a film called Chicken Soup and Scouse a documentary about the Liverpool Jewish community. Produced by Michael Swerdlow, it was both entertaining and informative, and the film became a great source of information for me, giving a really good insight into the Jewish community and of where they lived around the Brownlow Hill area at the turn of the century, which was not far from Little Italy. I watched it and briefed the members of FTF:

Most of the Jewish people who were interviewed for this film tell a similar story, that Liverpudlians seemed to welcome all immigrants, including Jews. There seemed to be little anti-Semitism here until the outbreak of WW1 and the sinking of the Lusitania, killing 1,198 passengers and crew, mostly a Liverpool and U.S. crew. It was then that riots broke out against anything that even hinted of being German. Jews from Russian put signs in their widows 'Russian Jews' in an attempt to protect themselves and their businesses. The rioters were mostly grief stricken angry mobs. Then, when WW2 kicked off, anybody from Germany or its allies who had not naturalised were considered enemy aliens and interned in camps, as were many Italian immigrants.

There were a few distinguished people named Cohen featured in this film from the world of retail and medicine, who were descendants of Liverpool Jewish families. I wonder if any of them could be descended from my grandmother Rebecca.

The people interviewed told candid stories of personal hardship and Liverpool's community spirit and during WW2 the synagogue was used to hold Mass on Christmas Day, after an incendiary bomb hit the local Catholic church.

One lady talked about the local Jewish dairy shop that kept a couple of cows in the backyard in the middle of a row of terraced houses in the city; not a blade of grass for miles! People would take a jug to the dairy and the cow was milked to order and the milk still had froth and hair floating about in it. But they survived and they're here to tell us these stories. I don't think my generation could get through two world wars. I don't think I could!

One guy told this next story of his youth and it really made me laugh. Quote:
'Some non-Jewish kids would shout after me and me mates . . . "You killed Jesus Christ."
And well, you see, we didn't even know who the gentleman was.' Unquote.

He didn't know who Jesus Christ was, and yet he told his story so respectfully. But I couldn't help but giggle.
Wallaby

Sometimes I would spend hours in the Liverpool Records Office until I felt nauseous watching the microfiche moving along. It had the same effect as reading in a car and it gave me motion sickness. I would often come home excited with stacks of notes and information, and then other days . . .

I have zero results from today's record office search. I have come to the conclusion that my father's family were just as poor as my mother's family had been and they could not afford to buy gravestones or pay to place an obituary notice in a newspaper. I suppose, unless you had money or you were a pillar of the community, or were a bad person who did something that became newsworthy, then there was no need to record what the family did, as they were a family of no importance. Sorry everyone, I've failed miserably today.
Wallaby

No stone was left unturned; the *Lusitania*, the *Titanic* and other outgoing passenger lists, naturalisation records, orphanages and hospitals, institutions, cemetery records, electoral rolls, school admissions and Kelly's street and business directories were all searched either online, or on foot. I spent one day each week at the Liverpool Records Office and then typed up my findings onto FTF, being careful not to post any information relating to people who may still be alive, which is a rule of most websites to protect a person's privacy.

We turned our attention to the marriages of Louis' two eldest sons. A marriage for Gedaliah was found in the name of Dal Freeman. I also found him listed in Hebrew school records as Darley. So he had been: Gedaliah, Daniel, Darl, Darley and had morphed into Dal. The members suggested I ordered Dal's marriage certificate. I found Hyman had married in the same year. Without telling the members, I ordered Hyman's marriage certificate too:

The postman's been and I have something interesting! You wanted Dal's marriage certificate?
Wallaby

Screams with excitement A hit at last. Come on Wal', what's the surprise? If that's the right marriage, I'll enter it on the tree and also the possible children of this marriage. One child has a wonderfully unusual name, which I will not put on the thread as he may still be living. Now, one wonders what Wallaby is doing?
OC

Well, although you asked me to order Dal's marriage certificate, I noticed Hyman married in the same year. Hyman on the 13 March and Dal, the 11 August 1924. So I thought it would be interesting to see what Louis' address and occupation was. I also wanted to know if both brides, Annie and Sarah Cohen, were sisters or from the same Cohen family and if they were linked in any way to my grandmother Rebecca Cohen. So I ordered Hyman's too.
Wallaby

When I say I've found a birth, marriage or death, I'm of course talking about the GRO listings of births, marriages and deaths – the General Register Office BMD indexes. If you have never looked at these indexes, I'll explain the information that can be found in them, as birth and marriage entries from 1912 onwards contain more information than the previous years.

An example would be if we were looking for the marriage of, let's say, a Peter Bloggs and we found a possibility in the index. It would tell us that his spouse's name was, let's say, Brown, and from this we can then find her first name. Armed with this information we can look for any possible births of children of this couple, with the surname Bloggs, mother's maiden name Brown. That's *if* the mother's name had been listed in the birth index; some of the earlier births don't list the mother's maiden name. The other fly in the ointment is when two brothers have married two women with the same surname, like we had Sarah Cohen and Annie Cohen. You would then need to untangle the children to see which child belonged to Peter Bloggs, and which child belonged to his brother Joe Bloggs. There is a facility on the GRO website to apply without the index reference if you know the year of birth and you will then get the opportunity to give both parents' full names. This is how we eventually found the children of my father's many siblings. Of course, we had to find their marriages first.

Death indexes for pre-1969 deaths give the deceased's age at death and also an approximate birth year, but the accuracy of the age given when the death was registered depends on how well the informant, that's the person who registered the death, knew the deceased, or how calm and collected the informant was when giving the deceased's details. Informants often give wrong information – remember the confusion with little Jacob's age?

Sometime in 1969, exact birth dates were added to the death indexes, which in my father's case helped me to find the correct birth for him from the information that Joan of Archives had found that first night when I joined FTF. It was his date of birth that was given on his death listing, which tied Harry Freeman, who'd died in London on the 10 May 1984, to the Harry Freedman who was born in Liverpool on the 17 November 1907.

By the way, in case you're still scratching your head, Peter and his brother Joe Bloggs are not in my family tree, they were just an example.

Dal and Hyman's marriage certificates both gave their father as Louis Freeman, with Hyman's address being no. 48 Moon Street. This proved the link between my grandfather Louis and his two eldest sons. Dal had married Annie Cohen, giving an address of 29 Irvine Street, which was Annie's parents' address, and Dal's occupation was a master woodcarver.

Hyman's marriage certificate gave his occupation as a ship's cook in the merchant navy, which was a long way from his previous occupation, which was a tailor. Hyman's wife, Sarah Cohen, had a different father to Dal's wife Annie Cohen, so they were obviously not sisters, but I wondered if they had perhaps been cousins.

My big question was, were Annie and Sarah Cohen connected to my grandmother Rebecca Cohen? Unfortunately, their marriage records gave no answer to that question and we shuddered at the mere thought of researching the trillions of Cohens, the Smiths of the Jewish community.

But at least we could now breathe a sigh of relief, with the knowledge that although Daniel had morphed into Gedaliah, Darley, Darl, and had now become Dal, at least Hyman was still Hyman. Little did we know what was waiting around the corner . . .

18 Hyman Was Still Hyman

I could have wallpapered our living room with the amount of electoral rolls I printed out to trace my father's siblings. We seemed to have too many Harrys, and we didn't know who was who. They seemed to be multiplying all over Liverpool like Russian dolls! We knew about the two Harry Freedmans whose marriage records OC had found in 1926 and 1947, and we knew neither of them was my father. We also had a *Henry* Freeman, who was shown as Hy Freeman in the electoral rolls, and he was a machinist living in Teck Street and belonged to another of the Friedman/Freedman families who had settled in Liverpool and whose names had also evolved into Freeman. Then I found another Henry Freeman who was a baker. We matched each one of these Harrys and Henrys to their families, so they were all accounted for. But then, another Harry Freeman began to emerge in the electoral rolls and we couldn't find a family to pin him to. So who was he?

I practically camped out in the Liverpool Records Office and went through electoral rolls for no. 48 Moon Street year-by-year. In 1919, 1920 and 1921 Hyman and Samuel showed up, as they were then both old enough to vote. Isaac, Samuel and then a new name, David, popped up in 1922 and 1923. Who was this David? In 1924, Isaac and this David guy was listed again. In 1925, Isaac *appeared* to be there alone. In 1927, Isaac along with yet another new name, Edward. Who could this Edward be? Then finally, a drum roll for Harry! At long last, my father Harry had finally surfaced when he was of age to vote. But who were these two new names, David and Edward? And where was my grandmother's son, Abraham? We had not seen Abraham since 1911!

We suspected that Gedaliah had probably morphed into David, after being Daniel, Darley, Darl and then Dal, as it began with D. So had Abraham changed his name to Edward? Or could Edward have been Elias, or perhaps my father's full brother Teri?

Confused? Well, now you know how we felt!

Louis and his third wife Rosie never showed on the electoral rolls, which indicated that neither of them had naturalised. So they were probably still living at Moon Street too, but remained invisible. Perhaps Russian-born Abraham was invisible for the same reason. Many immigrants did not bother to naturalise because of the cost. Nellie could not vote, as women below the age of thirty were not allowed to vote until, thanks to the suffragette movement, the law was changed in 1928. Unless they were a householder or married to a householder, or held a university degree. So there was no chance of finding Louis' eldest daughter Nellie in the electoral rolls. There was no mention of Abraham, Elias or Terrence either. But I had found Isaac, Hyman, Samuel, my father Harry, plus this David and Edward.

I looked at the cemetery list and spotted a death for Eli Freeman in 1921. Eli was probably Elias, so I ordered his death certificate. Eli Freeman died of kidney failure on the 5 March 1921. He was just twenty-two years of age. The address where he died was given as, 144a Brownlow Hill. This was the address of the Workhouse Infirmary. Eli worked in the docks, and his home address was given as no. 48 Moon Street, which confirmed he was *our* Elias. His elder brother Samuel registered his death, providing further proof.

Eli's death reminded me of the death of my mother's younger brother Billy, who died of TB at a similar age, and it struck a sad chord. My Jewish grandfather Louis' life seemed to be filled with as much sorrow as my Catholic nan Annie's life had been.

Later, we also found the death of Isaac on the 2 March 1940. Isaac's age on his death certificate was given as thirty-eight, but his birth certificate gave his birthday as being the 18 July 1900, so the age on his death certificate was wrong. Isaac died of muscular sclerosis shortly before his fortieth birthday at Belmont Road Hospital, later Newsham Hospital, and his home address was given as no. 150 Bamber Street. This address had not shown before. Isaac had been a baker, and again, it was his brother Samuel who had registered his death. Samuel appeared to take on a lot of responsibility, registering deaths and filling out the 1911 census form. So my father's two half-brothers, Elias and Isaac, had died young, and it appears neither had married.

Meanwhile, it was back to the Liverpool Records Office for me, to try to solve our latest mystery – who was this extra Harry who had appeared from nowhere? Weeks went by with no sign of a clue. Then one night, when we were all falling asleep at our keyboards, OC woke us all up when, figuratively speaking, she blurted out: 'Harry *is* ... Hyman!'

The impostor was Hyman. My father Harry's half-brother Hyman, for some peculiar reason, beknownst to none other than himself, had decided to change his name to Harry!

Why on earth would anyone in their right mind want to call himself Harry, if he already had a brother named Harry? Trying to separate two Harrys within the same family to prove OC's theory took weeks. Eventually, I found two Harry Freemans at two different addresses in the same year, proving there were indeed two Harry Freemans within the same family. To save confusion, I will continue to call my father's half-brother Hyman.

As we were now starting to get a handle on Hyman's family, we stayed with him. OC had already earmarked four children's births: first a son Raphael, who was born in 1930, then another son Gerald, a daughter Hilda and another son Sydney, who had died before he had reached his first birthday. Further research found that Gerald never married and had died in 1981 at the age of fifty-three. Hilda had married but she didn't have children and had also passed away.

We discovered that Hyman's eldest son, Raphael, had married out, and although both Raphael and his wife had now both died, we found that they had a son, Arthur, with an unusual middle name, which helped Moggie to trace him in the online electoral rolls using tracesmart.com. Arthur was now in his sixties and we found he lived in Cheshire. At last we had found a living descendant of my father's siblings! Arthur, although a few years older than me, was the grandson of my father's half-brother Hyman. I needed to be scraped off our ceiling! I was ecstatic, and the excitement on FTF was bouncing off the pages. It was just like the first night of my thread when I couldn't keep up replying to all the posts and private messages from well-wishes. I calmed myself down and composed both myself and this message of thanks to all the lovely people who had helped me to find my father's family:

May I just say to everyone here on FTF . . . members, moderators, administrators and to anyone reading these posts, that . . . I became a member of this website on the 14 of Feb 2009, after starting and stopping for many years with the overwhelming task of tracing my father after my mother died in 1989. I can't believe that here we are, just a few months later, having all this information in our hands, of not only my father, but of most of his family too! And now, we're having a discussion about the best way to make contact with a living relative!

It's just unbelievable and so surreal. I make jokes and try my best to keep all this light and less emotional than it really is for me. But inside, I'm shaking at the thought of actually making contact with a member of my father's family. I can't thank each and every one of you enough, for the help and the interest that you have all taken in my mother's story.

Wallaby x

Of course this is emotional for you, how could it be anything else? If we are going too fast for you, just say so. But believe me, we will all be just one teardrop behind you on the day you make contact with a living relative!
OC

Well, that did it . . . I was in floods.

I wrote to Arthur. About a week later he rang my mobile, but it was on charge, so he left a message on my voicemail confirming that he was Raphael's son, but he didn't leave his number! I wrote back to Arthur the next day and explained far more than I had dared to do in my first letter, and he rang me back.

At first he was naturally apprehensive and he actually knew very little about his grandfather's family; in fact, he didn't know his grandfather Hyman, who he only ever knew as Harry, had such a large family, and he was quite surprised when I explained the full story. He had no idea why Hyman changed his name to Harry, and he had no idea his grandfather had a younger brother who was also called Harry.

Men always take one step back and a sharp intake of breath when something feels a bit uncomfortable. But once it sank in that his grandfather Hyman had not been playing away from home, and he really did have a brother with the same name, Arthur bent over backwards to help me. He sent photographs of his parents and gave me the information to acquire merchant navy records for his father Raphael and also for his grandfather Hyman.

But Arthur didn't remember very much. He told me that I needed to find a female descendant who was more likely to remember things and to have kept mementoes and photographs, or to trace the Cohen side of his father's family, who he knew a lot more about. He explained that his grandfather's brother-in-law, Louis Cohen, had jeweller's shops in London Road many years ago, and another somewhere around the Walton area of Liverpool. *The Times* cryptic crossword was far easier to solve than trying to untangle the Freeman family, so I dreaded the thought of starting on the Cohens, especially as I had no proof that Sarah Cohen, Hyman wife, had any link to my grandmother Rebecca Cohen. But I spent many happy hours talking to Arthur, and he always ended his call with the same words, 'Goodnight an' God bless, sweetheart.' Arthur told me story after story about his father Raphael, who was known as Ray and then before he ended his call he talked to Brian about football. Some stories were so funny, but one had me in tears, and that was the story of how his grandparents, Hyman and Sarah, ended their days.

Arthur told me about the many war medals his grandfather Hyman had won and that he was captured and shipwrecked twice, in both the First and Second World Wars. Hyman became paralysed from his waist down and spent the rest of his life in a wheelchair. In the mid-1970s, he and Sarah moved into a ground-floor flat of a tower block. It was February 1977 and their neighbours became worried as they had not seen them for a couple of days. Noticing the milk was still on their doorstep, they raised the alarm. Arthur was first to arrive at their flat and when he kicked their door down, he found his grandparents.

Sarah had suffered a massive heart attack and was lying on the hall floor, dead. Hyman was lying beside her and was barely alive himself. He had tried to get out of his wheelchair to help his wife and had flung himself down onto the floor next to her, but he was unable to crawl to the telephone or the front door for help. All that he could do was to cradle Sarah in his arms, trying his best to keep her warm. They both were taken to hospital in separate ambulances and Hyman died three weeks later on the 7 March 1977.

I had never met these people, and yet I felt I had known them, having traced Hyman's every move since his birth in 1893 when Louis and his first wife Rachael had moved from Leeds to Liverpool. I had Hyman's birth and marriage certificates. Annswaby, who was always on standby to help with my research, was a regular visitor to Kew and she kindly obtained Hyman's merchant navy records for me and I sent copies of these over to Arthur. His father Raphael and his grandfather Hyman had been cooks on the Cunard liners and they had travelled the world. I wondered if Hyman had ever sailed with my Uncle Tommy. He might have been one of the sailors who gave me pear drops and dandelion and burdock when my Uncle Tommy took me to see his ship when it had docked at Liverpool. I'd followed Hyman's younger days in tailoring and I'd spent weeks looking at electoral rolls trying to untangle him from his half-brother, my father Harry. It was so sad to hear the tragic way in which Hyman and Sarah had ended their lives.

People like Hyman, my grandfathers Louis and Will, my dear father-in-law Frank and that entire war generation fought for us to live a life of luxury, in comparison to their humble beginnings. Their lives of austerity have paved the way for our freedom and prosperity. They had no welfare state to take care of them when they were out of work, or if they became ill, only the workhouse and its adjoining asylum, which stood at the top of Brownlow Hill casting its dark psychological shadow across Liverpool's inner-city community. Its entire image felt threatening to people as they passed by, even its architecture instilled fear into the community, and yet it was their only safety net, their shelter and their NHS.

Many people I talked to during my research tried to hide any indiscretions that they felt could now be misunderstood. They need not have worried or been ashamed, because I felt nothing but pride for my mother's family, and for my father's family too.

People from that generation – like my father-in-law Frank, who went AWOL from his Royal Naval post as a gunner during the Second World War to stay just a few more days with his wife Nell, when she nearly died after giving birth to stillborn twins – we have so much to thank that generation for.

I had never been able to find Hyman's death in the GRO index. I now realised that this was because his death had been registered under the name of Harry Freeman, not Hyman. When I later found his grave, his stone was inscribed 'Harry Freedman'.

I remembered when I first joined FTF, Night Owl explained how some Jewish families cast-out their children and treated them as if they had died if they married-out. Then I thought about what Naomiatt had explained about not naming a newborn after a family member until after that family member has died. If their name is given to a newborn while that family member is still living, it is seen as 'wishing that person dead'. And yet, Hyman had used my father's name? Did this mean something? Was this a sign that Harry had been cast-out and was seen as dead? Was this why Hyman had taken my father's name? And if so, had my father's memory been cherished by his half-brother? Was this a mark of respect? Or a mark of disregard?

Or was I reading too much into this? Was it simply that Hyman's shipmates had called him Harry when he joined the merchant navy? Or perhaps he purposely changed his name to protect himself after being shipwrecked and captured twice, to hide his Jewishness from the Nazis? But still, why had Hyman chosen the name Harry? I couldn't think any more, so I took a couple of aspirins and went to bed before my head exploded.

Arthur was not able to help me answer these questions, as he didn't know his grandfather's family and sadly had no photographs of them. But Arthur talked to me and shared things with me as if I had always been part of his family, and I introduced Arthur to the deceased family that he never knew he had. Well, at least on paper, that is.

Everything Arthur talked about included the words 'our family', making it clear he meant mine, as well as his, and he did it without thinking, not in the least bit forced or false. He was not brought up in the Jewish faith and, like me, he was not religious. His father Raphael had married-out after his grandfather Louis had died. His mum was not Catholic, but she was Church of England, so same thing; she was a Christian.

Evidently, it was not only religion that stopped my parents marrying, at least not on my father's side, anyway. I felt that I would never know the true reason why my parents never married and yet always kept in touch with each other. Did my father love my mother? I might just as well pull petals off a flower.

But at least I had made a massive breakthrough in my research. I had found my first living descendant of my father's family and, even though, by his own admission, he was hopeless at remembering stuff and keeping mementoes, Arthur was not the can of worms I had worried so much about. Arthur was that box of chocolates.

19 The Can of Worms.

Most of the family had disappeared again from our radar screens during the Second World War. That was until we found a death for a Louis Freeman, which stopped us in our tracks. However, this death was as confusing as the death of little Jacob, and again, we were tearing our hair out. I had found a death in the cemetery records for a 73-year-old Louis Freedman, who had been buried on the 26 December 1940. The age fitted for him to be my grandfather Louis. But in the column marked 'home or place of death' was the address of Harrison Drive. The only Harrison Drive in Liverpool was in Seaforth, a couple of miles north of the city in the direction of Bootle docks. Had Louis moved from Moon Street?

The only death we could find in the listings was for Louis Freeman, not Freedman, who was thirty-seven, not seventy-three, when he died on the 20th, not the 26th December 1940. But this Louis Freeman's address was given as 18 Clarence Street, not Harrison Drive. Arnold Lewis came to my help again and kindly called into Broadgreen's Jewish cemetery where he was buried, and luckily the grave had a stone with an inscription, which gave *this* Louis Freeman's age as thirty-seven, not seventy-three. This time, it was the cemetery's records that were wrong. So my grandfather Louis was still alive in 1940. The assistant at Birkenhead's registry office kindly explained the confusion. Thirty-seven year-old Louis Freeman was killed at the Harrison Drive air-raid shelter in New Brighton after it took a direct hit just before Christmas. It took six days to retrieve the bodies of the many people who lost their lives that night. So *this* Louis Freeman died on 20 December, and was buried on 26 December, and had lived in Clarence Street. Another family had buried a hero.

Meanwhile, my grandfather had disappeared. According to pre-war electoral rolls, he was no longer living at 48 Moon Street, as a family named Evans was now living at that address. It would be many weeks later when OC finally found the death of my grandfather in January 1949 and posted this message:

Ladeez and Gennlemen! May I proudly present, for your delight and delectation, the one, the only . . . Louis Freeman! Died 1949 Qtr 1. Louis Freeman age 83. Liverpool North. Vol: 10d. Page: 422. Found him!

OC

It may sound a bit disrespectful to be celebrating, but we were not rejoicing *in* his death, only in the *finding* of his death, because we had researched everywhere but the moon for Louis when he went missing from Moon Street. We actually felt sad to lose my grandfather, or rather, to find his death listing. He would be missed in our research. What a remarkable man Louis must have been. I would love to have met him. He had buried three wives, and yet he still held his large family together, bringing up possibly eleven out of thirteen children, if Rosie's daughter, Betsy also became part of his family, which I expect she did, given that Betsy was only about seven years of age when her mother Rosie married Louis. Yet, only seven year-old Jacob and baby Bertie had died in infancy, at a time when Liverpool had one of the worst infant mortality rates in England. Maybe it was thanks to the chicken soup, often referred to as Jewish penicillin? Or was it the strict kosher rules of food hygiene that protected Jewish people from diseases? Perhaps it was also the fact that their homes were marginally better than the courts where my nan Annie Welsby raised her family. It was most probably a combination of all these things that protected his children. Whatever the reason, Louis had worked at whatever he could find to make ends meet and held on to his family.

It had been impossible to keep tabs on Louis with him not showing on electoral rolls. So we were keen to see what address would be on his death record and who had registered his death, as the family had scattered in the turmoil of the Second World War.

The information on Louis' death certificate revealed a heartbreaking ending to his long life. He had died on 10 January 1949. His age was eighty-three years. The place of death was 241 Westminster Road. I found this was the address of Westminster House Care Home. His home address was given as . . . no fixed abode.

Just the thought that my grandfather could have become homeless was disturbing, and images of a vagrant reduced us to tears. What had happened to my grandfather Louis? After all this man had been through, was this how his life had ended?

I researched Westminster House and found it was one of the earliest and also the largest care homes for elderly people in the country. This huge Gothic-style building was built towards the end of the 1860s, and was originally Kirkdale Industrial School, built for pauper's children. In 1904 it became Kirkdale Homes for the aged and infirm and it was run by Liverpool City Council. It was later renamed Westminster House.

After 1910, lunatics – the derogatory name tagged onto any person who suffered from *any* form of mental illness, from senile dementia or postnatal depression to psychosis or schizophrenia – were all bunched together and transferred to Mill Road Hospital. As a hundred years have now passed, the 1911 census reveals the column, which gives details of any disability a person may have suffered from. The cruel descriptive labels such as lunatic or imbecile were once common practice. How repulsive these terms appear to us today.

The definition of 'mental disability' was still unclear in the first half of the 1900s and, as unbelievable as it might seem today, being an unmarried mother was enough reason for a woman to be locked away in a mental institution, even up until the 1930s. If a women gave birth to a child 'out of wedlock' she could be considered neurotic and socially unacceptable. Cases were reported as recently as the 1970s, of unmarried mothers who were found living in mental asylums, having been kept there for decades.

By 1930 Mill Road Hospital, where I was born, closed that section and mentally ill patients were moved to Smithdown Road. Elderly people with dementia, and people who didn't have dementia but had no family to look after them, were split between Belmont Road Hospital, which took the female patients and Westminster House, which took male patients. So, for whatever reason, my grandfather Louis ended his life in Westminster House.

Age Concern pressured the government to improve care for the elderly. When the NHS was established in 1948, older and disabled people were divided into categories; *sick,* who went into hospitals, and *care and attention,* who were placed in residential homes such as Westminster House.

Researching into the history of the care of the elderly reminded me of when Joanie and I did voluntary work at St Joseph's Little Sisters of the Poor home for the aged, next to Newsham Hospital, formerly Belmont Road Hospital. We were about thirteen at the time, and we felt sorry for the elderly people living there. We noticed that few of them received visitors, and they reminded us of Old Biddy who lived in the garret flat with her nine cats. We worked at night after school and served their evening meal in the dining room, washed the dishes and then helped them up to their dormitories and put them to bed. On Saturday mornings our job was to polish the corridors of woodblock flooring with commercial-sized polishing machine. Sometimes we received chocolates or flowers from the old peoples' families. I worked there for only a few months until my nan's cancer returned.

These memories gave me some insight into what it must have been like for Louis living in such a place. He might well have suffered from some form of dementia – we cannot be certain at this point – but his symptoms might have been mild, similar to my father-in-law Frank who had multi-infarct dementia and was no danger to himself or to anybody else. But mental conditions such as Alzheimer's disease and senile dementia were not fully understood in those days and people were scared stiff of anyone who was mentally ill. Anyone who was suffering from a nervous breakdown, postnatal or menopausal depression or depression following a stroke – or melancholy, as my mother called it – were at risk of being sectioned and locked away in an asylum. Ignorance brought with it such cruelty too. Kids with learning difficulties were labelled as being backward. Something as innocent as a child being left-handed attracted ridicule, and they were mocked and labelled as being cack-handed, seen as abnormal and made to use their *correct* right hand, while people with epilepsy were given a wide berth. How life has changed. How lucky we are.

But my grandfather Louis lived in another lifetime and this was how he ended his life. Thrown in with other patients, many of them perhaps violent, with more serious mental health issues. It is the same reason we could not bring ourselves to put my father-in-law Frank into an EMI care home, even though care and nursing homes have now improved, it's still a heartbreaking decision for anyone to have to make. But back in those days, people had little choice or control of what happened to their parents. It could happen to anyone.

I ordered Louis' admission and discharge records for Westminster House from the Liverpool Record Office. The cost of these records was a steep £20, and OC didn't think it was worth my while spending the money, as she doubted that the records would hold much more information for my grandfather Louis than we already had from his death certificate. But I ordered the records anyway, just in case there was a bit more to learn. I just had to know why Louis' address was given as no fixed abode. Surly he didn't end up on the streets? It turned out that the information that these Westminster House records contained proved invaluable to my research. It was £20 well spent.

The records for Westminster House gave Louis' next of kin as Mrs *Blank* and his home address was *Blank* Street, which I found was the address of Louis' youngest daughter Eva, according to pre-war electoral rolls. From this we concluded Eva had probably cared for her father before he went into Westminster House. The records showed that for over five years up until he died, Louis was admitted and discharged a total of four times for home leave, and each time he stayed with Eva, anything from a few weeks up to eighteen months.

So my grandfather *did* have a home and family to go to! We discovered that the words 'no fixed abode' was sometimes used in place of a home address on a person's death record when that person was a permanent resident of a place such as Westminster House. So my grandfather's family did not abandon him. Louis was not a homeless vagrant, which was the impression given on his death certificate. My grandfather's family had cared for their father probably as best they could, given that the country was at war and most of his sons were away fighting when he was first admitted into care. I've since read messages posted by concerned researchers also unfamiliar with this term of 'no fixed abode'. It's nice to be able to explain and reassure others, to pay something back.

Louis' eldest son registered his father's death and gave his name as Dal Freeman, confirming the links between Dal, Louis and Eva. We now knew where Louis had gone after the Moon Street address and we also now knew Eva's married name, which you've probably realised is not actually *Blank*. I ordered her marriage certificate, which held a wealth of vital, interesting information, most of which I cannot reveal.

We found Eva and her husband had a daughter who was still living in Liverpool. We had now found a female descendant of my father's half-sister. I remembered what Arthur had advised about women being better than men at remembering and keeping stuff. I was on cloud nine, until Joan of Archives brought me back to earth:

I don't want to get your hopes up, but please be prepared in case Harry's family are not accepting of you should you find more of them.

My sister-in-law contacted her family's relatives and they didn't want to know. Her father was Jewish, but her mum was not. I don't know if that had anything to do with it, but it was very upsetting for her, as she was an only child just like you.
Joan of Archives

If I detect the tiniest hint of coldness, doubt, or animosity from any of my father's family, it would send me off in the opposite direction, Joan.
Wallaby

Louis' granddaughter, who I shall give the fictitious name of Caroline, was now in her mid-seventies. Surely she would remember my grandfather Louis, who was her grandfather too, as Louis had lived with Eva and Caroline before he was admitted in to Westminster House.

Caroline would have been about twelve years of age when Louis died. Being much older than Arthur and also having lived with my grandfather, she was more likely to have known Harry and all his siblings. Perhaps she also knew my mum and maybe she knew something about Rebecca's son Abraham.

I was excited, but at the same time, I was a bit apprehensive. I'd put all my thoughts and efforts into finding my father's family, and I had not given much thought about what to do when we found them! Suddenly I was stiff with fear. I had been lucky with Arthur, but I had a niggling feeling about approaching Caroline. I was worried about her reaction to me, how she would treat me, and if she knew anything about me. She lived about seven miles away from our home. What if she is not interested in me? What if she knows all about me and doesn't want anything to do with me? On the other hand her welcome could be warm, she might throw her arms around me and say: 'Oh, thank God. You have found us at last!'

I took a great deal of time composing the letter to Caroline. Brian was passing her road the following day on his way into town, and so he offered to post my letter through her letterbox after discreetly checking with Caroline's neighbours that she still lived at the address. He parked at the opposite end of the long road, some twenty or so houses away from her house. Two men were stood talking at the end of the road, and he asked them if they knew Caroline's family and if they still lived at the address. How unlucky could Brian have been for one of the two men to turn out to be Caroline's husband!

Brian was thrown in at the deep end and, placed in an awkward position, he then found himself having to explain the story unprepared. But he did his best, and Caroline's husband was actually quite friendly. Without hesitation he invited Brian along to the house to meet his wife. All seemed to be going well.

Caroline's husband was a tall man in his seventies. He seemed a nice, quietly spoken person. He opened his door and quickly disappeared into the house, leaving Brian standing on the doorstep. After a few minutes, Caroline appeared at the door.

Brian usually gets on really well with older women, and if anyone can worm their way out of an awkward situation such as this, it's my better half. So after apologising for disturbing her and explaining his unplanned visit, and the gist of my story as best he could, he then offered Caroline my letter.

She listened without saying a word until her family was mentioned, and then she just went ballistic. Throwing her hands up in the air, she roared that she wasn't interested in her family or their history, and without further ado she slammed the door in Brian's face.

As soon as he walked through our door, I knew something was seriously wrong.

'You know these brick walls you keep going on about hitting?

'Yes . . . yes. Just tell me, what's happened?'

'Well, I think this time the brick wall has hit us.'

'Oh Christ, NO! What went wrong?'

'EVERYTHING!'

I was mortified. The following night, I bought some flowers and decided to go to see her by myself. I didn't tell Brian, as I knew he would have tried to stop me. I had my bunch of flowers and my letter on the passenger seat beside me, and as I drove to Caroline's house, I rehearsed what I was planning to say to her. Her husband opened the door, and I explained who I was and that I wanted to apologise to his wife for Brian's unannounced visit. Without a word, he disappeared into the front room leaving me standing on the doorstep, and within two minutes Caroline appeared in the hall. I introduced myself and explained that I wanted to apologise for any upset. She said nothing - just stared into me. I outlined my twenty-year search for my father, who was her mum's half-brother. She listened, her face totally void of expression. I offered her the flowers and letter. She looked at me, still without saying a word. Then, after taking a deep breath, she kicked off. With her hands clasped behind her back, she coldly and bluntly told me that she didn't care about any of the family . . . dead or alive. Suddenly, I was back in school again and my new-found cousin had mutated into Old Tooie:

'There's been a big fall-out with my family. So I'm not in the least interested in you. I'm not in the least interested in whoever your father was. I understand that you know nothing about my family fall-out, and that you don't know the family. But nobody wanted to know my mother when she was alive and now everybody's interested in family history!'

It appeared that I had walked into a serious family argument, and this tiny woman, who wasn't much bigger than a garden gnome, was still bitter about whatever problems had gone on within her immediate family. She fired off all this dialogue at me like a fully loaded machine gun and she didn't stop once to reload, or to draw breath.

I tried to get a word in edgeways, but it was perfectly clear that the garden gnome wasn't remotely interested in anything I had to say. By this time, curtains were beginning to twitch and I contemplated shutting her up by saying something along the lines of, *So, are you not interested in a share of the £2 million that you could be entitled to?* Then watch her gob hit the floor before I walked away from her. Oh Christ . . . this was my worst nightmare. I'd opened the can of worms!

When I offered her the flowers and my letter she didn't even look at them, no doubt preferring to concentrate on what she wanted to say next. With a dismissive, condescending wave of her hand, she continued the bombardment and by this time, I had smoke coming out of my ears.

'NO! I'm allergic to flowers – take them away, they give me hay fever. I'm not in the least interested in your flowers, or your letter, and I am not interested in you or your father. My mother was a loner. She had nothing whatsoever to do with her family. Our ancestors are up there looking down on us all. We all have to live with our problems and you have to live with the fact that you never met your father, just like I have got to live with all my problems. We all have our problems, and yours are no worse than mine.'

BANG ... (that was the door).

I felt like planting both her and the flowers in the plant pot that stood on her step, but this woman was in her mid-seventies and at least a foot smaller than me, and I'm only five foot! I could do neither. I had to respect her age. Besides, I'm a defender, not a fighter.

During the whole of this performance her husband was standing next to her in the long hallway. He was as tall as she was small, towering above her like a motorway lamppost. He looked embarrassed, and he never opened his mouth once. The garden gnome held all the cards and she seemed well aware of this. I could do nothing but walk away.

Besides, I got the impression that even if she did have a photograph of my father she would realise the power she held and perhaps want money for it. Or worse still, as I didn't have a clue what my father looked like, she could have just shown me a photograph of any Tom, Dick or ... Harry!

So after a long search and the build-up and all the excitement of finding a person alive who knew my father, who had actually lived with my grandfather and may have had a photograph of both of them, she turned out to be full of bitterness, waiting to off-load it onto some soft dope who happened to be passing by, and who just happened to be me. Oh God, what was I going to tell the members of FTF? They were waiting to see photographs!

I didn't notice that the sky had turned black and, as I scurried back to my car, the heavens opened. It was like Caroline had sent the wrath of God down on to me. I drove home at about 20 mph. The rain was horizontal and the windscreen wipers were banging from side to side and my head was pounding. Everything she had said to me was going around in my mind and I was feeling so sorry for myself. If only Big Annie Oakley had been with me! As I opened our front door, I was met by my other half with a face like thunder.

'Where've you been?

I muttered my reply.

'WHAT! I told you not to go. I told you what she was like. You never listen to me.'

Blue murder ensued for at least an hour. Feeling sorry for myself, my body crawled up to bed to lick its wounds in peace and quiet, and my fingers tried their best to type a heavily censored explanation of my disastrous meeting with my nearest and dearest new-found cousin to the members of FTF, who had put so much effort into helping me to find her. Meanwhile, my head was still arguing on Caroline's doorstep, saying all the things that I had been dying to say to her and would have done, if she had been twenty years younger *and* a foot taller. What on earth had stopped me from hitting her with the bunch of flowers and posting the letter through her gob, I'll never know. My Aunt Annie was back in my head again. The snakes on Medusa's head were hissing and spitting.

I was brought back from my imaginary fight when I heard Brian muttering away to himself as he walked into our bedroom. We weren't speaking, and I was in a sulk, so I kept my head down and typed. I had been still clutching onto the flowers when I walked through our front door. When he walked into our bedroom he was carrying a tray full of goodies with a mug of hot chocolate and a couple of aspirins for me as a peace treaty, and he had put the flowers into a vase of water on the tray. I looked at the flowers and we both fell into a heap. They were his favourite sunflowers and I remembered that I had squashed them in my car door when I slammed the door in temper. The poor things didn't have a head left on them. They were in tatters. I knew exactly how they felt.

20 Rose Bush Court

In the post-mortem analysis of my encounter with the garden gnome, the members of FTF shared their experiences of what they referred to as cold-calling, i.e. knocking on a relative's door without first sending a letter of introduction. It's never advisable, as it often gets a knee-jerk reaction and can provoke a negative response, although none of the members had ever encountered anything as negative I got and they agreed it would not have made a bit of difference with Caroline. Nevertheless, people get scared; they worry that this new family member who has just materialised out of the blue might have an ulterior motive. Or maybe Caroline wanted to conceal her Jewish roots and that accounts for her reaction to me?

The members of FTF suggested we move on swiftly. Arthur was a lovely person, and they were certain that I would find more nice family members. I wasn't listening. I was still licking my wounds and more interested in searching backwards to find my roots. The dead couldn't fight with me. I was safe. The members of FTF didn't take a blind bit of notice to me.

Completely ignoring my reluctance to search for more descendants of my father's siblings, the members rallied around to give their support, rolled up their sleeves and began researching for more living relatives.

By now I had most of the birth certificates for Harry's brothers and sisters, and we knew that his two brothers, Elias and Isaac had died and had not married. I grew fond of my father's eldest brother Gedaliah, who, out of his string of many names, I preferred to call Dal. He seemed solid and reliable, as you would expect the eldest brother of a large family to be. I found that he remained in Irvine Street with his wife Annie and they had no children. Eventually they moved into Rex Cohen Court, which is a Jewish sheltered housing complex on Croxteth Drive near to Sefton Park in Liverpool. We found Dal had passed away in 1974 at the age of eighty-three. His death was registered as Dal Freeman and his life, for me, was only a few bits of paper. I never met him, and I felt sad to think that I never would meet him.

Rex Cohen Court was built in 1968 by the Jewish Board of Guardians for the elderly people of Liverpool's Jewish community. Looking into its history, started some of FTF's members thinking about Rose Bush Court, while others looked for more living descendants.

Slowly but surely, we began to make progress. We found Samuel had married Annie Levi in 1923 at Hope Place synagogue. Annie Levi was born in 1902. Her parents, Morris and Leah Levi, lived at 14 Trafalgar Street, off Brownlow Hill. By 1911 Annie Levi had been adopted by Max and Sarah Waterman. Max Waterman had a glazing business in Netherfield Road. On the 1911 census we discovered that they had also adopted another girl, Rosie, who was born in Hull two years after Annie. I later learnt that Rosie died of cancer in her thirties. The census gave both girls' surnames as Livi-Waterman (sic). This made me wonder if the girls were sisters or maybe half-sisters. No death was found for Annie's parents in Liverpool, so perhaps they moved to Hull. We found Samuel and Annie living in Adcote Road, Dovecot, and then later Litchfield Road in Wavertree. But still nothing was found of my father's full brother Terrence or half-sister Nellie, and absolutely zilch for Rebecca's son Abraham, who would still have been classed as a Russian national and so would not show on electoral rolls if he had not naturalised. We wondered if Abraham had changed his name back to Abraham Cohen after his mother Rebecca died in 1911. He was the only link I had to my grandmother Rebecca, so what had happened to Abraham? Had he naturalised under a different name? Could he have been the Edward I had found on the electoral rolls?

When I thought about it, Abraham must have had such a tragic life. His father had died pre-1904, presumably in Russia, and his mother Rebecca, brought Abraham and his baby brother Jacob to Liverpool where she married my grandfather Louis, himself also a widower with six children between the ages of four and thirteen years. Did they all get on? Maybe this marriage had been arranged, as many marriages were in the old days. In 1907 Abraham lost his little brother Jacob. Then in January 1911 he lost his half-brother Bertie, and by April 1911 he had lost his mother Rebecca too. He was still only thirteen years of age, and lurking in the shadows, just three years ahead of him, lay carnage; the First World War. He would have been about sixteen years of age when war broke out. Now, as documentaries are shown in commemoration of the Great War's centenary, the full horror of trench warfare has been brought into our sitting rooms. Vast improvements in technology has given old film footage colour and corrected the speed. Our grandparents now look like real people to us. The expressions shown on their faces can now be read and understood. We can sit warm and comfortable as we watch what they went through when they fought and died for us.

According to the movinghere.org.uk website, about 50,000 Jews enlisted for the First World War. Many were from Allied countries who had come to Britain as young children. They formed their own unit, the Zion Mule Corps, fighting in Gallipoli in 1915. The Jewish units of the 38th, 39th and 40th battalions of the Royal Fusiliers joined the Jewish legion in Palestine. Many eastern European Jews were in the Pioneer Corps, working as labourers or digging trenches, repairing roads and railroads, guarding POWs and also burying the dead. The Victoria Cross was awarded to five Jewish soldiers. Jews in the Labour Corps in Belgium and France worked unarmed close to German guns. Whether Abraham naturalised and was then eligible for conscription, or perhaps volunteered into one of these Jewish battalions, is something that remains a mystery. After Russia withdrew from the First World War in 1917, Russian nationals living in Britain became eligible to serve in the British Army, so if he didn't naturalise or enlist, he would have been called up for service eventually. In the Liverpool Hebrew School records, I found admissions dated 22 August 1904 for two boys who were both named Abraham Cohen. Samuel Freedman was also admitted on the same day as them. To distinguish the two Abraham Cohens from each other, the letters (a) or (b) were placed after their names. Abraham Cohen(b) looked tantalisingly interesting. His address was no. 48 Gill Street. His parent was listed as Betzy Cohen (sic). Occupation: dressmaker. Abraham Cohen's date of birth was listed as ?-?-1897. (sic)

Usually it's the father's name listed as the parent. So could this Abraham Cohen's father have died? Rebecca's death certificate recorded her first name as Becky. So could this Betzy have been my widowed future grandmother, Rebecca, admitting her son Abraham into school? Abraham Cohen(b) is listed in the withdrawal column of the school records in 1911. Nothing has been found of him since. What happened to you, Abraham?

Meanwhile, the members who looked into Rose Bush Court where my father had lived before he died, brought back the following information about the apartments. They were owned by the British Humanist Association (BHA). I wondered if that was significant. I found it was not easy to get a flat at Rose Bush Court at that time. The apartments nestled in an affluent area of Hampstead and were much sought after by retired people within the community. We wondered if Harry had been a member of the BHA, which perhaps had given him a foot in the door. I had previously tried obtaining information several times from Rose Bush Court, without success. I even tried to obtain details using the Freedom of Information Act. But the apartments were managed by SP Housing Association, who were not obliged to abide by this act. So I contacted the BHA directly and, after explaining my story, I received a reply from Hanne Stinson, who was the Chief Executive at the British Humanist Association. Hanne kindly checked their memberships and found zilch for Harry. She explained that this didn't necessarily mean he was not a member of the BHA, only that they failed to find him in their records, but added that their records were incomplete.

However, Hanne gave me some information about Rose Bush Court, and also on how their housing projects began. This, at least, gave me some insight into how their residents were selected and also the general set-up of facilities at the apartments. I also knew who Harry's neighbours had been, thanks to a brilliant piece of detective work by Peppie, who photographed the full list of residents' names on the 1984 electoral roll at Camden library. From the electoral rolls, Peppie found that Harry had lived at the apartments since 1969, which was when Rose Bush Court was built. But we could not find where Harry lived after 48 Moon Street up until he moved into Rose Bush Court. So there was still a big gap in my father's life to fill.

The apartments were comfortable, compact one-bedroom units, the majority of them being built for single occupancy. There was a resident warden and a communal lounge, and at the rear of the building was a garden with parking and a heated ramp for easy access in winter. This area around Parkhill Road was, and still is, a desirable place to live, being close to Belsize Park and not far from Primrose Hill. It's an area that is home to some prime property. It's also a popular area with Jewish families, so Rose Bush Court had a high ratio of Jewish residents, and it still has to this day. There are many kosher shops and pavement cafés dotted about the leafy, tree lined lanes, and many notable people live in this area of Hampstead. Local electoral rolls probably read like a *Who's Who*, featuring artists, poets, playwrights and interesting people. Another member of FTF, whose username is 'Jill on the A272', took a tour of the streets when she was visiting her own relatives and emailed me some photographs of the apartments. So, I was able to see what my father looked out onto from his window, and this at least gave me an idea of how he spent the latter part of his life. Contacting the BHA directly also opened some doors for me, and I found the warden at the apartments knew Janet Scott, who was the warden who had written to my mum in 1987. Although she couldn't give me her address, she offered to pass a note to Janet on my behalf. So I wrote a letter to Janet asking her a string of questions and enclosed a copy of her letter, which she had written to my mum over twenty years before, telling her of *Henry* Freeman's death. I heard nothing for a couple of months, and had given up all hope of receiving a reply from Janet, but when her reply arrived, it was both helpful and informative . . .

I came to Rose Bush Court as a Duty Warden in October 1983 and I do remember your father. He was a very private person and never spoke about family or friends. I remember he enjoyed ballroom dancing and would go to the afternoon tea dances now and again with one of the ladies who shared the same interest, but she also passed away many years ago.

Harry became poorly and was taken to New End Hospital in Hampstead where I visited him a couple of times, but that hospital has now closed. I attended his funeral with my late husband and Mrs Schrier, his ballroom dancing friend. He was buried in a North London cemetery, a Jewish service. I'm afraid I can't tell you anymore, as it's many years ago.

Good Luck with your search

Janet Scott

Rose Bush Court, Parkhill Road, Hampstead. Courtesy of FTF member, Jill-on-he-A272.

I assumed Harry had been transferred from New End Hospital to the Royal Free Hospital. He had become friends with a Mrs Schrier and they went to afternoon tea dances together. This information gave me many new avenues to pursue. I wondered if my father was related to Mrs Schrier in some way. There must have been a reason why he settled in this area.

From the list of residents that Peppie had photographed on the 1983 electoral rolls, I was able to see that Mrs Eva Schrier had lived at no. 6 Rose Bush Court. We found that she had died in 1998, which meant that she had still been living at Rose Bush Court when I first asked about my father when I found the letter after my mum died in 1989. Yet, I had been told on several occasions that nobody living at Rose Bush Court could remember my father! It was a lesson too late. Do not be fobbed off. Always ask more than one person. Be polite, but be persistent.

It didn't take us long before we found that Eva Schrier's granddaughter Stephanie had a page on Facebook. Stephanie lived in Maryland, Virginia. Her mother, Sylvia, was Eva Schrier's daughter, and Sylvia had recently retired from Virginia to Florida. After explaining my story to Stephanie, she promised to pass my details on to her mother, and sure enough, the following night Sylvia rang me from Florida.

The main thing I needed to know from Sylvia was, had my father and her mother Eva been related in any way? Sylvia was very helpful and we talked for a couple of hours. She explained that she had met my father just once in the communal lounge at Rose Bush Court, on one of her visits to her mother. Sylvia confirmed that her mother and my father went to tea dances together in the afternoons, but she was not related in any way to him. Sylvia remembered Harry being a nice man, very charming, but she knew nothing more about him, other than her mother had said he was funny and a good dancer. She was surprised when I explained that my father was from Liverpool. I wondered if Harry had lost his Scouse accent.

I've been thinking about Harry's time in Rose Bush Court. He lived at Flat no. 13. I've managed to find three things in the Guardian from 1969 and 1973, which may be interesting. One is a letter from a resident living at no. 16 about moral education and religion in schools. The content probably isn't relevant other than Harry may have known this person.

The second is a death notice for J. B. Coates of no. 14, Rose Bush Court, leader of the Personalist Group. Mr Coates may have been Harry's neighbour, with Harry living at no. 13. Perhaps my imagination is running away with me, but I'm starting to build up a picture of a group of educated, deep-thinking people.

Lastly, in a 1973 article entitled, 'Who cares about the elderly', the journalist visits the Humanist Housing Association's block in NW3, which I'm sure must be Rose Bush Court. It describes the type of accommodation and how people are selected to live there. I can't post them on FTF because of copyright but Wallaby, if you could PM me your email address I'm happy to send them. They make interesting reading.
Night Owl

Just had a quick read about the Personalists. This Mr Coates, who died, was a leading light in the group and a most intelligent and cultured man – Harry certainly had some interesting neighbours, if nothing else.
OC

At that time, I only had a vague idea about what it actually meant to be a humanist and about what they believe in, or rather, what they *don't* believe in, as it is more what they do not believe that distinguishes a humanist. I knew that humanists were agnostics, but I learnt that many prominent people belong to this association. The BHA's website explains that humanists take the view that we all have this one life and they believe that it is our duty to share this life and to also take responsibility for it, and also for what we leave behind in this world for others. They also believe in social cooperation, mutual respect, individual rights and freedom. Humanists are positive thinkers, taking inspiration from life, art and culture, and they feel that it is the responsibility of the individual to make this one life a good life, for the benefit of themselves and for others too. They think that we can make sense of the world using our experience and shared human values and that we can still live a good life without superstition or religion of any kind. What very refreshing thinking. Obviously, the word faith isn't used much in their vocabulary. Looking back, I think my Uncle John was a humanist without joining the club. John wouldn't join a club; he was a man with questions rather than answers, and he was very much the wait-and-see type who kept his mind wide open.

It was while we were engrossed in analysing the intellectual leanings and activities of the residents of Rose Bush Court and trying to find out if Harry had moved away from Judaism and joined this bunch of deep-thinking intellectuals he'd lived amongst from 1969 until he died in May 1984, that we made our most important breakthrough of the search. And this time, there wasn't a red herring in sight. Moggie had been quietly searching in the background and she had found a descendant of Samuel's. He had a daughter named Shirley!

To recap, Samuel and his wife Annie Levi-Waterman had moved from Adcote Road in Dovecot to Litchfield Road in Wavertree. We found that Samuel died in 1951, just three days before his fifty-fifth birthday. His death certificate told us that he had worked at the Ministry of Pensions Hospital in Liverpool. These hospitals were set up after the First World War to cater for the ongoing medical needs of those who had fought in the Great War. Samuel and Annie had two children, a son, Raymond, and a daughter, Shirley, who married jeweller, Louis Bodansky, in 1954. We had lost the family again until Moggie found Shirley Bodansky on the 2008 online electoral roll. It turned out that Shirley, who, by this time would be in her late seventies, lived only about a mile away from our home! Oh, please, let her still be alive. I dreaded the thought of her perhaps having senile dementia or maybe being too frail to be interested in me. I'd lost my confidence after opening the can of worms, and so I scrutinised all the details we knew about Shirley before I carefully drafted yet another letter.

It's difficult to write a letter to a person when you have no idea what they already know of you, if anything. The letter needs to give enough information, but not *too* much information, just in case you have contacted the wrong person, and then, if they are the right person, you don't want to appear to be a crank and hold back information either. There are many hoaxes going around, and people are naturally cautious. So the letter needs to be open and honest. It's a fine balance, and it's important to get it right, as you don't want to frighten the person you're writing to and you don't want your letter to be binned. I remember how I felt when I got that telephone call from the London couple when they refused to give their details. If only they had written, explaining things properly and giving me all the details about their friend Harry in a letter, so that I had something to mull over and take my time to digest, things could have been very different. If only I had something written down on paper to refer back to, I would have known if my mother was not telling me the truth. Or, perhaps she only knew my father as Henry and genuinely didn't know anyone named Harry and, like me, didn't associate the two names. If only they had given me his full name, address and telephone number, I could have contacted Harry Freeman myself without telling my mum and I could have met my father before he died. If only . . .

But it's no good crying over spilt milk. So I drafted my letter to Shirley. Every single word I wrote was so important. It was now that Samuel's amputated fingertip came in handy, for me at least, as I used Samuel's war injury to identify him to his daughter Shirley, so that she could see I had found the correct family, and I was open about myself, about who I was and where I lived. There was no more anonymity for me; it was now time to come out.

Revealing my details would allow Shirley or her family to check me through Google, telephone directories or just by word of mouth, as we lived so nearby that it was entirely feasible for her family to make enquiries about me within the community. Plus I had been in business for nearly thirty years, so this would give them confidence that I was genuine. I felt that this was the last throw of the dice. So, I took a deep breath and I wrote this letter:

Dear Mrs Bodansky,

I am currently researching my family tree on my father's side and wondered if you could help me. My father was Harry Freeman & he was born in 1907 & had many brothers. One of his brothers was called Samuel Freeman who married Annie Levi-Waterman & I've learnt that Samuel & Annie had a daughter named Shirley. Mrs Bodansky, I wondered if perhaps Samuel & Annie would have been your parents?

If your father was the same Samuel Freeman who was part of my family tree, it may help to identify him by the fact that he lost part of his finger during the Great War.

If you are Shirley, the daughter of Samuel Freeman & Annie Levi-Waterman, you may be interested to know that I've done a great deal of research into the Freeman family & if you, or your family are interested in family history, I would be more than happy to share this with you & perhaps exchange some family history information.

I have given my address above & my number & email below & I would be happy to hear from either yourself or your family.

However, if I've made a mistake, & your parents were not Samuel & Annie Freeman, I do sincerely apologise for taking your time & I would be very grateful if you would please return the stamped addressed envelope I have enclosed with a quick note to explain this, so that I may move on with my research.

Yours sincerely . . .

21 Shirley

It was just over a week before my self-addressed envelope was returned, and enclosed I found a handwritten note on beautiful personalised notepaper. Shirley confirmed to me that her parents were indeed Samuel and Annie Freeman and that her father had been injured in the war as I had mentioned. She enclosed her telephone number and invited me to call. I could see from Shirley's steady handwriting that she was sensible, astute and a hundred per cent lucid. In fact, despite her advancing years, I soon realised that I need not have worried, as Shirley's mind was sharper than my own.

I made notes of things to talk to Shirley about in case I dried up, and I could have done with a couple of diazepam that day, but I took a deep breath and dialled her number. When Shirley answered, she sounded very together, and then when I explained who I was, she seemed slightly taken aback, but only for a moment. Then, she collected herself and we talked and talked and talked. Shirley seemed as excited to talk to me as I was to talk to her.

She knew absolutely nothing about me or my mother or that her Uncle Harry had a daughter, so I explained my story and she was amazed. It was such a relief for me to hear Shirley utter the words:

'Did you know there were two Harrys in the family?'

I laughed and replied: 'No . . . but I soon found out!'

Shirley had no idea why her two uncles were both called Harry; it was just the way things had always been when she was growing up. To think of all the time I had spent in the Liverpool Records Office and the hours and hours of researching that the members of FTF had done online, trying to untangle Hyman from Harry, only to find that one of the Harrys we had found *was* Hyman, and Samuel and Annie's 's daughter Shirley lived only around the corner from me and could have explained all these complications and saved us months and months of work.

I hung on Shirley's every word as she talked about my father and explained that he was a regular visitor at her house.

'He came every Sunday to visit us until about the mid-1950s, or soon after, and then he just disappeared! We often wondered what had happened to him!'

This cracked me up.

'Well Shirley . . . I think what happened to Harry . . . could have been *me!*'

We both laughed and then Shirley said: 'Well, I would love to meet you . . .'

It was only a little thing, but Harry's disappearance around the mid-1950s made sense, and it also solved a mystery for Shirley too.

We agreed that she would come to our house the following Wednesday night, which was one week away. We talked some more and I asked her to make notes of all the things she could tell me about my father. I wanted to know every tiny detail about him, and I asked Shirley not to polish him up. I wanted to know the bad and the good. I was now rabbiting on ten to the dozen, nerves left far behind me. Then, I heard Shirley say quietly, almost as if she was thinking aloud:

'Uncle Harry was at my wedding and he is on my wedding photos.'

I had waited twenty years to hear somebody say those words and I froze. It was so, so surreal and neither of us spoke. 'Hello . . . Hello . . .'

'Yes . . . yes I'm here. Shirley, did I hear you say that you have a photo of my father? Harry . . . not Hyman? Do you have a photo of Harry? Are you absolutely certain it's Harry . . . your father's *youngest* half-brother, Harry?'

'Oh yes, it's definitely Harry. Hyman was in the merchant navy, and so he wasn't at my wedding. It was definitely Harry who came to my wedding, and Uncle Dave, who you call Dal or Gedaliah. Uncle Dave gave me away, because I got married in 1954 and my father Syd, who you call Samuel, died in 1951. Harry is on the wedding photograph standing next to Uncle Dave. It's only a small photo, but it's definitely Harry . . . your father!'

For the rest of my life, I don't think I will ever forget those words. Shirley had no idea what this day meant to me and I couldn't speak. I wanted to jump into my car and drive to her home that minute to see the photograph of my father. I stood up and paced the floor.

'Shirley, I've never seen him. I've never even seen a photo of him! All I've ever wanted was to put a face to him. Will you be able to find the photo?'

Shirley assured me that she knew exactly where her wedding photographs were and she would bring her wedding album.

Shirley told me that she'd had her knee replaced and was waiting to be admitted to have her other knee done and found it difficult to walk. Smiling, I told her to take good care of herself; after taking so long to find her, I didn't want anything to happen to her now!

Shirley laughed and told me that she was fine but couldn't manage the stairs, and so since her operation she had been staying with her partner Monty at his flat, which was only a few minutes' drive from our house. She also told me that her daughter Linda was listening into the conversation with a smile on her face that stretched from ear to ear. I suggested that Monty and Linda come along too.

I later learned that Shirley wore a hearing aid and needed to have her telephone on amplifier, so everyone in the room could hear every word I said. I imagine I sounded like an excited hyena!

Shirley was so natural and easy to talk to. I could hardly wait to meet her. I just couldn't believe my luck. What a contrast after my encounter with the garden gnome. The members of FTF were ecstatic and pulled my leg about hiding in our garden and bugging the house to listen to all the things Shirley could tell me about my father and his family, so I made a list of questions. I was 99.99% sure what the answer would be to my first question:

Did my father ever marry?

Do you recognise my mum in her photograph?

What was my father's work? Was it in scrap metal?

What was my father like as a person?

Did my father serve in the war?

What happened to Nellie?

What happened to Abraham?

Who happened to my father's full-brother Teri?

Do you know where Louis came from and if he had any other family here?

By the following week I had about three pages of notes and questions to ask my very special visitors.

I had joined FTF on 14 February 2009. As the next few months went by, my 'Hospital Records' thread had acquired a following of members who had bent over backwards to help me find my father and to learn as much as possible about his family. Along the way, many members sent me private messages of support through the FTF website. By the time Moggie had found Shirley in June 2009, my Hospital Record thread had accumulated over 120,000 hits in only a few months, and as I write this chapter it is now approaching 300,000 hits.

This was a record for FTF's website, and each time the thread reached over 1,000 posts I was asked to open a new thread, because it becomes too slow to download. I named each new thread 'Hospital Records Part 1, 2, 3, etc . . . By the time Shirley and her partner Monty were due to visit us at our home, I had come to the end of 'Hospital Records Part 5' and planned to open 'Hospital Records Part 6' with my father's photograph, and promised the members of FTF to do this the minute Shirley and Monty left that same night, no matter how late. The members of FTF wanted to see Harry as much as I did.

As the week went by, I learnt as much as possible about Jewish culture and kosher food. Although we had Jewish friends, they were not strictly kosher and would eat anything put in front of them, whether it was kosher or not. So off I went to Roseman's Jewish deli, which was not far from our home, and I bought all kinds of wonderful kosher delicacies, many of them surprisingly familiar. I didn't know how *frum* my special guests were; they might only eat kosher food from a kosher kitchen, but at least I had made a special effort.

I don't really know what I was expecting Shirley to look like. But when our doorbell rang at eight o'clock on the dot, Brian opened the door to the most attractive, tiny little Jewish lady with snow-white hair. It was a lovely, balmy summer night and Shirley looked tanned and was dressed in a turquoise jersey-cotton top, embellished with beads and silk flowers, and a long, white linen skirt. She was so stylish, warm and approachable. Shirley's partner Monty was eighty-three, and he didn't stop talking from the moment he walked through our front door, which broke the ice. Monty was tall with thick white hair and he was smartly dressed, wearing blue, jean-style trousers, deck pumps and a blue striped blazer. I could tell Monty knew how to wear his clothes and I suspected he had been a tailor in his working life. They explained that they had both been widowed for many years and known each other their entire lives. Shirley's late husband, Louis Bodansky and Monty had been great friends, and Monty was actually the best man at their wedding.

Shirley opened her wedding album and handed it to me. The page showed a family group wedding photograph of Shirley and her late husband Louis Bodansky, traditionally surrounded by both their families. There were many men in the photograph. I asked Shirley not to point my father out, as I wanted to see if I could recognise him myself. Immediately my eyes fell onto a tall man who was standing next to a much shorter man at the end of the group. There was something about his face that was familiar to me.

'This is him here . . . isn't it?'

Shirley looked up at me, smiled, and quietly said, 'Yes . . . yes that's him.'

Wearing a black tuxedo, my father was tall, dark and handsome, just as I had always imagined my father to be, because my mum's screen idol had been Tyrone Power, the 1940s Hollywood movie star. She thought he was the most handsome man in films, and when I first clapped eyes on my father's photograph, I thought to myself, *this is my mum's Tyrone Power.* Of course, he would have been well into his forty-eighth year at Shirley's wedding in July 1954 and I would have been just nine months old.

My father's eyes were half closed, as if he was focusing on someone or something in the distance rather than looking straight at the camera, and he had a shrewd look about him, as if he was streetwise and as sharp as a razor.

Standing next to my father was his eldest half-brother, Gedaliah aka Daniel, Darley, Darl, Dal, or Uncle Dave, as Shirley called him. So we had guessed right, Dal had been the David I had found on the electoral rolls. Uncle Dave was a much shorter man than my father and he was nearly nineteen years his senior. They looked as different as chalk and cheese. Uncle Dave had a kind face and looked solid and reliable, just as I had always imagined my father's eldest half-brother to be. I wondered if I had ever met my father or any of his family when I was a baby. I would have loved to have met Uncle Dave. There was just something about him that looked like he would understand everything.

In another photograph my father was standing behind Shirley and her veil was concealing the bottom half of his face. His head was slightly bent down and to one side and his eyes were wide open looking up. It was then that I could see myself in my father's eyes.

I asked Shirley if any other family members were in the wedding photographs.

'Yes, this is Auntie Lil.'

'Auntie Lil? Who's Auntie Lil?'

'She was your father's half-sister.'

'Ohhh . . . do you mean Nellie?'

'Yes that's right, Nellie. Her name was Helen-Lillian. But we called her Auntie Lil.'

'Well, no wonder we couldn't find Nellie!'

Shirley went on to explain: 'Auntie Lil married a man called Jack Holden, who was not Jewish, and they moved to Blackburn. Sadly, Jack died in the late 1930s, but they did have two daughters, Renah and Margaret. Renah married Allan Bennett and they had a daughter Natalie and a son John. Their younger daughter, Margaret, emigrated to Australia with her husband Fred Farrer, I think that was about 1950. Auntie Lil followed them out to Australia about 1958/59. After being widowed for over twenty-years, she met and married

Harry Armstrong, but I can't remember whereabouts they actually settled, it was possibly Melbourne. My mum and Auntie Lil's second husband, Harry Armstrong, often wrote to each other, but then Harry died and we lost touch with them. I would love to know how they are.'

I asked Shirley about my father's work but she knew nothing about any scrap metal business in the family and doubted that information. She remembered her father's brothers had worked at an array of jobs; woodcarving, tailors, hawkers and ship's cooks and she was told there was also a brother who had died young and he was a baker. She had some vague recollection of him having a terrible accident at work with something falling on to him. She explained how people needed to work at anything and everything in those days, but she was quite certain that nobody in the family worked with scrap metal!

Before I found FTF I had traced every pre-war scrap metal business that had traded in Liverpool! Now it looked like Steptoe and Son needed to be deleted from my search notes. I asked Shirley if she knew anything about my father's full-brother Terrence, who, according to his birth records, had been registered as Teri.

'Teri . . . who's Teri? Oh, you must mean Teddy? His name was Edward and we called him Uncle Teddy. Yes, he was your father's full-brother. He married Annie Blair, who was not Jewish, and they had two daughters, Joyce and Olive, who were about the same age as me, but I've not seen them since we were young children. I would be delighted if you could trace them. But you know it's really strange, because I thought Uncle Harry and Teddy's mother's name was Eva. I've never heard of this Rebecca who you have mentioned.'

Although I said nothing to Shirley, I thought to myself, *so far, at least two of Louis' children had married out, and yet although my parents had kept in touch with each other, they had not married and my father was kept a secret?*

So Terrence was the Edward I'd found on the electoral rolls. That left only Abraham unaccounted for from *the boys*, as Shirley referred to her father's brothers, but Shirley had not heard of Abraham. It turned out that Shirley knew nothing about Louis' third marriage to Rosie, and their daughter Eva or Rosie's daughter Betsy. We then realised that Shirley was remembering the name Eva as being the mother of Teri and Harry. When in fact, Eva was their half-sister not their mother. Of course, my grandmother Rebecca had died twenty years *before* Shirley was even born and Rosie had died when Shirley was only four years old. Maybe Shirley remembered Eva as being the woman of the household when she was a child.

Shirley explained that she didn't see much of her grandfather Louis in his later years. He had died when she was only about sixteen, but Jewish children didn't go to funerals back in those days. She remembered Louis always called her his little Rohel, pronounced Rockel. This was Hebrew for Shirley's second name Rachael, which was her grandmother's name.

I showed Shirley some photographs of my mum in her younger years, and although she thought she was beautiful, she did not think she had met her. She told me that, as far as she was aware, my father never married, at least not before the mid 1950s, which was when she had last seen him. She talked about him always being full of fun and told me that he loved children. I asked Shirley if Harry had served in the Second World War. Shirley didn't think he had served in the war but added that she and her brother Raymond were evacuated during the war, so she was not certain, and wondered if perhaps Teddy's daughters, Joyce and Olive, or Nellie's daughter Margaret could remember more.

So that would be my next assignment, to find Joyce and Olive, wherever they were, and Nellie's daughter Margaret, who was somewhere in Australia. They were also my first cousins.

Shirley told me that her brother Raymond had passed away only last year and he would have loved to have met me. She explained that Nellie's other daughter Renah had also died many years ago, but she remembered that her daughter Natalie lived somewhere in the south of England. So I had a shopping list, and although I didn't have a clue where to look for Joyce and Olive, at least I knew where to search for Margaret and Natalie.

We now had a total of three Annies in my father's family. Why am I not surprised? My father's eldest half-brother Dal, who we now know as Uncle Dave, married Annie Cohen, Samuel had married Annie Levi-Waterman, who was Shirley's mother, and now my father's full brother Teri, who became known as Uncle Teddy and was the Edward I had found on the electoral rolls, had married Annie Blair. At least this counterbalanced my nan Annie Welsby, my aunt, Big Annie Oakley and her youngest daughter, who we called Ann. I had now found Harry's entire family, apart from Abraham, who had gone AWOL.

Shirley had years and years of stories to tell and it helped that Monty remembered my father too. Monty was so easy to talk to, warm, open and straightforward, and Brian got on really well with him.

When I talked about Louis, I always referred to him as Shirley's grandfather, until Shirley interrupted me, and I will never forget what she said to me:

'Louis isn't *my* grandfather. He's *our* grandfather! Don't forget, he's your zayde too!'

It was the way she said it that was lovely. I don't know how I didn't burst into tears.

'I can't get used to calling him grandfather, I feel like I'm pinching him from you!'

If I could have painted a picture of how I wanted my first cousin to be, Shirley could not have been more perfect and I loved her to bits. I felt so comfortable with these people. I'd always worried about detecting some hostility, the slightest of which would have caused me to back away immediately. But Shirley seemed as delighted with me as I was with her, and after all my worrying about opening up another can of worms, it had turned out to be another box of chocolates with a lovely cream centre. I had worried for nothing.

I had expected to meet Shirley's daughter Linda, but she was working nights in ICU at Aintree Hospital and so Shirley promised to bring her along on her next visit. At one point, Monty asked Brian if he could see our garden, and when Monty walked past my chair he stopped, put his arms around me, gave me a big hug, and then he whispered in my ear.

'You do realise that you're half-Jewish . . . don't you, dear?'

'That's fine by me.' I replied.

Monty was so laid-back and full of fun, but this was just a bit of banter. According to the Torah, a person needs to be born to a Jewish mother to be recognised as being Jewish. I was a half-breed, which suited me down to the ground. At least after all those years, I now knew what I was half of. I had no wish to become Jewish, but now that I had introduced myself to my father's family and it had been confirmed that he did not have a wife, I would never again feel the need to hide my father or conceal my Jewish roots.

Before Shirley and Monty left, I had one final question. I asked Shirley if she knew where about in Germany Louis came from and if he had any parents or siblings in Liverpool or anywhere else. Shirley looked puzzled.

'Germany? I thought zayde came from Russia! Louis didn't seem to have any family, at least as far as I can remember. He just seemed to be one on his own.'

Louis claimed to be a German national on his marriage records and all the censuses that he was listed on. I hoped Shirley was right.

Shirley left her wedding album with me, which I thought was a lovely, trusting thing for her to do. So I scanned my father's photograph and also the photographs of Uncle Dave, his wife Annie and his sister Nellie, who was known as Auntie Lil, to upload onto FTF, as they were all deceased and I knew the members wanted to see the people they had helped to search for, especially my father Harry.

After midnight, there would usually be no more than a handful of members viewing my 'Hospital Records' thread, as it was the change-over between one side of the world going to sleep and the other side waking up to begin their day. But that night there were members from Italy, Spain, Canada, the US, Australia and New Zealand as well as all over the UK, and from that boat, wherever it had now sailed to, and the *craic* between them was hysterical. They all knew as much about my father's Freeman family as I did, and they all said the same, they felt like the Freeman family was their family too. In only a few months, I had found my father with the help of a bunch of complete strangers who didn't even know my first name, nor I theirs, and still don't! These people were not professionals, they were unpaid amateurs who were completely addicted to family history research and who became totally enthralled with my mother's story. Where do I begin to thank these people . . . whoever they are?

Before Shirley and Monty arrived that night, I had already written my first post for my next thread, which I was about to start: 'Hospital Records Part 6'. I always wrote the first post of a new thread as an introduction post or a recap to enlighten a new reader and to bring all the members up to date on where we were up to with the search, as it got rather confusing, as you can imagine.

It was shortly after midnight when Shirley and Monty left us that first night and as soon as their car disappeared around the corner, I scanned, cropped and resized my father's photograph and uploaded it onto the FTF website. This is how I introduced my father to the lovely members of FTF who had worked relentlessly to help me find him . . .

Welcome to Hospital Records Part 6 . . .

Hospital Records Part 6 marks a catalyst of change from what seemed an impossible search for my father . . . into reality.

All my life I have tried to imagine what my father was like. I have longed to sit and talk to him, or for someone to sit me down and tell me what kind of a man he was, what he looked like and what was important to him. Of course, I didn't think I had a cat in hells chance of finding out who he was, until my mum died in 1989 and I found a letter giving me a name and an address. It was a clue; a very misleading clue . . . but at least I had something.

Now, after twenty-years, thanks to relentless help from members of FTF, who, since February this year have not left their keyboards, in what has been the most remarkable team effort imaginable, from a bunch of people who have never met each other – nor me!

Everybody, I would like to introduce my Father . . . Harry Freeman

Thank you

Wallaby x

My Father Harry Freeman: Circa 1954
1907–1984

22 Margaret – 'Your Father Was My Hero'

I enlarged and printed my father's photograph and put it into a retro-style frame matching one that I had my mum's photograph in, and I hung it on the wall next to her's, alongside one of my Russian violins. I could hardly take my eyes off my father's photograph, I felt like I had finally brought him home.

Up to this point, Brian and I still hadn't told anyone about my father apart from my two closest friends, Linda and Shelagh, and Jo and Lisa, who manage the daily running of my business. These people are like family to me. But I wanted to introduce myself to my father's family before I began talking openly about him. Meanwhile, I had great fun picking the brains of my Jewish friends who hadn't an inkling of what I was about to announce. So after meeting Shirley, I began telling a few close friends as and when I met up with them. Besides, I thought it was better to wait until this book was finished to let people read the full story for themselves, as it would take me another twenty years to try to explain every little detail. So, I decided to remain *schtum*.

It's easy to lose all sense of time when researching your family's history. Holding a person's birth or marriage certificate in your hands seems to bring that person to life again and it throws things completely out of sync. OC warned me that I would now go through a sort of mourning period, and I didn't understand what she meant by this. I soon found out.

I had found my father and his family, but of course, he was dead and so were all his siblings. He was only a stoneless grave at the end of my long search, and although I knew that before my research began, it didn't hit me until I found his family, and he was not there.

I soon returned to earth, dried my eyes and blew my nose, and began gathering up all my notes and information to begin the first draft of this book. Up to now, I had not mentioned the book to Arthur, or Shirley and her partner Monty, as I wanted to see how it all pieced together first and to prove to myself that I could do it. So, while my attention was turned to writing this book, the members worked on the information that Shirley had provided and began the search for Nellie's daughter Margaret in Australia.

They found Margaret's birth in 1922 in Blackburn, and her marriage to Fredrick Farrer in 1946. We now had the name Farrer to search for, and while we slept, FTF member Mary from Italy found a Mr and Mrs Fredrick Farrer sailing to Melbourne on 12 July 1950 on board the HMS *Cheshire*, under the ex-servicemen's scheme. But then the trail went cold and Margaret was lost to us somewhere in Australia. So Margaret and her husband Fred were placed carefully back on to the shelf, and we turned our attention to Nellie's eldest daughter, Renah Holden, who had been born in 1920 in Blackburn. Shirley told me that Renah had married Allan Bennett and they had a daughter Natalie and a son John before she died in 1994. We also discovered that Renah had owned a successful dance school and still, to this day, the Renah Bennett Cup for Ballet is awarded each year in Crawley. We then turned our attention to her daughter Natalie. It wasn't long before Moggie found Natalie's marriage and found her living in Surrey, and when Shirley and Monty invited Brian and me for supper, I updated Shirley with our new findings. She felt sure that the Natalie that we had found must be Renah's daughter. It took me not much longer than ten minutes to draft a letter to Natalie. By this time I knew exactly what to say without even thinking about it. Besides, it was much easier to write a letter now that I could mention Shirley. I included the details of Natalie's grandmother Nellie and her various names, and I mentioned about her going to Australia in the late '50s. The following night, I went out for a couple of hours and I left my mobile phone at home. Brian had arrived home before me, and when I walked through our front door I found him deep in conversation with Natalie, as if he had known her all my life.

As I walked into our kitchen I overheard him saying to Natalie:

'Well, do you know Brad Pitt? Well, I look like him.'

I grabbed my mobile off him.

'Hi Natalie, take no notice to my other half. He suffers from delusions. Believe me, he looks nothing like Brad Pitt!'

Within two minutes of talking to Natalie I knew we were on the same wavelength. She was delighted to receive my letter and we talked for ages. She explained that she never knew her grandmother's name was Nellie; she only knew her as Helen-Lillian or the family called her Auntie Lil. Natalie told me that her grandmother had been a tailoress and she once made her a rag doll, which she still keeps on her dressing table. When she gave Natalie the doll, she told her that the doll's name was Nellie. So to now be told over fifty years later that her grandmother's name had actually been Nellie made sense to her, and she was in tears. The last thing Natalie remembered of her grandmother was waving her off at the station when she was leaving for Australia.

Natalie told me about the delicious egg custards that her grandmother often made and, what a good cook she had been and how hard she worked as a tailoress. She went on to tell me that her grandmother, Aunt Margaret and Uncle Fred had first settled in Melbourne, then later moved to Brisbane and were now living in Noosaville. Her aunt and uncle had only recently moved into a retirement apartment complex and she would get their address from her brother John, who also lived in Australia. Despite their advancing years, Natalie told me that they were both as fit as fiddles in both mind and body, and still swam and played golf every day. Natalie explained that after her grandmother's second husband, Harry Armstrong, died, she later remarried for a third time to Lance Simpson. She died in 1987 at the ripe old age of ninety-three.

I explained the story of my parents, and Natalie said that she would search the attic as she was sure she had a photograph of her Uncle Harry somewhere and possibly one of her great grandfather Louis too. True to her word, Natalie actually found a much younger photograph of my father when he looked to be in his early twenties, and he looked even more like Tyrone Power.

My father Harry Freeman
Circa 1930s.

Natalie also found what we think could be the only photograph of my grandfather Louis in existence and he looked nothing like what I had imagined. In fact, I was surprised to find that my grandfather Louis appeared far more prosperous and distinguished than I had ever envisaged in this 1935 photograph, given that he was then approaching his seventieth year. Far from the image I had in my head of a hawker, my grandfather was nothing short of a hunk. Donned in his **dark three-piece suit with crossover necktie, pocket watch and chain,** Louis reminded me **of the Hollywood actor Spencer Tracy.**

Below:
My grandfather
Louis Freeman.
Taken at Nellie's home,
Blackburn. Circa 1935.

Above: Back row (left to right)
Margaret, Shirley's mum Annie,
holding Shirley's brother Raymond.
Shirley's grandmother Sarah Waterman.
Middle row:
Louis, Shirley age 5-years and Nellie aka Auntie Lil'
Front row:
Natalie's mum Renah and possibly Hyman's son,
Raphael. Circa 1935.

Louis was sitting in Auntie Lil's garden surrounded by many members of his family. The day looked warm and sunny. Auntie Lil was sitting next to Louis with her two grown-up daughters, Margaret and Renah. Shirley, then five years old, was sitting in the middle, with her mother Annie standing behind holding her little brother Raymond. Another photograph, which appeared to be taken on the same day, was of my father, Harry with his two nieces. These photographs were a fantastic window onto my father's life.

Natalie told me that her mum Renah had researched the Freeman family many years ago before the age of computers, and she had even travelled to Salt Lake City to research the Mormon records. Unfortunatley, Renah's notes had not survived, but Natalie remembered her mum telling her that the name Freeman may have originally been Freemanowitcz, or something sounding like that. The nearest names that we could find were Formanowicz or Furmanowicz, which were both of Polish origin. Without Renah's notes to refer to, it was impossible to know if Renah was speculating or if she had found some evidence to prove this. So I made a note of these names in my laptop for future investigation.

Natalie's brother John kindly provided Margaret's new address so I drafted a letter to my new first cousin enclosing all my details including email. I was excited to find Margaret, as she was eight years older than Shirley and might remember more.

I hadn't written this many letters for years, as most of my business is done through email now and most of my friends have email, so I've lost patience with snail mail, and rarely use it. The day I posted my letter to Margaret, the snails went on strike! So it was many weeks before I received Margaret's reply, which I was surprised to find, came in the form of an email, expressing her surprise and informing me that she had posted a letter that same day. A couple of weeks later, I came home with my arms full of groceries and when I picked our mail up off the hall floor, I found a four-page, beautifully handwritten letter from Margaret, which was jam-packed with stories and information about my father.

I stood in the hall, my arms still juggling shopping bags. Our cat Bimbo had entwined herself around my ankles and was meowing loudly for attention. I ignored her while I read Margaret's letter, hanging onto every word. Margaret was now eighty-eight years of age. She remembered my father very well and had so much information to tell me. These are just a few snippets from Margaret's letter, a letter that would be the first of many more to follow.

The first line of Margaret's letter immediately had me in tears. She had a lot to tell me and spoke about my father warmly. She began her letter in such a lovely way, a way that I will never forget . . .

My dear cousin,

What a lovely surprise I got today, it was like a bolt out of the blue. Before anything else I would like to tell you what I know about your father Harry, because, my Uncle Harry was my hero . . . .

He was so different from the rest of the family, tall, slim with thick, black shiny hair, which he swept back off his face using Brylcreem. His suits were well cut with wide lapels and good material. He was a good dancer and I always thought of him as someone who enjoyed life.

He bought and sold gold until the war, then he became a fireman. When the Tate and Lyle factory was bombed, he worked on that fire and I remember it upset him greatly. He always made us laugh. He was a loveable person and my family thought the world of him.

I never met my grandfather, Louis, until I was twelve years old. He banned my mother from his house because she ran away to marry a non-Jew and it was twelve years before he relented.

I never knew the family name had been originally Friedman, then Freedman before it became Freeman. I can't be certain, but I think I remember my mother telling me that her father Louis came from Poland . . .

Poland? Louis claimed he was from Germany. Shirley thought Louis was from Russia and now Poland had been thrown into the pot. I needed to take Louis' place of birth with a large pinch of kosher salt.

This news that my father had bought and sold gold meant that OC had been right all along. Harry's work had nothing whatsoever to do with *scrap* metal. It was *precious* metal! Before I found FTF I had researched every *Steptoe and Son*-type of scrap metal firm that was in business in Liverpool between 1930 and 1950. Harry was not a Harry H. Corbett after all. Margaret had confirmed Shirley's information and OC was right, my father traded in gold!

*TOLD YOU TOLD YOU! I just KNEW he traded gold and not scrap metal. Jews often played things down. Oh, what brilliant news and your new-found Australian cousin sounds lovely. To think you were once so worried to approach anyone in case they rejected you or were suspicious of your motives. Now you have found a lovely family, apart from one, that is. *Dances across thread, doing an elderly restrained sort of jig**

OC

Arthur had told me that Hyman's brother-in-law, Louis Cohen, had been a jeweller and I also knew that Shirley's husband Louis Bodansky was a jeweller, so my father had good contacts in the business, but maybe he played down his work, as OC had suggested.

I later read a book called *Diamond Street: The Hidden World of Hatton Garden* written by Rachael Lichtenstein, about the jewellers of Hatton Garden. It gave me a good insight into the strict secrecy and security in which the jewellery and diamond business operated. Rachael wrote that deals were done on a handshake; trust was everything in this village-like neighbourhood where everyone knew each other. I began to understand the need for all the secrecy between the wholesalers, retailers and brokers, who were the middlemen of the industry. They thought nothing of carrying pocketfuls of precious stones, gold and silver to trade. Perhaps Harry was more at the 'cash for gold' end of the business. Or maybe higher up the ranks; a broker or middleman and he had gone to London to work in Hatton Garden, which was then the epicentre of the industry, and was dominated by Jews at that time.

Meanwhile, the information Margaret had provided about my father being in the fire service during the Second World War was enough to order his service records from the Liverpool Records Office after first obtaining permission from Jean Crimmins, a very helpful archivist at the Merseyside Fire and Rescue Service, as these records were closed.

A call to Simon Ryan at the Auxiliary Fire Service Archives gave me some idea of why my father had joined the fire service. Simon took the time to explain that there could be several reasons why my father had not been called up. If he wasn't in a reserved occupation, which he was not, he could have failed the medical with something that appears trivial to us today, like flat feet or a perforated eardrum, which, together with his chest condition, a perforated eardrum was what disqualified my Uncle John from active service when he tried to enlist. In that situation many otherwise fit men joined the fire service to do their bit for their country. Or if my father had passed the medical, given his age of thirty-two when war broke out in 1939, he certainly would not have been one of the first to be called up. In which case, many men joined the fire service or the Home Guard while waiting for their orders.

Several books have been penned about the heroic work of the Liverpool fire bobbies. With pathetically little training or equipment, they protected Liverpool and were seen as heroes. They saw just as much action as the men on the front line, and many lost their lives during the relentless bombing of the city and its docks. I felt like I was now uncovering the other side of the story; a story of two Liverpool families whose religious backgrounds were completely different, and yet their struggles and fears were just the same.

Harry's fire service records gave me a wealth of information about him. The records gave another address for my father which we had never seen before. In 1939 he was living at no. 27 Mulgrave Street in the south end of Liverpool where my cousin Mary had thought he had lived. His service records also told me that he had been stationed at the Essex Street division whilst with the fire service and between 1926 and 1932 Harry had been in the Liverpool King's Regiment TA. These records even gave his uniform measurements. So from not knowing a thing about my father, I now knew his height, hat size, boot size, and even his chest measurement!

Above: Liverpool's Fire Bobbies and Water Pump at North Langton Dock.
Both Photographs Courtesy of the Auxiliary Fire Service Archives.

Right: Example of basic equipment.
*Coventry Climax Trailer **Pump**.*

Reading the lovely words in Margaret's letter gave me the best feeling in the world. I have no interest in money, except that it gives me independence, which is important to me, and the pride I can take in knowing I have earned what bit I have after starting with nothing. But what I treasure more than anything else are photographs, and the photograph Shirley gave me of my father is, to me, the most valuable possession I have. The other thing that I will always treasure is this telegram, which Margaret sent to me. She received it in 1946 on the day of her wedding. It was from her Uncle Harry.

Reading my father's words in his telegram was equal to seeing his photograph for that first time. Although this is not his handwriting, it is the next best thing; these are his words, which he chose to compose his telegram to his niece.

MISS M HOLDEN 95 RILEY ST AUDLEY RANGE BLACKBURN   3:49PM LIVERPOOL LGS 55

TO MY DEAR NIECE MARGARET AND HER HUSBAND. I AM SENDING MY VERY BEST WISHES ON YOUR WEDDING DAY AND IN THE YEARS TO FOLLOW MAY YOU BOTH LIVE WELL AND BE HAPPY. SORRY I COULD NOT BE PRESENT. GOD BLESS YOU. KISSES. YOUR UNCLE HARRY.

Above: My father's telegram to his niece Margaret, on her wedding day, 21 December 1946.

Words say a lot about a person, and my father seemed to have been a sentimental, caring person. But I could also see from the younger photograph Natalie found of him that Harry was also a charmer, and he cared about how he looked and dressed, so I nicknamed him Flash Harry. I imagine my mum had a lot of competition.

The Mulgrave Street address on my father's fire service records intrigued me and I was inspired to go back to the Liverpool Records Office and check the electoral rolls to see who else had lived at that same address, but according to the records, Harry appeared to have lived there alone. By all accounts, he seemed to be very much a loner, but I was determined to find him and fill that gap in his life. So I decided to search the electoral rolls for every single year, going through them street by street, and moving out of the city from the direction of Brownlow Hill and surrounding area and heading south through the Sefton Park area, which was the route the Jewish community travelled over the years as they prospered and moved to the suburbs, eventually settling around the leafy areas of Allerton, Mossley Hill, Childwall and Woolton. Liverpool's Jewry peaked at around 11,000 at the beginning of the First World War, but since then it has slowly declined, and in 2004 it fell short of 2,700. I can only hazard a guess that it would be no more than a couple of thousand today, as the general population in Liverpool has declined, despite the short-lived economic boost of later years.

I had a planned work strategy and took a few streets each week, then went onto another year. I did this week after week, until one week, I got lucky. I found him living at no. 10 Princes Avenue on the 1951 electoral rolls and he was still at the same address in 1954. But then the fog descended again and he was lost. To this day, I don't know anything of my father's life from 1954 until he moved into Rose Bush Court in 1969. Some London electoral rolls are online, but although I've spotted a couple of possibilities, there are too many Harry Freemans in London to single him out. I would love to hear from anyone who knew him. Shirley remembers he had a friend, obviously now deceased, who had lived somewhere on Queens Drive in Liverpool, but although she cannot remember this friend's name, she recalls meeting his friend's wife many years ago, and his wife enquired about Harry as he had disappeared so suddenly. So neither my father's family nor his friend knew where he'd gone. And yet, my mum knew where he was.

We saw Shirley and Monty regularly and Shirley often brought photographs with her that she'd found and I copied, repaired and laminated them for her. My guess about Monty being a tailor was correct. However, I learnt that Monty was no ordinary tailor, but a well-regarded master tailor, and he had premises in Stanley Street for many years. Throughout the 1950s and '60s, Americans would cross the pond especially to have a suit made by master tailor Monty Fagin.

When Shirley was going into hospital to have her other knee replacement operation, we took some flowers and called in to see them at Monty's flat before she was admitted. We thought it was best not to visit her while she was actually *in* hospital. I was delighted that Shirley had welcomed me into her family, but I was also mindful of not overstaying my welcome. When Shirley was discharged, her daughter Linda sent a text to let me know that her mum was home and she was fine. After a few days I rang her and Monty answered the telephone. Immediately he wanted to know where on earth we had been and why had we not called sooner. When I explained that we didn't want to intrude, as it was a time for close family, I will never forget what Monty said to me.

'We're all one family now. So we don't intrude on each other's business.'

Monty had a lovely way about him and they were so good for each other. It was heart-warming to watch them together. They were in the autumn of their lives and they were making every day count. They always had something planned – a holiday, a night out, a weekend away – and they looked after each other. Monty's wife Cybil had passed away many years before, and Shirley's husband Louis Bodansky had died over thirteen years earlier.

Monty explained that Hyman's brother-in-law, Louis Cohen, who Arthur mentioned had two jeweller's shops, was not related to Dal's wife Annie Cohen, and he didn't think they were linked to my grandmother Rebecca, either. However, they didn't know anything about Rebecca. So, I needed to keep my mind open to the possibility of my grandmother Rebecca being linked to Hyman's wife Sarah Cohen or to Dal's wife Annie Cohen. And I still didn't have a clue where Rebecca's son Abraham had gone. Shirley and Monty had never even heard of Abraham.

By this time, I had persuaded Mary, my cousin's daughter, to get herself a computer and some lessons so that she could keep up to date with the research on FTF. We often talked about her mum's brothers and sisters, but, like me, Mary had lost touch with them all. I worried if perhaps they had all passed away, as Mary explained that none of them had attended her mum's funeral. She had been close to Kathleen, her mum's younger sister who was deaf, until Kathleen died of cancer, and she knew that her mum's brothers, Tommy and Billy, had also died many years ago. But she had not heard from her mum's younger siblings Brian and Ann for a long time.

My cousin Brian had inherited his father's black hair and I remember him being tall, dark and handsome. He had lived in Ditton in the 1960s after his marriage to his wife Laura and he worked as a miner around that area for the first few years of his married life. My mother often talked about how hard he worked down the pits. At Christmas he bought me the *Girl's Own* annuals, and one year he bought me a silver plated bracelet, which I treasured for years. Mary remembered her mum and Kathleen visiting their brother Brian back in the 1990s, and they were then living somewhere around the Widnes area, but she had not heard anything of him since. Ditton and Widnes were only thirty minutes drive from where we lived in Woolton. I was relieved to find there was no death listed for my cousin, who would be in his mid-seventies by now, so I searched 192.com for him. It wasn't long before I found him, and when I looked at his address on Google Maps, he lived near a close friend of ours.

It was then just before Christmas 2009, so I sent my cousin Brian a Christmas card enclosing a note and my telephone number. I had not heard from him since John's funeral in January 1993!

A few days later he rang me and we talked for ages, and the following week he was sitting in my kitchen. My cousin had no idea that my father had been Jewish, but he was able to tell me some surprising things that he himself could now make sense of, and he also had a surprise for me.

'I remember you were christened at St Columbus church in Huyton and for the first six months after you were born, you and your mum lived with us. There was a problem with some neighbours, one family in particular. I remember being in John's car one day with you and John, and this family attacked us and tried to turn the car over. I was only eighteen then, and you were just a toddler. I used to visit a lot in those days, and I remember being there one day when two men came to the door asking for your mum. Your mum's cousins Paddy and Jimmy Hill were still living there at that time and Jimmy had answered the front door. When I asked Jimmy who the men were, he told me that the tall, dark man was your father. He also told me that Auntie Katie wouldn't marry him.'

'Oh my God! You're telling me that it was my mum who refused to marry my father?' I remembered OC's words from an earlier post . . .

'. . . *have you ever considered it was maybe your mum who refused marriage? When Jewish people married-out, they lost their family. But when Catholic's married-out, they faced eternal damnation! Well, they did then . . .* '

I thought to myself, *OC was right again. The woman must be psychic!*

'Yes, but I wasn't told why. People didn't talk about stuff back then, especially not to kids, and I would still have been just a kid in their eyes. I never knew your father was Jewish. I can't believe our Mary kept this to herself for all those years!'

This news that it was my mother who refused to marry my father was a shock to me, and I was reminded of a message posted in the early days of my thread by Janet in Yorkshire, who was another helpful researcher on FTF, when we were discussing why my parents never married. And, for the first time in my life . . . I felt sorry for my father.

I don't think Harry was as worried by the religion issue as Wallaby's mum. We are now finding that some members of his family did marry out. To marry Harry, Wallaby's Catholic mum would face a huge dilemma having to cut herself off from family, church, culture, life as she knew it. Once her family knew about the pregnancy and it was clear she could count on their support, perhaps she felt that was the way to go. It was security for her and Wallaby.

To choose Harry probably carried too much uncertainty, the marriage might not last, and then what? Where would she go, who could she count on? I think she probably made the decision and Harry, with sadness, accepted it. After all, we now know he never married or took up with anyone else. Perhaps as Wallaby grew older, it became more difficult for Harry to maintain physical contact (who was that man, Mummy?) and so, he moved away. He could have had a job transfer, been retired from active service, etc. There's a lot we don't know yet. Moving away probably tore the poor man apart. When you think about it, Wallaby's Mum had Wallaby – poor Harry had nothing.

Janet in Yorkshire

It was now clear that my father had not done a runner and cleared off to London as I had always assumed. He had wanted to marry my mum, and it was clear from that mysterious telephone call from the couple with the London accent that he'd kept an eye on me from a distance; and Shirley told me that he loved children.

My mother believed in a God, but she never went to Mass. I don't think it would have been religion that bothered her. It was more likely to have been the risk of the marriage failing, and the fear of being left alone to face the backlash of anti-Semitism with divorce added to her list of sins. Another Catholic taboo. As Janet in Yorkshire had suggested in her post, my mum chose security. I poured my cousin another coffee and quizzed him further.

'Can you remember what my father looked like, that day when he came to our door?'

'He and the man he was with were just starting to walk away from the door, but I do remember he was tallish, but not as tall as me, and he had thick black hair that was swept back off his face. I remember his hair more than anything. But that's all I can remember. Don't forget, it was well over fifty years ago!'

My cousin was at least 6 feet 2 and he was still quite fit and agile, looking ten years younger than his years. He was still handsome, but his thick dark hair, had turned white.

I showed him Shirley's wedding photograph on my laptop and I asked him if he could point my father out from the other men in the photograph. Brian's eyes started looking at the men from the left side of the photograph and my father was standing on the far right, but I said nothing and waited quietly until his eyes moved along the rows, studying every man in turn. He pointed to a small man with a moustache and thick black hair swept back off his face.

'This man here looks a bit like him, but he was **much taller and he was clean-shaven,** he definitely didn't have a moustache.'

I kept quiet. Then his eyes moved along to the **opposite end of the photograph, and** he pointed to Harry.

'Yes, that's Harry Freeman . . . that's my father.'

*My Father Harry with Uncle **Dave***
*aka Gedaliah, Dal **Freeman.***
*Circa **1954.***

23 Joyce

We turned our attention to my father's full brother Teri, who was known as Teddy and was the Edward listed on the electoral rolls. I wanted to trace his two daughters, Olive and Joyce. We found Olive had married Philip Brown, but sadly, I had missed her by only one year; Olive had died in 2008 and her husband Philip had also died only a few months before his wife. But they did have a son, who I have yet to trace. We didn't have a clue who Joyce had married. So I decided to introduce myself to Olive's neighbours in the hope that they might know something about her sister Joyce. One lady remembered Joyce's surname and that she lived either in, or close to Wales. Eventually, I found Joyce living in Halkyn, Flintshire, which was only an hour's drive from our home. I found her address and telephone number and I don't know why, but I decided to take the direct approach this time, which I would never advise as you risk opening a can of worms, but by this time I had my confidence back.

I rang her number and, after making sure I had the correct person by confirming Joyce's maiden name and her father's name, I explained my story. It was a big chance to take and I can only blame my impatience and excitement. Plus, it's such a long story to explain over the telephone and a hell of a lot for anyone to take in. But I had worried for nothing. I only needed to explain everything once to Joyce and she followed every word I said, jotting the entire story down in shorthand. Joyce was one year older than Shirley and, like Shirley, her mind was as sharp as a razor. In fact, at one point, I confused Louis' first wife Rachael, who was Shirley and Margaret's grandmother and his second wife Rebecca, who was Joyce's grandmother, as well as mine, and Joyce read her shorthand notes back and corrected me! Impressive, given that Joyce didn't know anything about Rebecca until I explained about our grandfather Louis and his three wives.

Joyce asked how I had managed to trace her and I explained about talking to her late sister's neighbour and how sorry I was to have not met Olive before she died.

'WHAT!... our Olive is... DEAD? When did this happen?'

'Errr...y yes. Olive died last year, in 2008. Did you not know?'

'NO! I didn't know! We hadn't seen each other for many years. But I don't understand why her husband Philip hasn't rung me?'

'Errr...well, I'm afraid that Philip died just a few months before Olive died. Oh Joyce, I am so very sorry to bring this sad news to you like this.'

'WHAT!... Philip is dead too?'

Have you ever just wanted to put the phone down and pretend you had been cut off? I was absolutely mortified! But Joyce was lovely and we talked for hours about her late sister Olive and her family. Joyce told me that she had done a genealogy course at her local school and had been tracing her family tree for the last three years. She had done some work on her father's side until she hit a brick wall, so she researched her mum's Blair family. Joyce explained that she could not find her grandfather Louis after she had found him at the age of nine with his parents on the 1871 Liverpool census. It was my turn to be dumbfounded.

'WHAT!... You've found Louis' parents!?'

'Yes, but I can't find him after or before the 1871 census.'

'Joyce, are you absolutely sure? Because I, along with an army of other researchers from all around the world, have worked 24/7 and we could not find our grandfather Louis before his marriage in 1890, and we've never managed to find his parents!'

Joyce emailed the 1871 Liverpool census to me, and what Joyce had found was a German Jewish family and their surname was spelt 'Friemann'. The parents were Joseph Friemann and his wife Sarah and their address was York Street, Liverpool. They had a nine-year-old son Louis, born about 1862, and a seven-year-old son Jacob. My grandfather Louis was born about 1867 and his father's name was Tobias, according to his marriage records. But although a few things didn't tally, we decided to investigate this Friemann family, if only to rule them out. It also made sense to learn about families with similar names just in case another link was later found. What worried us was that we couldn't find *this* Louis *Friemann* anywhere in the UK on the 1891 census, until Tilly Mint found a notice of a betrothal in the *Jewish Chronicle*'s archives for the daughter of a prominent Jewish family to Louis Friemann of South Africa. Further details proved that he was the son of Joseph and Sarah Friemann. This confirmed that he was not my grandfather Louis, but only another coincidence. I had only been in Joyce's life a few weeks and I felt like the grim reaper bearing bad news. Now, I had to tell her that she'd been following the wrong family for the last three years!

But this just goes to show how complicated family history can be, and how nothing must be taken for granted without solid proof. By the same token, nothing should be overlooked. Because the tiniest clue, the most unlikely link, often opens up a whole new avenue to search and gets you onto the right path to find your roots.

Shirley was delighted to hear I had found our first cousin Joyce. There was only one year between them in age and they had not seen each other since they had both worn their hair in ringlets over seventy-five years earlier. So one sunny afternoon we collected Shirley and Monty and set out for a day trip to Halkyn, a few minutes drive from Holywell in Wales. Joyce had a beautiful home built on a hillside overlooking the Dee Estuary and surrounded by farmland. It was a clear day, and from Joyce's living-room window we had stunning views across the estuary and the River Mersey to Liverpool's waterfront.

Joyce was lovely – so natural, warm and friendly – and it was wonderful to reunite my two first cousins. Brian and I enjoyed listening to them reminiscing. There were plenty of family photographs in Joyce's album. One photograph was of her father's half-brother, who Joyce referred to as Jack. Shirley took the words right out of my mouth.

'Who's Jack?'

'Well, I only ever knew him as Uncle Jack. He was my father's half-brother. I think he had something wrong with his spine.'

Joyce explained that Jack came to live with her family when she was about six, so that would have been 1935. She remembered that he didn't get on with his stepmother. Jack's stepmother was Louis' third wife Rosie at that time, and she would have raised Jack, from the age of about twelve. Given that Rosie died in 1935, it didn't make sense that Jack moved out to live with Joyce's family after Rosie's death. It seemed more likely that Jack moved out because he didn't get on with his half-sister Eva.

'Then one day he was suddenly gone! They never told children about death back in those days. But I remember Uncle Jack always sat in a long wooden chair, which seemed too big for our living room.'

The photograph brought a lump to my throat. I realised exactly who Jack was.

'I think Jack, must be Isaac. He had muscular sclerosis and died just before his fortieth birthday, in 1940. That's according to his death certificate.'

This jogged Joyce's memory.

'Yes, that's right! I remember now, my father sometimes called him Yitzhak!' Yitzhak was the Hebrew name for Isaac. It meant laughter. Another mystery had been solved.

Left: Isaac aka Jack Freeman b:1900 - d:1940
Right: Joyce's Father Teri, aka Teddy/Edward Freeman b:1905 - d:1965.
(Photograph circa mid-1930s)

I was mesmerised by Isaac/Jack's photograph. It looked to have been taken around the mid-1930s and he was clearly the most handsome of all my father's family with his dark rugged looks and thick mop of wavy black hair. The Freemans were certainly a good-looking bunch, and not least our grandfather Louis. Joyce remembered Louis being a very smart man who came to visit them every Sunday and gave her and her sister Olive a shiny new penny from the bank. As OC said, the reference to hawker covers a multitude of occupations. Jewish people lived in fear, so they played down what they did for a living, hence my father's claim to dealing in scrap metal when he was dealing in precious metal.

I now had photographs of all my father's siblings except for Hyman, Elias, their half-sister Eva, Rosie's daughter Betsy and, of course Rebecca's son, the mystery Abraham.

Joyce made us some lunch and afterwards she showed us a sepia photograph of a young soldier in First Wold War uniform. Joyce explained that the soldier was also Isaac/Jack in his younger years but there had been some confusion about when and how he'd died. On the back of the photograph were some notes that Joyce's mum Annie had written many years ago. There was also a note added by Joyce herself in 2006 before her mother had died.

The notes read . . .

'*Uncle Jack Freeman, Teddy's bro. Died of war wounds (14–18). Soon after we moved to College St.'*

Then the additional note, **which Joyce had written herself in 2006, which said** . . .

'*No mum. Annie says he died of cancer. 1916.'*

Right:
Reverse of the young soldier's photograph showing confusing notes.

Left:
Mystery soldier of the Great War. Could this be Abraham? His uniform and cap badge are possibly Army Service Corp, but his battalion has not been confirmed.

We were now certain that Isaac/Jack had died of muscular sclerosis in 1940. Not of cancer or war wounds in 1916. Elias had died in 1921 of kidney failure, so the young soldier could not have been either Elias or Isaac/Jack. So who else could have died in 1916 . . . Abraham?

The problem I had with this photograph of the young soldier was that I didn't think he looked remotely like the dark, rugged looking man standing with Joyce's father in the 1930s photograph. The young soldier in uniform looked completely different. His eyes were not dark; in fact, they looked more grey or perhaps blue. His complexion looked fair and fresh, and although his hair was mostly hidden beneath his army cap, I could imagine it being fair, judging by his fair complexion, his fair eyebrows and the snippet of sideburn, which was barely visible. But it was difficult to compare a sepia and black and white image, and there was probably a twenty-year gap between when the two photographs were taken.

I asked Joyce which Annie she had been referring to in her note, and Joyce explained it must have been Shirley's mother, and that her parents had moved to College Street from Bengel Street just before she was born, about 1928/29. This information didn't tally, and it was tantalising to wonder if Joyce's mum was not entirely wrong about this young soldier. Maybe half of this story was correct. Perhaps this young soldier *did* die in 1916 of either war wounds or cancer. If that was the case, then this young soldier could not possibly have been Isaac/Jack, so maybe this soldier was Abraham.

I had another reason for suspecting that the young soldier could have been Abraham. Natalie had found this next photograph, which was taken at Gale's Photographic Studio in Liverpool. Don, who is a member of FTF, kindly dated the lady's fine black clothes to around 1900–1905. The young girl's body language looks restless and the two boys look shy and apprehensive. The younger boy, with his mop of blond, curly hair looks to be about four years old and the older boy, with fair cropped hair could be around six years. In contrast, the young girl is quite dark and she looks like Nellie in the photograph we found of Nellie when she was in her late teens. In my eyes, the older boy had more than a striking resemblance to the young soldier. So, could these two boys have been Abraham and his little brother Jacob? Was the woman dressed in black because she was still in morning for the loss of her first husband? Given that Louis' first wife had died in February 1904, I wondered if this woman could have been Rebecca. If so, then this lady is my grandmother.

Notice the way her hands are resting on the little boy's shoulders, as if to reassure him. The boys had already lost their father. How sad that Jacob died in 1907, followed by Bertie and their mother Rebecca in 1911, and then possibly Abraham in 1916.

I strongly suspect this is my grandmother Rebecca 1875-1911. Her youngest son Jacob 1900-1907.
Her eldest son Abraham 1897-1916? Louis' daughter Nellie aka Auntie Lil' 1894-1987
Taken at Gales Photographic studio Liverpool. Circa 1905.

We had really enjoyed our afternoon and before we left for our journey home, Joyce asked if I could find her father's grave, as she couldn't remember where he had been buried. He had died suddenly in 1965, at the age of only fifty-nine, after collapsing in the street from a heart attack. It was sad to hear how my father's family ended their lives. I was beginning to understand why it was thought that Harry had no family. Apart from his eldest half-sister Nellie, who was living in Australia when my father died, his younger half-sister Eva, who seemed to be estranged from the family, and perhaps Abraham, who may or may not have died in 1916, my father must have thought he was the only survivor of all his siblings.

So now for some grave-hunting. I knew little Jacob had been buried in Broadgreen cemetery and my grandmother Rebecca, along with Elias and Isaac/Jack were buried at Rice Lane, cemetery. Each one of them resting in an unmarked grave. At least now they are all immortalised in this book, and their lives have been acknowledged. Night Owl had found my father's grave at Bushey cemetery on United Synagogue's website, but I didn't have a clue where the other members of the family were buried, and Shirley couldn't remember either. So this was my next task.

I checked all the Jewish cemeteries, and then turned my attention to Liverpool City Council's cemeteries. I discovered that the records of all burials at council cemeteries are kept at the lodge within the grounds of Allerton cemetery and they charge a small fee for a grave search. As I live not far from the lodge, I popped in and was lucky enough to speak to a nice man who kindly looked at the records while I was there. Because I was able to provide him with the names and exact dates, this gave him a good idea where their graves would be, and within minutes he found the plot numbers in his record book. It turned out that they had been buried under my nose all along, at the Jewish section of West Derby cemetery. The cemetery our flat had overlooked and where my mum's washing had blown from the line onto the graves. I had buried my mum and Uncle John in the general section of the same cemetery. How strange that our paths had crossed in so many ways.

I asked permission to visit the closed cemetery but sadly Louis' grave had no stone, which was a shame as it would have given me his Hebrew name and his father's Hebrew name. I was at least able to make notes of the grave number for Joyce's father who was also buried in the general section of the cemetery.

We had now found all the living descendants of my father's siblings. Now it was time to turn the search around and head in the opposite direction to find where in Germany Louis actually came from. That's *if* he came from Germany.

24 Roots

Although I've travelled to many of the far-off lands that I had marked with blobs of pink chewy on my Uncle Tommy's plastic globe, including Hong Kong, Singapore, Bali, Thailand and nearly every state in America, I have seen little of Europe, apart from France, Spain and Greece. So to educate myself on pre-war eastern Europe, my head was buried in more books.

Geographically, the kingdom of Prussia was vast around the time that Louis was born and at different periods in the kingdom's history, I leant that parts of Poland, Lithuania, Denmark and the Czech Republic also came under Prussia's jurisdiction. The unification of what became known as the German Empire took place in 1871.

The countries of eastern Europe seemed to be constantly at each other's throats in this period of the continent's history, so it's understandable that there was confusion about Louis' birthplace. I thought I stood more chance of finding life on Mars than finding a birth record for my grandfather, without first finding proof of the *shtetl,* or at least the province where he was born. So far we had found no family whatsoever for Louis or his three wives, other than the family he had begun in Leeds and completed in Liverpool.

In terms of years, I was completely out of sync with my Jewish grandfather. He was born about 1866/7, going by his age on his civil marriage record. It was a time when most of my friends' gt. gt. grandfathers were born. Charles Dickens was still alive, Edison had not yet provided the world with electric light, and Alexander Graham Bell was still waiting to make his first call. This is the world my grandfather was born into, and I found it fascinating.

Margaret had written that she thought our grandfather had come from Poland, and Shirley thought Louis came from Russia, while Joyce remembered being told that he was a German immigrant and every census stated that Louis was a German national. Yet, he had married three Russian women, and I had always had this *thing* about Russia. So my blob of pink chew was still stuck on Russia and it was staying there until I could prove otherwise.

I needed to narrow Louis' place of origin down. But how? Months went by and I was running out of inspiration. One night we rechecked the United Synagogue's website and found the marriage authorisation certificate listed for Louis and Rachael's marriage in Leeds in 1890. This was an important find. The marriage authorisation certificate, gives a couple permission to marry, and sometimes it holds a wealth of information. I was keeping my fingers crossed that it would give the country of origin in more detail for Louis, his Hebrew name, and if I was really, really lucky, it might reveal details of an unmarried brother of Louis' if he attended the wedding. Remember the old custom; in attending the service, the unmarried brother of the groom was accepting responsibility for his brother's (the groom's) widow, in the event of his death, and agreeing to raise any children from the marriage. I'm not sure how that worked in practice if the brother had since married himself, but the marriage authorisation certificate is vital if you have no gravestone from which to get this information. So I ordered a copy of the MA certificate, as we called it, but when it arrived it gave little more information than the civil marriage certificate had already provided. It had only the country of origin as Germany for Louis and Russia for his wife Rachael. No *shtetl* or province was mentioned. But it did give Hebrew names for Louis and Rachael and also their father's Hebrew names. My grandfather's Hebrew name was a bit of a mouthful.

Groom: Louis Freedman. **Hebrew name:** Yehuda Lieb Aryé. **Age:** 23 years. **Address:** 52 Copenhagen Street, Leeds. **Occupation:** Hawker - own account. **Place of origin:** Germany. **Father's name:** Tobias Freedman. **Father's Hebrew name:** Tobiah. **Father's Occupation:** Hawker.

Bride: Rachael Simon. **Hebrew name:** Rohel. **Age:** 25 years. **Address:** 37 Back Byron Street, Leeds. **Occupation:** Tailoress. **Father's name:** Isaac Simon. **Father's Hebrew name:** Yitzhak. **Father's Occupation:** Master Tailor. **Place of origin:** Russia. **Wedding witnesses:** Morris Cohen and Morris Rosenberg.

Finding no parents, siblings, aunts or uncles for my grandfather in Leeds, Liverpool or anywhere in the UK and no family for his first wife Rachael née Simon, my grandmother Rebecca née Cohen and formerly Cohen or for Louis' third wife Rosie, we decided to turn our attention to the two wedding witnesses, Morris Cohen and Morris Rosenberg. We had several reasons for doing so. I have already explained the complicated issues with Jewish names, the many given names and anglicised family names, and if this book was fiction I could just make up names for ease. But as the very nature of this book is family history, I can't make it up as I go along, and I can't make up the names to make it easier for you to read or for me to write. So you might need to read these next two pages a few times before the complicated details sink in, and eh . . . it might be a good idea to take a couple of aspirins.

On their marriage records, Rachael had given her address as 37 Back Byron Street, Leeds. One of the wedding witnesses, Morris Rosenberg, also lived with his family at that same address, according to the 1891 Leeds census. Now, this is where it gets complicated . . .

When Rachael registered the birth of their first son Daniel (aka Gedaliah, Darley, Darl, Dal and morphed into Uncle Dave), who was born in Leeds in 1891, Rachael gave her maiden name as Rachael née Rosenberg, and yet, her marriage records had given her name as Rachael née Simon, the daughter of Isaac Simon a master tailor.

When Louis and Rachael moved to Liverpool and had their second son Hyman (aka Harry) in 1893, it was my grandfather Louis who registered his birth, and he gave Hyman's mother's maiden name as Rachael née Simon, matching the name given on their marriage certificate. So given the conflicting information, could it be that Rachael was related in some way to the wedding witness Morris Rosenberg?

Annswaby found Morris Rosenberg's naturalisation records at the National Archives at Kew. These records gave Morris Rosenberg's place of origin as Chotel, Kovno, Russia. I could not identify the place of Chotel, although there are a few possibilities on JewishGen's 'shtetl names' section of their website. I mentioned earlier that Kovno is now known as Kaunas and is part of Lithuania, the area where many Jewish immigrants who settled in Leeds were from. Morris's 'nat records', as we call them, also gave his date of birth and his parents' names. But there was no evidence to link Morris Rosenberg to Louis' wife Rachael. So I ordered birth certificates for two of Morris's children to see if perhaps his wife was connected to Rachael. But his wife's name was Rebecca née Taylor, not Simon.

Rachael's maiden name became even more baffling each time that Louis registered the births of the other children he had to his first wife, and the plot thickened and thickened.

When Nellie (aka Helen-Lilian/Auntie Lil) was born in Liverpool in 1894, Louis gave Nellie's mother's maiden name as Rachael née Cohen. Not Rachael née Rosenberg or Simon. Then, in 1896, Louis registered Samuel's birth giving Samuel's mother's maiden name as Rachael née Jacob! I hope you took them aspirins because it gets worse . . .

For Elias, who was born in 1898, and Isaac/Jack born in 1900, Louis registered their mother's maiden name as Rachael née Cohen, again?

Whatever Rachael's maiden name was, she died in February 1904. We have found no evidence to suggest that there was more than one Rachael, and other details confirmed that we had the correct birth certificates for all of their six children.

So Rachael née Simon was aka Rosenberg, aka Cohen and possibly also aka Jacob, although we suspect that maybe the name Jacob was just a mistake.

The second wedding witness was another Morris – Morris Cohen. He was from Germany and he had lived next door to my grandfather at no. 50 Copenhagen Street, Leeds, according to the 1891 Leeds census, which was the same street Louis had lived in before he married Rachael. Number 52, where Louis lived, appeared to be a boarding house, judging by the number and assortment of people living there on the 1891 census. Morris Cohen was also a tailor, and he was the only person who signed his name on their marriage certificate. Louis, his wife Rachael and the witness Morris Rosenberg, all signed with their mark . . . X So, could there be a link to both wedding witnesses? Nobody has been able to get to the bottom of this mystery, up to now. But I wonder if . . .

Could it be that Rachael née Simon aka Jacob aka Rosenberg aka Cohen, and Louis' second wife, my grandmother Rebecca née Cohen and formerly Cohen, were tied together in one big kosher knot? Could it be that my grandfather Louis, married his dead wife's sister? In other words, could it be that Rachael and Rebecca were sisters with surnames, Cohen?

It's hard to get your head around, but remember the old tradition that when an unmarried man attends his brother's wedding, he accepts the responsibility of marrying his dead brother's widow, in the event of his brother's death? It was common practice for widowed relatives to marry each other and bring up children and both Louis and Rebecca were widowed. Perhaps my grandmother Rebecca had previously been Louis' sister-in-law?

We researched Morris Cohen and found that he had married in Leeds in 1885. His marriage records gave his wife's name as Becca née Bromberg. The marriage authorisation certificate gave their parents' Hebrew names, and gave Germany as their place of origin. No town in Germany was given; however, there is a place called Bromberg in Germany, and Jewish family names are often taken from the town where the family originated. Morris and Becca Cohen both signed their names in an educated hand, and Morris' signature matched his signature on Louis' marriage records. For my own research, I've now drawn a line under the wedding witnesses. At least, until I'm released from my padded cell.

Above: (L to R) My father Harry, a family friend and Shirley's mum Annie. Circa 1950s.

Above: Dal aka Uncle Dave with wife Annie. Circa 1920s

Right:
Shirley's father Samuel,
aka Syd. In his twenties
at TA training.
Circa 1920s.

Below: Samuel Freeman in his forties.
Circa 1940s

Above: Shirley's brother Raymond
at Boots Pharmacy. Circa 1960s.

Below: A young Nellie (sitting)

aka Auntie Lil' Circa 1920s

Above: Nellie with her 1st Husband

Jack Holden and their Daughters

Margaret and Renah. Circa 1920s

Above: Nellie with her 2nd Husband

Harry Armstrong. Circa 1970s

Above: Nellie with 3rd husband

Lance Simpson. Circa 1980.

Above: My father's full brother Teddy, with his wife Annie and daughters, Joyce (left) and Olive (right).
Circa 1940s

Left:
Teddy and his wife Annie at
The National, Aintree Racecourse.
Circa 1930s.

Right:
Joyce's father Teddy
(end left) Circa 1926.

Above: Nellie's daughter Renah, Natalie's mum. Circa 1940

Above: Nellie's daughters, Renah (left)
and Margaret. Circa 1950s.

Above: Nellie's daughter Margaret
on her 90th Birthday.

25 *Mazel Tov!*

Over the following year we met up with Shirley and Monty regularly. In May 2010, they went on a cruise for Shirley's eightieth birthday and when they returned home Shirley's two daughters, Linda and Susan, hosted a birthday party for their mother at Susan's home. We really enjoyed the company of Shirley and Monty's family and friends; they were all lovely people and they made us very welcome.

We met Lucy, who was soon to marry Shirley's grandson Michael; my husband Brian and I were invited to their wedding. Neither I nor Brian had ever been to a Jewish wedding before and I had always wanted to go. So we were delighted and felt honoured to be invited as day guests to such a close family function, and I was looking forward to taking part in all the Jewish traditions at Lucy and Michael's wedding.

I had a lump in my throat as we drove along **Princes Avenue, past no. 10, the flat** where I found my father had lived in the 1950s, to **my first Jewish wedding. The weather** was perfect and the Old Hebrew Congregation syn**agogue, which stands at the end of** Princes Road, was magnificent. Built towards the **end of the 1870s, this Grade I listed** building, which is an eclectic mix of Moorish design **with** Byzantine and Gothic overtones, is thought to be **one of** Europe's finest examples of this type of architecture. **The** interior was strikingly colourful, and a complete sur**prise** after the sandstone exterior. Pillars painted vibrant co**lours** of jade decorated with gold leaf supported two mezz**anine** seating galleries on either side of the pulpit, stretching **the** full length of the shul, and the barrel-vaulted ceiling **was a** photographer's dream.

Right: Alter at Old Hebrew Synagogue.

Above: Stunning interior of Old Hebrew Synagogue at Princess Road, Liverpool.

At the beginning of the 1900s the area of Princes Avenue was affluent. This tree-lined boulevard was one of the main roads into the city's centre and it displayed the wealth of Liverpool's merchants. Handsome white three-storey Georgian mansions stood cheek-to-cheek, giving visitors a hint of the stunning architecture that the rest of the city had in store. Many people are surprised to find that Liverpool is home to so many listed buildings – in fact, more than any other city outside of London. Sadly, Princes Avenue, which continues along from Princes Road and is now a busy dual carriageway, had fallen into disrepair by the 1970s. Now it has been painstakingly restored to its former glory. For over a century the road has been home to numerous places of worship, with practically every religion represented. Greek Orthodox and Welsh Presbyterian churches can be found close to the synagogue, alongside various Christian denominations, with Hindu and the Sikh temple and the mosque all standing close by, complementing each other's architecture. Nestling among mature trees are the stunning mansions of the avenue, most of which have now been transformed into stylish modern apartments, only visible when you walk through the doors. But with a bit of imagination, horse-drawn carriages can still be heard clip-clopping along the cobbles transporting their passengers into the city, while over the rooftops the Anglican and Catholic cathedrals can be seen standing at opposite ends of a street called Hope.

My first Jewish wedding was all that I could ever have wished it to be. It was very traditional, and Shirley's daughter Susan explained each part of the service as it progressed. The bride and groom stood beneath the *Chuppah*, the canopy that represents the home, surrounded by bridesmaids and close family and friends. Men and women were separated, so I stood alongside the rest of my father's family in the perfect position to see and hear the entire ceremony, and Brian stood with Monty, who had brought along an extra *Kippah* for Brian to wear. It was so funny to see him standing alongside the men wearing a *Kippah*, but Monty made him feel at ease and explained each step of the service, which was similar in many ways to a Catholic wedding. I could see Brian was fascinated by everything and enjoying himself. I could also see that Monty was enjoying himself too, and amused at the idea of educating a Catholic ex-choir boy into the rituals and traditions of a Jewish wedding ceremony. One ex-choir boy teaching another ex-choir boy, in their different religions.

The entire service was beautifully atmospheric. Lucy had filled the shul with candles. To add to the atmosphere, an elderly gentleman played traditional Jewish folk songs on a harp, and when the cantor sang 'Sunrise, Sunset' in his beautiful baritone voice, everyone was holding back their tears.

While I stood in the synagogue alongside my father's family, I began to think about and compare the traditions of Catholicism and Judaism. I had been brought up to keep my mind open, ask questions, take an interest in and have respect for other people's beliefs.

As I listened to the service, I thought about the stuff Old Tooie tried to ram down my throat at primary school. The 1950s Catholic curriculum had taught me Catholicism, but zilch about other people's beliefs, only about our differences. I suppose, it was the same for other religious teachings. As I listened to the service, I became conscious of our similarities, the many things that our different religions had in common with each other.

The Jewish Sabbath is known as *shabbat* or *shabbos* and is observed as a day of rest, which begins an hour before sunset on Friday evening when *shabbos* candles are lit and prayers recited. Friday night dinner begins with *Kiddush*, a blessing recited over wine and loaves of *challah*, which is a Jewish braided bread made from eggs, fine white flour, water, yeast and sugar, sprinkled with sesame seeds and blessed. It is similar to brioche, but unlike brioche it contains no dairy.

I had done some research for Edward David Luft, a retired tax lawyer, author and genealogist who lives in Washington DC, and Edward gave me lots of invaluable advice and sent interesting information from the *Avotaynu Guide to Jewish Genealogy* from the Library of Congress in Washington DC. This was of great help to me, and I found many similarities within the Irish and Jewish cultures, many of which reminded me of my childhood. For example, the Irish wake. Sitting with the dead to cheer them on their way to meet their maker– like the wake we held for my nan Annie, even providing her with a little drop of stout and not leaving her alone or out of the conversation. The Irish wake is similar in many ways to the Jewish tradition of sitting *shiva*, although I imagine *shiva* to be far less alcoholic. In order to prevent evil spirits from taking over the body of the deceased, Jews keep their dead company until interment. The word *shiva* means seven. Traditionally, the family of the deceased mourn for seven days. During this time readings from the Torah takes place each day, usually at the home of the deceased or the deceased's family. It's customary for the immediate family to sit on low *shiva* stools, or even on the floor. This is to symbolise the emotional reality of the loss, of being brought low by the grief. During the seven days of *shiva*, friends and neighbours provide comforting food for the grieving family, in much the same way as our neighbours laid a table of food at my nan's wake. We covered our windows and mirrors with white sheets, and it's also a Jewish custom for mirrors to be covered. Old customs bring comfort in times of loss.

Although some comparisons can be drawn between the Irish wake and the Jewish *shiva*, unlike a Catholic funeral, where the family lavish whatever they can afford on the deceased's casket and funeral, there's no display of wealth whatsoever at a Jewish funeral. After a service given in Hebrew at a prayer hall within the cemetery's gates, the deceased's body is given back to the earth in a basic coffin to encourage nature to do its work. Both the coffin and prayer hall are purposely unadorned to signify that no matter how rich we may be lucky enough to become in our life, we leave all that wealth behind us when we pass away, and return to our maker in the same way as we came into the world. With nothing. Ashes to ashes, dust to dust. As my mum used to say, 'There are no pockets in shrouds.'

Kaddish, the prayer for the dead, is recited in classic Hebrew usually by a close male relative of the deceased's. After the eulogy, the coffin is then wheeled slowly to the grave on a basic and quite ancient wooden cart. The cart, which most probably was the same one that carried the deceased's parents, grandparents and gt. grandparents, is stopped several times on its journey to the grave, signifying the mourners' reluctance to part with their loved one. Women wear no make up. Men don't shave. Every detail is taken care of by the deceased's family. Even the grave is filled by male relatives of the deceased, each taking their turn to lay their loved one to rest.

Reading the traditions of the Jewish funeral provoked some deep thinking. I found it very moving and, at the same time; chilling. There was no false comfort gained from picking a quality casket and surrounding it with flowers. This was a stark, poignant reminder that nature was about to take charge, and from now on all material possessions were immaterial.

I also read a charming Irish story about the legend of the Hebrew princess. To quote from the *Avotaynu Guide to Jewish Genealogy*:

> In Irish mythology, a Hebrew princess came from the East, bringing with her the harp that is Ireland's national symbol and for which many beautiful melodies have been composed to accompany a rich collection of Irish folk songs. The princess also brought the Stone of Destiny, accredited with having been the pillow on which the patriarch Jacob rested his head on the night when he wrestled with the angel. This stone was moved to Scotland when some Irish tribes conquered that country where it became known as the Stone of Scone. On it, Scotland's kings and, later, British kings have been crowned ever since.

The Stone of Scone last did its duty at the Queen's Coronation and was featured in the film, The King's Speech. As for Michael and Lucy, their wedding ceremony was coming to an end and the celebrations were waiting to begin, but for me, the best part was still to come: standing alongside my father's family in a synagogue, where he had probably stood himself many times during his earlier life in Liverpool, to see the breaking of the glass and shout . . . *Mazel Tov!*

With the ceremony now over, we made our way to the stunning Palm House in Sefton Park, which was a short drive from Princes Avenue. This beautifully restored Victorian, octagonal glasshouse is Grade II listed, and it was a perfect setting for a wedding reception, and the harpist played while the photographs were taken alongside Peter Pan's statue in the manicured gardens. While we were introduced to guests, and to Manny, the young Rabbi who had conducted the ceremony, champagne and mouthwatering appetisers were served, until it was time to sit down to a delicious kosher meal and listen to family speeches. As night fell we took part in the traditional Jewish *Hora* and danced to *Hava Nagila*. I expected to see familiar faces, and of course, I did. Many people came up to me and said:

'Well . . . I never knew you to be Jewish!'

To which I replied: 'No . . . neither did I!'

The music was too loud for me to explain my story, so I told everyone the same thing:

'It's a long story, Shirley will explain later.'

By the end of the night, Shirley was surrounded by ladies who were hanging on her every word, while Monty, Brian and I sat close by and listened as she told her story.

'Well, completely out of the blue, I received a letter.' Then an hour later, ending with, ' . . . and all these years we've lived only around the corner from each other!'

Then Monty said something to me, which I will never forget:

'You know, we are very lucky to have found you.'

'No, Monty. I'm the lucky one . . . lucky to have found you and Shirley.'

Brian and I had been to our first Jewish wedding. Little did we know then, that less than a year later, we would be going to our first Jewish funeral.

Shirley with Monty 2010.
Photograph Courtesy of Shirley Bodansky.

26 Eureka!

Natalie gave me some dates when she was able to come to Liverpool, and after a bit of organising we agreed on Sunday 22 August 2010 for a family reunion at our home. To me, that day represented the culmination of twenty years of searching for my father's family.

Brian met Natalie at Lime Street station. She had given me a brief description of herself and told me that she would be wearing pink and carrying a pink overnight case. I told Natalie that Brian would be there waiting for her when she got off the train but advised her not to bother looking for a Brad Pitt lookalike as she would be standing there all day!

Natalie and I had spent the previous weeks telling each other our girly problems, so from the description she gave me of herself I don't really know what I expected to meet that day! But I didn't expect the tall, stunning blonde lady who walked through our door, wearing a pink linen dress and clasping pink roses in one hand and a bottle of pink champagne in the other. She burst into tears when we met, and she had forgotten to bring Nellie, the rag doll her grandmother made for her. She also had loads of photographs and it was like I had known her all my life.

Brian set off to meet Joyce, her son David and his wife Jill at West Derby cemetery. We arranged to meet Joyce at the cemetery because Joyce wanted to visit her father's grave on the way to our reunion. Unfortunately her daughter Ruth could not change her nursing shift and so was unable to come, but David said I had his sister's eyes.

After weeks of torrential rain, the weather had finally broken to provide us with warm sunshine. While Joyce and Monty serenaded us, we shared photographs and stories.

For me, it was a great sense of achievement to reunite my father's family. The only person missing was Arthur, and of course Margaret and her family in Australia, and I didn't want to leave them out, so I made a DVD of the family reunion, including all the old family photographs and finishing with Michael and Lucy's wedding, the future generation.

Our Family Reunion. 2010
Back: (L to R) My Husband Brian, David's Wife Jill. Natalie, Joyce's Son David and Monty.
Middle: Me, Joyce, Shirley's Daughter Susan, Front: Shirley's Daughter Linda and Shirley.
Photograph Courtesy of Shirley's son-in-law Kevin Banning, who is behind the camera.

Above: The day we met Joyce. (L to R) Joyce, Shirley, me and Monty.
Brian is caught in the mirror behind us taking the picture.

By that time, I had made a lot of headway with this book, and on the FTF website I had now started 'Hospital Records Part 11'. My biggest worry was how the hell I was going to end this book. Although I had seen it more as a family memoir than an actual family history book, nevertheless, I still wanted to finish it with at least the finding of my grandfather's parents and some concrete evidence of his birthplace. I still had this gut feeling that my grandfather Louis also had Russian origins, regardless of his Germanic claim. But we had nothing to go on. Louis and his birthplace were still a total mystery.

We knew from Louis' marriage records that his father's name was Tobias Freedman. But we could find no trace of a Tobias Freedman/Friedman/Freeman anywhere in the UK. It seemed to be an unusual name combination, as I found no other person with that name in the censuses. I looked up the name Tobias and found that it is derived from the Hebrew biblical name Toviyah or Tuvya, meaning the Lord is Good. It's also often used as a surname. This was at least much better than there being hundreds with the same name to untangle. The research was starting to wind down on FTF. We were all beginning to feel like we could take it no further. I began drafting an assortment of endings for my book, none of which I was happy with. I couldn't let the book fizzle to an end like the research seemed to be doing.

Then one day, Wanda Houghton, one of the members of FTF, who, up to this point had been quietly following my thread in the background, found a 1902 death for a Tobias Freedman in Dublin on the Mormon's familysearch.com website, which is updated regularly. At seventy-two years, he was the right age to be a strong candidate for Louis' father. Well, we didn't have another candidate, so even though no connections with Ireland had ever arisen before, no stone should be left unturned. In fact, you need to look under every stone at least twice in family research, and if you get stuck, shelve that stone, try another route, and then go back to it later. Don't ever throw that stone away because you might later find a niche for it, which helps everything else to fit into place.

Ordering Tobias Freedman's death certificate from the Dublin General Register Office was a bit of a long-winded palaver as they had no online ordering service for 1902, which was the year Tobias Freedman had died, although they might by the time you read this book. I needed to download and fill in a form and fax or send it via snail mail to the Irish Records Office in Roscommon, enclosing a cheque. It took over four weeks for his death certificate to arrive. The information it gave was that Tobias Freedman had lived at 2 Emorville Square, Dublin. His age was seventy-two. Solomon Benjamin, who we learnt was a Jewish social worker of sorts, registered his death, which unfortunately gave no clue to any family.

I traced Tobias on the Dublin 1901 census at the Emorville Square address and this threw an Irish spanner in the works. The household transcript had his name listed as *Julia Freedman*: male; age 65 years, with, I assume his wife, 64-year-old Faiga Freedman; both Russian. When I looked at the original transcript, I could see that the name Julia looked more like Tubia, another version of Tobias, so I concluded his name had been wrongly transcribed, as his name on the death certificate was clearly Tobias. His age was different, but I had learnt that ages were often wrong on Irish records, especially on Irish censuses, and given that the address was the same we felt that the information could be trusted.

Tobias and Faiga were listed as boarders. In other words, they were renting a room from the Masliansky family, who are mentioned in James Joyce's *Ulysses*, although Joyce has spelt the name Mastiansky. Also mentioned in the novel is T. Freedman. I found no other T. Freedman in Ireland around this period, so it was tantalising to wonder if this tiny mention could be Tobias Freedman who was likely to be my great grandfather, given that the Jewish community living in Dublin at that time was small, and Joyce borrowed many of the names for his fictional characters from individuals in the Jewish community around the area of South Circular Road, including St Kevin's Parade, Lombard Street West, Clanbrassil and Emorville Square, in the city where that famous day in the life of Leopold Bloom was spent. This prompted me to read everything I could about the history of the Jewish community in Dublin, and one book in particular; *Jewish Ireland in the Age of Joyce* written by Cormac Ó Gráda was not only interesting reading but also of great help to me in understanding what life was like in the early part of the 1900s for Tobias and Faiga. I needed to know if there was any link to this Masliansky family. We found the name had changed to Maslam and some of the family went to America. Naomiatt found a helpful Rabbi who was a descendant living in Texas. Although the Rabbi didn't know if his family had any link to Tobias and Faiga Freedman, he took the time to give me some good advice and told me of other books about the Jews of Ireland where the names of his family, along with many other Jewish families, were mentioned. I also contacted Stuart Rosenblatt at the Jewish Museum in Dublin. Stuart had compiled no fewer than nineteen volumes of information on over 52,000 Jews who had settled or passed through Ireland; many originating from the Lithuania area. Stuart was a great help and we exchanged information.

I have already mentioned the problems of researching Irish ancestors. Many Irish records have not survived for one reason or another. According to the National Archives of Ireland, the first full Irish census was taken in 1821, and then at ten-yearly intervals through to 1911. No census was taken in 1921, because of the War of Independence. Then the first census of the Irish Free State was taken in 1926, and that census will not be released to the public until January 2027. I would later find that the 1926 census could be important to my research. With fifteen years to wait, I may well have joined my parents by the year 2027, in which case I hope a member of my father's family will carry on with my research and fill in any remaining gaps that I might need to leave unfinished.

The original census returns for 1861 and 1871 were destroyed shortly after the censuses were taken. Those for 1881 and 1891 were pulped during the First World War, likely because of the paper shortage. The census returns for 1821 through to 1851 went up in smoke in the 1922 fire at the Public Record Office at the beginning of the Irish Civil War, with only a few charred remains surviving for some of the counties. Although a request was made to the population of Ireland imploring them to provide the Record Office with a copy of any certificates they may have in their possession, as you can imagine, many were lost.

What this means for us researchers is that the only complete Irish censuses available to search are those for 1901 and 1911, along with a few bits that have survived for some of the counties for 1821, 1831, 1841, and 1851. All of these censuses are available to search online, free of charge at census.nationalarchives.ie

As if that wasn't bad enough, many people didn't even bother to register a death. They didn't see the need, and it cost money that many didn't have. After fines were imposed, births or deaths were registered late when people could afford to. So little Paddy Leahy could have had a full set of milk teeth before he was officially born. It's this lack of records or wrongly transcribed records that makes both Jewish and Irish roots really difficult to trace. And now I was tracing both.

I needed to find descendants of Tobias Freedman and to find Tobias' wife Faiga after the 1901 census. But we found no trace of Faiga on the 1911 census for either Ireland or the UK, and found no death, nor evidence that she had ever left Ireland or remarried. In those days, Jewish people often remarried even late in their lives to look after each other in their old age, as these were difficult times for everybody, and it could be that she remarried under a *Stille Chuppah* and later died, and her death was perhaps registered under another name. So, Faiga Freedman had disappeared without a trace.

Eventually, I found a family headed by Isaac-Jacob Freedman living close to Emorville Square in Lombard Street West. Naomiatt found another researcher on jewishgen.org who had Isaac-Jacob Freedman in his tree, and he'd lived in Dublin from about 1880 until 1892.

So I contacted this researcher, whose name was Maurice Freedman, through the free message service provided by jewishgen.org and we exchanged details. Maurice lived in Melbourne, Australia, and he explained that he was the great-grandson of Isaac-Jacob Freedman. Over the following few weeks Maurice provided me with many pieces of vital information, such as a copy of his great-grandfather's naturalisation records, which gave Isaac-Jacob Freedman's parents as Tobias and *Fege* Freedman (sic) and Isaac-Jacob's place of birth was Sweksna, Kovno, Russia, which we took to mean Sveksna; a small *shtetl* about thirty-five kilometres from the German border, and which is now a part of Lithuania.

The names of Faiga and Fege are the same, so I emailed a copy of Tobias's death record to Maurice in Melbourne, as Tobias was his gt. gt. grandfather and Maurice had not been able to trace him, most probably because his name was shown as Julia. The only fly in the ointment was that Isaac-Jacob was from Sveksna, Kovno, Russia and his parents Tobias and Faiga/Fege were also from Russia, and my grandfather *claimed* that he was German. Although my mind was wide open, I needed proof that Louis was Tobias and Faiga's son.

A complicated investigation then followed and I shelved Tobias and Faiga Freedman many times because I found no further evidence. But Dublin and Liverpool are so close and historically connected, so I couldn't get Tobias and Faiga Freedman out of my head. We were mindful of how confident we were that the Louis from Lomza was my grandfather, and he ended up in New York. So it was entirely feasible that Louis' father never set foot on UK soil and that the Tobias Freedman who died in Dublin might have nothing whatsoever to do with *my* family, given that we didn't have a scrap of evidence that Louis had crossed the Irish Sea. So, we needed proof. We needed a document that told us Louis' mother's name, or evidence of where in Germany or wherever Louis was from, or proof that he had a Dublin connection.

Maurice explained that his father Victor was the son of Morris Freedman, who was the eldest son of Isaac-Jacob Freedman, and his story was fascinating. He told me briefly that Isaac-Jacob and his family emigrated from Dublin to Cape Town, South Africa in 1892, where his eldest son, Morris, decided to change his name to Maurice Freeman and he became very successful. The family worked hard in the goldmines, and through their hard work they prospered. In 1934 Maurice Freeman became the mayor of Johannesburg. His grandson, Maurice in Melbourne, sent me a video link of his grandfather giving a speech alongside Ouma Smuts, who was the wife of Jan Christiaan Smuts, the Prime Minister of South Africa at that time. The resemblance of Maurice Freeman to my grandfather Louis was enough to spur me on. I just knew I was on the right track.

It was a family anyone would be proud to be a part of, but this made me all the more careful of finding solid proof that we were connected. Tobias and Faiga were undoubtedly the parents of Isaac-Jacob Freedman, but were they also Louis' parents too? If so, then this meant that Isaac-Jacob Freedman, who was born in 1854 in Sveksna, Kovno, Russia, was my grandfather's elder brother.

Above: Maurice Freeman Mayor of Johannesburg 1934.   *Above: Isaac-Jacob Freedman, Louis' Brother.*
Photograph Courtesy of Maurice Freedman.   *Photograph Courtesy of Lynn Neiman.*

The thing that niggled me was that my grandfather had named one of his sons Isaac, with the nickname of Jack, and he was born in 1900. But Isaac-Jacob Freedman was still alive and living in South Africa in 1900, so this broke the Ashkenazi strict rule of not naming a newborn after a close member of the family. Naomiatt explained that she had come across this situation many times in her own family research and found that the Hebrew names were different, so even though they were both named Isaac on their birth certificates, their Hebrew names were most probably different from one another, and so this was acceptable. Also, on his nat records and on a shipping list heading for Cape Town, which FTF member Christine in Herts found for me, Isaac-Jacob Freedman had called himself Isaac Freedman. Yet on the birth records of six of his nine children who were born in Dublin, he stated his name was Jacob Freedman; it was his address and his wife's name, Dorah Harris, which helped me to recognise that we had the correct birth certificates. The fact that Isaac-Jacob Freedman had fathered twin boys strengthened that proof.

I subscribed to the many special interest groups, known as SIGs, on jewishgen.org and I received daily emails. These SIGs are free to join and they allow researchers who are interested in a specific area such as Russia, Germany, Lithuania, Poland, South Africa, the UK and America to post messages pertaining to that particular area in the hope of finding a link to another researcher tracing the same family, in the same way that Naomiatt had found Maurice in Melbourne was also tracing Isaac-Jacob Freedman in Dublin. The problem I had was that I wasn't sure where Louis was from, so I joined *all* the SIGs. These areas were vast and home to thousands of Jewish *shtets*, and their borders seemed to change by the minute. Kovno had now popped up a few times in my research and, as I explained earlier, is today the modern, vibrant city known as Kaunas and, although it was under Imperial Russian rule for over a hundred years, it is now a part of Lithuania. Kovno was also the area where the wedding witness Morris Rosenberg and many of the Jews who settled in Leeds were from. But Morris Rosenberg's nat records stated that he was from Chotel, Kovno and we were never able to pinpoint this *shtetl*. OC suggested that perhaps Chotel had been *shtetl* and was lost in translation! Anything is possible in Jewish family history research.

Over twelve months went by with no sign of the proof I needed to confirm where Louis originated from. I sent over 1,200 blanket messages to all the other researchers on the jewishgen.org website researching the names Friedman/Freedman/Freeman, and also the names Simon, Rosenberg and Cohen. Amazingly, I received over 380 replies, which kept me busy for many weeks corresponding and exchanging information, but alas, to no avail. However, I did receive some good advice and I exchanged emails with many helpful and interesting researchers and got myself involved in other people's research along the way. Sometimes looking at another person's tree helps you to progress with your own tree as it clears your mind and you learn from each other, with tips and advice about new websites or new records that have been transcribed and come online, as this happens continually.

By its very nature, family history attracts caring people and it is so interesting to communicate with people from all around the world. Many have fascinating stories to tell of how their ancestors arrived at their chosen destination, often penniless and unable to speak the language or to even write their own name. Yet many ended up wealthy just from sheer hard work and tenacity, working at whatever they could find, and many were hawkers just as my grandfather Louis had been. One researcher told me that after his great-grandfather arrived on Ellis Island, he was put on a train in New York bound for Chicago with only his fare and a banana in his pocket and a sign around his neck saying 'Chicago'! He sold needles and threads on the streets and became wealthy, only to lose it all in the Wall Street Crash. Picking himself up again, he eventually owned the street where he had sold his wares.

Meanwhile, I was getting nowhere in finding the proof to link my grandfather with Isaac-Jacob Freedman and his parents Tobias and Faiga/Fege from Sveksna, Kovno, Russia. Months and months went by and I was going around in ever decreasing circles and wishing I had never committed myself to writing this book, as I could see no ending to my research and no ending to this book!

Then one day I got a telephone call out of the blue from Stuart Rosenblatt at Dublin's Jewish Museum. He left a message on my voicemail, but the line was crackly and I could barely understand a word, but he mentioned something about my grandfather Louis, so I listened to the message again and heard him saying that he had found some interesting information and could I ring him. So, with pen in hand, I rang Stuart.

There is just something about the combination of being both Irish and Jewish that provokes a spontaneous smile, as it seems almost a contradiction in terms. But of course, Jews have settled practically everywhere on this planet, so why not Ireland. Stuart is lovely, and has the most beguiling Irish drawl accompanied by all its charms, with its quirky little mannerisms and comical sayings. Scousers and Irish people, especially Dubliners, have always felt at home in each other's company, being almost seamlessly integrated, and enjoy pulling each other's leg. Much of Stuart's conversation flies over my head at the speed of light, because he never seems to begin at the beginning with the usual pleasantry of 'hello'. Or, as the Irish say, 'Ahhh, it's yourself then. How are you?' Stuart just dives in, talking ten to the dozen as if he has been in conversation with you for the past hour and has merely paused to draw breath. If you can imagine a dark, strong pint of kosher draught Guinness, if there is such a thing, well, that is how I would describe Stuart. It has taken him years to put together nineteen volumes of records of Irish Jewry dating back to 1664. These are available to view in the reading room of the Dublin National Archives and list the births, marriages, deaths, burials, school records and census information of the Jews of Ireland. I've never met Stuart, but for the last few years there's not a brain cell of his that I have not picked. So Brian and I look forward to taking a trip over to Dublin to meet Stuart, and to meet all the Irish people who have helped with my research.

After firing a string of questions at me to clarify his information, Stuart nonchalantly revealed to me . . .

'I've come across yer Gran'pappy Louis in my records. Didn't he go an' sign the alien register at the Dublin police station in June 1917. So there, your instinct was right after all. Sure, yer man was here!'

27 Little Jerusalem

Louis went to Dublin! Was I excited? Is the Pope Catholic and the Chief Rabbi Jewish? Finally, a Dublin connection for Louis had been found. I was on cloud nine! This new discovery gave me many new avenues to go down.

Not wanting to pester Stuart any further, I put a message on the Dublin section of the rootschat.com website asking if some kind person could obtain a copy of the original entry for Louis in the Dublin Metropolitan Police's alien register, which I found was held at the Dublin National Archives. Although I trusted the information in Stuart's records, I wanted a copy of the original document or a transcript of it for my book. Asking for a *look-up,* as it is known, is common practice in family history research, and it's genealogy etiquette to also offer to reciprocate the favour. Many people need look-ups at the Liverpool Records Office because it was such an important port for immigration and emigration. Practically the entire world and his wife passed through Liverpool at some time, to or from somewhere. Most record offices in the UK offer the first look-up free for people who live a good distance away, but that free look up is time-sensitive and the time varies for each record office.

Many people replied to my request, but I needed someone who fully understood the records at the Dublin National Archives. That person was Steven Smyrl. Steven turned out to be a professional genealogist who ran a company called Massey & King, which specialises in legal genealogy such as probate research. Luckily, he was based in Dublin and he knew the archives like the back of his hand.

Steven explained that he wanted to familiarise himself with the alien registration records, because although he was aware of their existence, he had not needed to look at them until now and he felt they would be beneficial for any research he embarked upon for future clients. So Steven offered to do the research for me *pro bono* and he didn't need me to return the favour. This was my lucky day!

Steven was a pleasure to work with – a quick-minded, fast-talking, no-nonsense kind of guy who had the ability to digest information in seconds. He knew most of the archivists at the Dublin National Archives. Within a few minutes of talking to Steven it was obvious that he knew his business inside out. A few days later, a typed transcript of the original entry from the Dublin Metropolitan Police's alien register, giving the entire details of my grandfather's visit to Dublin, appeared as if by magic in my inbox, and I didn't even need to cross the Irish Sea.

At last, this was the proof I had been waiting for; this record gave me documental evidence of the place of birth for my grandfather, and not a German town or *shtetl* in sight! Just look at the birth place for Louis: SWEKSNA . . . KOVNO . . . RUSSIA!

This was the same place that Isaac-Jacob Freedman was from! I was thanking every saint in heaven for Stuart Rosenblatt and his remarkable achievement of recording all this information about the Jewish immigrants who had settled in, or passed through, Ireland. Shirley had said that she thought Louis was from Russia, and she was right. Actually, I found Margaret was also right, as this area was known as Russia-Poland when Louis lived there.

I now had evidence that Isaac-Jacob Freedman was my grandfather's elder brother and Tobias and Faiga Freedman were his parents and therefore my great-grandparents. Most researchers would be more than satisfied to accept that this was enough evidence to prove the link, and in my heart I knew that there were now too many coincidences to deny that I had indeed found Louis' family and his true place of origin. But to me, solid proof is not solid proof unless it is an official document, such as birth records for my grandfather Louis and his elder brother Isaac-Jacob, which would give their father's name as Tobias and their mum's name as Faiga/Fege. So although I was 99.9 percent sure that they were all from the same family, I would not be satisfied until I had that evidence in my hand and to get that document I would need to take my research to Sveksna. That was far easier said than done, so I focused on Dublin for now.

The alien record stated that my grandfather had arrived in Dublin on 28 June 1917. He was with his third wife Rosie, whose name was spelt Rosia, and also five of his younger children: Elias, then nineteen years-old; Isaac, seventeen; Terah, twelve, who had to be Teri/Edward; my father Harry, then ten years of age; and Louis and Rosie's youngest daughter Eva, who was only a three-year-old toddler. The alien register also revealed the initial E, hinting at a middle name for my grandfather Louis, which had never materialised before. They were lodging with a Mrs Levin at no. 12 St Kevin's Parade, Dublin.

Register of Aliens

Police Registration District of:	**Dublin Metropolitan**
Police Division of:	**A**
Serial Number. Date of Entry:	**8000. 28.6.1917**
Surname:	**Freedman**
Christian Name:	**Louis E.**
Nationality and Birthplace:	**Russian/Sweksna, Kovno**
Postal address: a) Residence, b) Business	**a) 12 St Kevin's Parade, Dublin**
	b) None

Trade and Occupation and Name of Employer, if any:	**None**
Date of Birth and Sex:	**1867 / M**
Houseowner, Lodger or Servant:	**Lodger with Mrs Levin**
Particulars of Family:	**Rosia, wife, 35, born Russia**
Children:	**Eli (1898) Isaac (1900)**
	Terah (1905) Harry (1907)
	Eva (1914) born England

Date of Arrival in District, Previous Place of Residence:	**28-6-1917**
	48 Moon Street, Liverpool

Remarks:	**Identity Bk 63012**
	issued at Liverpool on
	31-5-1916
	5 ft 3 ins; medium build;
	grey hair

Signature of Alien:	**X**
	Louis Freedman
	His Mark
	Witness T . . .

This posed many questions, the main one being, was Mrs Levin a relative of Louis or Rosie? And why had my grandfather taken five of his younger children across what was then known as U-boat Alley? It was only one year after the *Lusitania* had been sunk off the coast of Ireland. Louis must have had good reason to take his family to Dublin. What was it?

I read that conscription in England was enforced in March 1916. All men between the ages of eighteen and forty-one years were called up unless they were married, widowed with children, working in a reserve occupation or a religious minister. Two months later the Military Service Act was extended to include married men, and in 1918 the age limit was extended to fifty-one years. Although 140,000 Irishmen volunteered to fight in the First World War and over 30,000 lost their lives, conscription in Ireland was never implemented, so I wondered if Louis had taken his family to Dublin in an attempt to protect Elias and Isaac from conscription. Shirley had told me that Louis' eldest son, Dal, had failed the medical and so had joined the Home Guard, but his second-born son Hyman, and Shirley's father Samuel were then fighting overseas, and it was possible his stepson Abraham was too. So perhaps Louis thought having two sons, plus a stepson, in the First World War was enough, and maybe this was his reason for taking his sons to Dublin? Especially given the note on Joyce's photograph of the young soldier. If my gut feeling was correct, and this young soldier was Abraham, and he had died in 1916 of war wounds, as the note suggested, then maybe Louis didn't want to lose another child to the enemy. Or perhaps it was simply that Isaac/Jack and Elias were medically unfit for war, given that Elias died of kidney failure in 1922 and Isaac/Jack died of MS in 1939. Was this why they were all in Dublin with Louis and not at war? Until I found answers, I could only guess.

But at least my gut feeling about my grandfather was correct. The little fibber was not German as he had always claimed, which was why he was not classed as an enemy alien and interned in a camp; he was a friendly alien. He was allowed to leave Liverpool as long as he reported to the police. Louis was then in his fiftieth year. What was he doing in Dublin?

To find answers I needed to know if there was a link to this Mrs Levin who Louis stayed with at no. 12 St Kevin's Parade. This was close to where Tobias and Faiga Freedman had lived in Emorville Square, and to where Isaac-Jacob Freedman had lived in Lombard Street West, before he went to Cape Town. The area was known as Little Jerusalem, and was home to about 2,000 Jews at that time. Most of them were Litvaks from the *shtetls* around the Kovno area of Lithuania such as Ackmene, Veisknai or Sveksna and many of them were related to each other. The wedding witness Morris Rosenberg was also a Litvak and all of them being Litvaks would in itself have given them a connection to each other, even if they were not related or from the same *shtetl*.

The 1901 Dublin census gave Mrs Levin's first name as Edith, while the 1911 census had her name as Ada and her husband's name was Morris. I posted another message on jewishgen.org and this time I was contacted by Morris and Ada Levin's great-grandson who explained that his great-grandmother, was one of eight children born to Mendel and Chana Harris and that originally, the family name had been Zorochovitz, but had changed to Harris when the family arrived in the UK, and that they came from Karkelan, Paura, Kovno, Russia. Ada ran a boarding house at St Kevin's Parade and she also had family in Manchester, South Africa and south Wales.

I found another descendant of Isaac-Jacob Freedman's, via Isaac's younger daughter, Sarah. Lynn Neiman was born and had lived in South Africa for many years before she came to live in London with her husband Selwyn and their family. They had done a great deal of research into Lynn's Freedman family and were able to provide me with birth certificates for some of Isaac-Jacob's children who were born in Dublin and these records gave Isaac-Jacob's wife's name as Dorah née Harris. Bells were starting to ring. Could this be the family link? Could Ada Levin née Harris be linked in some way to Isaac-Jacob's wife Dorah née Harris? The name Harris was a common name, so I was a long way from finding the answer to that. Isaac-Jacob and Dorah were already married with three children before arriving in Dublin, which was a pity as their marriage records might have given Dorah's maiden name as Harris aka Zorochovitz, and everything would have slotted nicely into place. But that would have been too easy-peasy. So Ada remained either a tantalising possibility or another wild goose chase depending on whether Louis was a paying guest at her boarding house.

At least I now had a handle on my grandfather Louis. He turned out to be a Litvak – the name given to Lithuanian Ashkenazi Jews with roots in the Grand Duchy of Lithuania. Over ninety percent of Lithuanian Jews who stayed behind – approximately 195.000, were wiped out within just six months during the Holocaust, from June to the December of 1941.

Meanwhile, I tried to get into my grandfather's head. Why did he persistently state that he was from Germany, when all along, he was from what was the Lithuanian area of the Russian Empire? One explanation could be that in the mid-1800s, many Jewish immigrants claimed that they were of German origin, because German Jews were well respected and seen as honest citizens. They were generally seen as more cultured and therefore more likely to get a decent job than the deprived Jews of the Pale of Settlement.

But when the political situation changed and the First World War loomed with Germany, many Jewish immigrants in the UK dropped their Germanic claim and became Russian or Polish Jews practically overnight, whether they were or not. Even though Jews hated Tsarist Russia because of the way that they had been persecuted by them for years, they did what they had to do to survive. Life was so bad for Jews under Tsarist Russian rule that some Jews felt they would be better off under German rule.

Perhaps this was why my grandfather Louis told porkies, although I'm sure they were kosher porkies. But why keep it up? There is so much we still don't know at this point. Perhaps this was a sign of early dementia, and Louis was unaware of the risk he was taking with his claims of being German and he stuck to his story. Or perhaps Louis *did* drop his German claim after the 1911 census. We have no records to enlighten us after 1911, apart from the alien record. Or perhaps before he came to the UK, Louis lived in Germany for a while – after all, the German border was only about thirty five kilometres from Sveksna, and many Jews fled to the countryside and earned the price of their ticket at whatever work they could find in Germany before making their way to the port of Hamburg.

Whatever the reason, people needed to survive; they faced many problems that we cannot comprehend in today's world, and like everybody else, my grandfather Louis got himself to safety, got through his life and raised his family as best he could.

I also got the impression that Louis acted soft. After all, he raised a dozen children and worked on his own account through two world wars and the Great Depression. He was obviously streetwise and an extremely capable man. So I was beginning to doubt that he was only able to sign his name with his mark and wondered if that was just a cover, as many immigrants were afraid of authorities and I was surprised how prosperous Louis appeared in the photograph Natalie found. Joyce had told me that she remembered her grandfather being a smart man who gave her and her sister Rose a shiny new penny from the bank when he visited them when they were children. Joyce was born in 1929, so she was a child during the depression of the 1930s. Not many people had a bank account in those difficult times. Louis was definitely not the street peddler or door-knocker I had imagined him to be.

I stopped trying to psych out my grandfather Louis and fathom out his motives and decided to read everything I could lay my hands on about the Dublin Jewish community. I found that it was very much a community of two halves, much like Liverpool's Jewish community at that time. One half were descendants of earlier immigrants who were well-established, often born in Ireland or England and already integrated into the community.

They were English-speaking Jews, who were middle-class, educated, and quite comfortable; some were relatively wealthy moneylenders. They were not as religiously observant, or *frum*, as the Litvak Jewish immigrants were, most of whom arrived between 1870 and 1900, with another wave following in the build-up to the Second World War.

The Yiddish-speaking Litvaks were mostly of a lower class and they were strictly Orthodox and dirt-poor compared to earlier Jewish arrivals, although not nearly as poor as their non-Jewish neighbours. The Greeners, as they were called, were nevertheless an unwelcome addition to the existing Irish Jewry of that era, and the social gap that formed between them sadly signified that they were worlds apart. It appears that class distinction was judged not only by wealth, but by the *age* of that wealth. I'm proud to say that my Freedman family were a part of the half that were seen by the wealthier Jewish community, as the underclass. My grandfather's family were among the later Litvak immigrants who were looked down upon by their affluent Jewish neighbours. They were mostly drapers, hawkers and artisans; no moneylenders to be found here. They would later rise up to break down that class system and give birth to future lawyers, doctors, writers, actors, politicians, political activists and pillars of the community. Liverpool's Jewish community was divided in a similar way.

The further any of us go back in our family's history, we will all find ancestors who were uneducated and unsophisticated. Given that compulsory education didn't begin until 1880, and even then, school was only from the age of five to ten years old. So it's inevitable. They are the raw fabric of all our roots and we should be proud of them, because you and I would still be uneducated and unsophisticated if not for the hard work and tenacity of our ancestors. Personally, I think we should never hide them and never forget them.

The houses in this area of Dublin were built around the 1870s and '80s, so they were only twenty or thirty years old when Tobias and Faiga lived in Emorville Square in 1901. Each home had running water and an outside toilet. They were better off than many of Dublin's non-Jewish communities, many of whom lived in the unsanitary, overcrowded open-door tenements where the infant mortality rate was much higher than in the Jewish community and also far higher than in England. The main artery of Little Jerusalem was Clanbrassil Street, which was lined with kosher shops, including butchers, bakers and drapers similar to Liverpool's Brownlow Hill. Some poorer Jews took in lodgers, and the better-off had a *shiksa*, a domestic servant, often Catholic, who could do the little jobs forbidden of Jews on their Sabbath, such as lighting the fire or turning on a light.

From what I've read, life for Ireland's Jewry appeared far less miserable than for Jewish immigrants who had settled in other major cities, such as Glasgow, London's East End, Liverpool and Leeds, at least in terms of living conditions. I'm sure they would have found Ireland's laid-back way of life far less perilous than Tsarist Russia.

Reading everything from *Dublin's Little Jerusalem* by Nick Harris, to James Joyce's *Ulysses*, gave me an insight into what life was like for my great-grandparents, Tobias and Faiga Freedman. Although my head looked for further proof to dot the i's and cross the t's, my heart was convinced and needed no further evidence that they were Louis' parents and therefore my great-grandparents. It was clear that some answers lay in Dublin.

The information on the alien records for Louis would have been partly provided by Louis and partly taken from his identity card as the alien records gave Louis' identity issue number with the date and place it was issued. This was another record that could provide a wealth of information, and while some members of FTF continued looking for a link to Ada Levin, I turned my attention to researching the identity records that were issued for aliens living in Liverpool during the First World War.

Annswaby enquired at the National Archives at Kew, while I contacted the Liverpool Records Office, and after we were both passed from pillar to post I found it was actually the Merseyside Metropolitan Police Museum that held the few surviving identity records for both enemy aliens and friendly aliens for the Liverpool area. In fact, only a total of about forty alien identity records have survived for Liverpool, and those forty records are from both the First and Second World Wars! Of course, Louis was not one of those forty. But I would never have known that those records even existed if I had not been persistent, as not much seemed to be known about them. You might have better luck than I did, and one of your ancestors might be one of those forty. I have been told that these alien identity cards hold a wealth of information including full birth address, parents' names including mother's maiden name and also a photograph. What a find that would have been!

I still had so many unanswered questions. I needed to know how long Louis was in Dublin and if he ever went to Dublin on any other occasion, either prior to, or after 28 June 1917, and if he did, who he stayed with. This would at least answer some of those questions. So to find out why Louis had crossed the Irish Sea slap-bang in the middle of the Great War, I would need to cross it too . . .

28 My Dublin Day Out

It's not much more than forty minutes' flying time to Dublin from Liverpool, less with the wind behind you. So on the 1 March 2011, I caught a cheap flight over to the Emerald Isle. I bought a same-day return ticket for only £9.99 plus airport tax. I emailed helpful archivist Aideen Ireland at the National Archives in Dublin and pre-ordered all six volumes of the original alien registers held at the archives, so that they would be waiting for me when I arrived, otherwise it meant waiting around until the archivist went to collect the records, which is usually only every hour or two. I planned to look through every page to see if there were any further entries that would show when Louis returned to Liverpool, or if he went to Dublin on any other occasion and, if he did, who he stayed with. I had a planned schedule of work and, as long as there were no delays at the airport, I knew it would take me no more than a long afternoon to look through the six volumes and photograph anything I might find.

I had over cautiously reconfirmed the order with Aideen twice in the previous week, and again the day before I left. But I received an out of office reply to my last email; Aideen had gone on leave. So, I forwarded my email on to the Dublin National Archives' main email address, to make absolutely certain that nothing would go wrong and the records would be ready and waiting for me on my arrival. What could possibly go wrong?

To save more time, I downloaded and completed a day-pass form. I took photographic ID, library card, iPhone, my laptop and I borrowed Lisa's compact digital camera, which Lisa had set to silent mode, and turned the flash off. Nothing more; not even a handbag. I got to Dublin about midday, but when I arrived at the archives, no records were ready for me!

One of the archivists in the reading room acknowledged my email and informed me that he would go and fetch the records on the next collection window, which, he told me, would be one o'clock. Archivists usually collect records from storage each hour or so, unless the records have been ordered in advance – which, I explained, is what I had done!

I didn't have time to waste arguing with him, and besides, I didn't see much point. This was a reconnaissance mission, and maybe it was a bit over ambitious. I had planned to stay until the archives closed at five o'clock, but the taxi driver who collected me from the airport advised me to leave before four o'clock for my return flight as the traffic was heavy because of roadworks. So my planned time at the archives was already cut short, and now I had nearly an hour to kill before the archivist even went for the records.

While waiting, I asked him if I could see Stuart Rosenblatt's books on the Irish Jewish community. He pointed to where they could be found and I selected a few volumes of interest. I found Stuart's entry of Louis' alien record on 28 June 1917 and looked for other possible entries of him returning, or if any record was made of him leaving Ireland, but there were none. I made notes of the page numbers of interest and then looked at Stuart's cemetery records for Tobias Freedman at Dublin's Dolphin's Barn cemetery where Tobias was buried. Still no alien records materialised, and I felt the trip had been a wasted journey.

The Dublin National Archives don't allow mobile phones, bags, pens or coats into the reading room. Free lockers are provided, and a clear plastic bag is given for the few items that are permitted, such as a small camera, change for any photocopying you might need, a notebook and pencil. All archives have similar rules, and for good reason. Photographing pages of archives is permitted, but in Dublin a time slot is allocated so as not to disturb other researchers. This was unexpected as their website had no mentioned of this. I was told that the time slot was between four and five o'clock. I needed to put my thinking cap on quickly, as I needed to leave for the airport before four o'clock to catch my flight home! Complaining would only waste more time, so I slowly turned the pages of the Dolphin's Barn cemetery records and I found Tobias Freedman's grave. Tobias had been buried in plot no. 02-A-11 (nts), which means 'no tombstone'. I quickly flicked through a few more pages and my eyes fell on to an entry for a *Feige* Freeman. Tobias lived with his wife *Faiga* Freedman at Emorville Square on the 1901 Dublin census and her name was spelt *Fege* on Isaac-Jacob Freedman's nat records. Could this Feige Freeman be Faiga/Fege Freedman?

Stuart's records gave her date of death as the 7 July 1927 and grave details as, plot no. 09-A-09 (nts). That put her age at death at about ninety! No further details were given.

Ah, sod it. This was such an important find, so I decided I just had to break the rules. I discreetly took out Lisa's camera and photographed the page. Well, it wasn't my fault that I had to wait for records that I had preordered. Nobody complained, so I took photographs of all the pages that listed all the names of Freeman, Freedman, Friedman, Cohen and Levin.

I was discreetly photographing everything of interest and began to feel better. It was not a wasted journey after all; I had found the grave of Feige Freeman, who was highly likely to be Tobias' wife Faiga, and my great-grandmother and I was well-pleased. I thought I was getting away with my audacious prohibited photography, as people appeared unbothered that I was blatantly breaking the rules. The flash was turned off on Lisa's camera and the shutter was on silent mode, so what harm could I be doing?

As I turned the pages of Stuart's book and focused on the next photograph, from nowhere, a shadow crept across the page that I was attempting to focus on. I looked up, and the same archivist was standing there with his arms folded and a look on his gob, as if to say, *I knew you'd be trouble.* He politely repeated their photography rules and reminded me of the time slot. Then he stood in silence and watched to make sure I put the camera away.

I politely explained my predicament, and although he listened and sympathised with my situation, he explained again that he couldn't allow pictures until the allocated time slot, and he didn't make the rules, so there.

In my head I said, *If the records I'd ordered had been ready for me, I wouldn't need to be breaking rules!* But I could see no point arguing so I put my camera away and sat there, face tripping me like a child who'd had a toy confiscated for being naughty. Eventually, the alien records were brought to me, but security only allowed me to look at one box at a time. I took the lid off the big brown archive box, and wearing white gloves to protect the fragile paper, I turned each page of the faded 1917 handwritten alien registers and made notes of all the information I found on each person whose name was a variation of Freeman. Every time I finished looking through one of the six volumes, I had to take that volume back to the counter and wait my turn in the queue for the archivist to sign over another volume to me. Making notes was slow and this was all eating away at my time and eating away at me.

The volumes were in date order, and I knew Louis' entry had been the 28 June 1917, so I looked at his details first. I wanted to make absolutely sure that I had seen the original information myself. I made a note of the page number and asked the archivist if I could see the volume again just before four o'clock to take a photograph of the record, and he agreed. I searched each page of all six volumes of alien registers, but found no more entries for my grandfather. So there's no way of knowing how long he stayed in Dublin, or if he went to Dublin, either prior to, or after the 28 June 1917. Louis was classed as a friendly alien, and although he was not an enemy to Britain, nevertheless he needed to abide by a strict curfew and report to the police station to sign the alien register whenever he moved more than eight miles from where he had initially registered. He was also obliged to re-register with the local police in the new place of residence or wherever he was visiting. But unfortunately no records have survived outside of Dublin, so there's no telling if he moved around Ireland while he was there. I imagine he would have needed to sign a register when he arrived back home in Liverpool, given that he didn't sign when leaving Dublin, but no such records have survived for Liverpool. So there's no way of telling how long Louis was in Ireland. I had been extremely lucky to have found what I had found so far.

I gave the last of the alien registers back to the archivist and looked at marriages and deaths in Stuart's books while waiting for the time slot, making notes of all the pages I wanted to photograph. Just before four o'clock the archivist brought the alien records back to me, and I began a frantic photo-shoot.

I flew out of the National Archives nearly twenty minutes behind schedule and was convinced that I would miss my flight. Luckily, I got a cheeky taxi driver who knew all the back roads to avoid the roadworks and he got me to the airport just in time to relax and unwind with a much needed cappuccino and a leprechaun sandwich - at least that's what the label said, at one of the many coffee shops at the airport. After discovering that Ireland's leprechauns tasted no feckin' different than corn-fed chicken, I concluded that perhaps the label was referring to the *size* of the sandwich, rather than what it was made of, but it was nice all the same.

While waiting for my flight, I imported my photographs into my laptop. The flight was so quick that it was hardly worth sitting down, and Brian was waiting for me at John Lennon Airport. I was home just before nine o'clock. I was really happy, but shattered, as there is a lot of walking to do at Dublin's huge new airport terminal and I was carrying a heavy laptop. Next time I'll take my trolley case.

I downloaded an application form on the Dublin GRO website and ordered Feige Freeman's death certificate, this time via fax putting my debit card details on the form, which I was a little nervous about doing at first, but I had no problems.

I had the details from the photographs I'd taken of Stuart's Dolphin's Barn cemetery records and I stated the three variations of her name, Feige, Faiga and also Fege, and also included all the Freedman name variations. The name Faiga means 'little bird', but sadly, this little bird had flown away, as a couple of weeks later, I received disappointing news from the Dublin GRO. They could not find Faiga Freeman's death listed, even though they searched the two years before and two years after the date I'd given. I applied again, this time taking ten years off the date. That is, the 7 July 1917, not 1927. I chose the date based on the theory that perhaps Louis went over to Dublin on the 28 June 1917 to see his mum before she died. This would put her age at death as eighty not ninety, which was more feasible for that time. It was a good theory, but alas, it didn't prove fruitful, and the Dublin GRO explained that they had searched from 1915 to 1919. Feige Freeman's grave is at Dolphin's Barn cemetery, so she must have died somewhere in Ireland to be able to comply with Jewish burial customs of burying the deceased before the sun goes down, but where and when she died remains a mystery to this day. So my great-grandmother's death was shelved for the time being.

The following week, we collected Shirley and Monty and took them for a meal at the Boot Room, a restaurant within Liverpool Football Club at their Anfield ground, and I told them all about my Dublin day out and the information I found on Louis in the alien register, giving the poof that he was from Sveksna, Kovno. They really enjoyed the Boot Room but we noticed that Monty seemed unusually quiet that night and we could tell he had something on his mind. He confessed that he was worried about the angina, which he had been recently diagnosed with, and was waiting for an appointment with a specialist.

They had previously booked their usual trip to Israel for Passover and I rang them when they returned home. Monty answered the telephone. I could tell he was not his usual chirpy self and Shirley was worried about him. She explained that they'd had long delays at the airport coming home, which was probably due to extra security for the royal wedding, but despite that, they had both enjoyed their holiday with Monty's daughter and her family.

Little did I know then that this would be the last time I would ever talk to Monty, as only a couple of weeks later, Monty was rushed into hospital and on 18 May 2011, just one week before his eighty-fifth birthday and the day before Shirley's birthday, Monty passed away, and with heavy hearts we attended our first Jewish funeral.

As we stood around Monty's coffin alongside his family and friends in the tiny, stark prayer hall within the cemetery's gates, we listened in silence as Manny, the young Rabbi who we had met at Michael and Lucy's wedding, recited the *Kaddish*, and as we listened, my mind drifted back to that night, when Monty said to me . . .

'You know, we're very lucky to have found you.' I can only repeat my reply:

'No, Monty. I'm the lucky one . . . lucky to have found Shirley and you.'

29 More Siblings

I didn't have the heart to do much research after Monty's death. And poor Shirley was lost. I visited her as often as I could at Monty's flat and it felt like he was still there. Shirley stayed until his flat was sold and then she returned to her home. It was the end of an era for us all. Monty was always so active, walking with his pals each day along the Mersey waterfront at Otterspool Prom' and he was always making plans for the future. He never wasted a minute of his life. I was thankful that only a few weeks before he died, Monty gave me a little strip of his labels to sew into Brian's suits: 'Monty Fagin – Exclusive Tailor'.

Instead of cutting the strip and sewing them into Brian's suits, I decided to drape them around the oval mirror on my dressing table, where they will be seen each day.

I was plunged back into research when a lady by the name of Esther (Herschman) Rechtschafner contacted me. Although Esther now lives in Israel, her grandfather originated from Sveksna. Esther gave me a link to an article that she had written for the jewishgen.org website about the *shtetl*'s history called *'Sveksna: Our Town',* which gave me a good insight into the hardship of *shtetl* life and it also gave a chilling account of the fate of Sveksna's Jews in the Second World War.

With an extensive record collection to hand, Esther searched for the births of my grandfather and his elder brother Isaac-Jacob, and records of their parents Tobias and Faiga, but disappointingly, she found no trace of them. Esther suggested that the Freedman name may have been something entirely different when the family lived in Sveksna, or it could be that Louis' family was from another Lithuanian place called Veisknai, which sounds very similar to Sveksna when pronounced with a Yiddish accent. Whilst I agree every possibility should be considered, Isaac-Jacob's naturalisation records and Louis' alien records both clearly state that Sveksna, spelt Sweksna on both documents, was their home, so surely this information would have been taken from their identity papers and was therefore reliable?

Surely when Isaac-Jacob Friedman applied for naturalisation in Dublin on the 28 April 1892, before leaving for Cape Town the following November, his background would have been scrutinised? He naturalised under the name of Isaac Friedman. He must have had genuine identity papers, which showed that Friedman was the original spelling of his family's name? It could be that birth records for Sveksna have not yet been transcribed for the period that my grandfather (b: 1867) and his brother Isaac-Jacob (b: 1854) were born. So, although I reluctantly placed this part of my search back onto the shelf at this point, it was not the end, not by a long chalk. There was still much more to discover in Dublin.

The one thing that is reliable in Jewish research are the Hebrew given names, so the more siblings I could find, the more Hebrew names I could harvest and that would help to identify the family, even if their family name was something completely different when they lived in Sveksna, regardless of the surname on Isaac-Jacob's nat records. Just like the Irish, Jews traditionally had big families and there was fourteen years between my grandfather, Louis, and his elder brother, Isaac-Jacob. I was sure Dublin would hold the key to unlock my grandfather's family history, so I searched for more siblings in Ireland to fill that fourteen-year gap. I call this, researching sideways. In other words, if you hit a brick wall finding proof of the birth place of your grandfather, try researching his siblings.

Ordering a copy of an Irish BMD certificate for genealogy purposes cost just €6 euros at the time, a bargain compared to UK certificates, which by now had gone up from £7 to £9.25 UK pounds. So I decided to speculate and ordered a few marriage records of people I had a *feeling* about. Of course, I ended up with some marriage certificates that were wrong, being a different family, but this saved months of work, as some marriages were right.

My first success was a sister to my grandfather Louis. Esther-Baila Fridman (sic) whose father's name was Tobias Fridman – notice the spelling of the surname! Esther married Maurice Abramson in Dublin in 1887. My luck soon fizzled out, as no children were found from the marriage, and my grandfather's sister, disappeared off the face of the earth with no death or census information for Esther-Baila found. Her marriage certificate gives the wedding witnesses as W. Goldwater and Michael Harmel. We found some of Michael Harmel's children had emigrated to South Africa. Tilly Mint found details of a descendant, Alan Michael Harmel; a political activist fiercely opposed to apartheid who had rubbed shoulders with Nelson Mandela, and his wife Ray made Winnie Mandela's wedding dress. Although I've found no obvious family connection to my Freedmans, so far, it's nevertheless interesting to find who my ancestors were friends with, or had links to.

My next find ran a little longer and led me on a fascinating journey, when I found another brother to my grandfather Louis. I discovered the marriage of a Ralf Freedman to Sarah Levy in Dublin on the 29 December 1880. The civil record gave Ralf's father's name as, T. Freedman. The MA certificate confirmed the initial T stood for Tobias, and gave Ralf's name as Philip Freedman, with Hebrew name Raphael. One of the wedding witnesses was Jacob Friedman, probably his brother Isaac-Jacob, who later went to South Africa.

Among the photographs I had taken in Dublin of alien records, I found an entry for Philip with a side note that revealed a moving story, which took me on a fascinating journey when some more records were found in Dublin, thanks to an Irish angel.

The alien record for Philip Freedman, which was entered on the 7 January 1915, stated that Philip arrived in Dublin in 1878. His occupation was a 'pedlar', and his birthplace was given as Kovno, Russia. His date of birth was the 13 March 1855 and he was lodging with a Mr Farrell at 46 Charlemont Street, Dublin. His five children listed on the alien record were Ellen, Minnie, Lillian, Eva and Ethel.

An additional note stated that Philip had been admitted into Donnybrook Hospital, which was called the Hospital for Incurables, much like a hospice today, on the 2 May 1917. I learnt that Donnybrook Hospital was a charity-run hospital, and I discovered that they have extensive archives and a knowledgeable and helpful archivist, Steven McCormac. Being able to provide Steven with an accurate date of Philip's admission into Donnybrook, along with his address, made his job easier and over the following weeks he uncovered several documents, which gave me fascinating information about my grandfather's brother, Philip.

After some security questions, Steven sent me copies of his findings. Four of these documents, which included the application for admittance into Donnybrook, were dated between April and August of 1915. Some of them were handwritten character references for Philip, who appeared to be having great difficulty being accepted into the Dublin hospital. A person needed to prove he or she warranted admission into this charity-run hospital, and for Philip, there seemed to be a big problem. However, the reason for Philip's difficulties in obtaining admission seemed to be more because Philip was a non-national than because of any doubt about his financial circumstances, as Philip was able to provide proof that he was in financial need. The admission declaration form revealed that he was scarcely scraping a living for his family as a shopkeeper dealing in antiques. Most probably the reality was that he had nothing more than a bric-a-brac shop carrying the sort of stock usually found in flea markets, rather than any valuable antiques, but people had their pride.

1915 was not a good time for aliens, given this was the middle of the First World War. The sinking of the *Lusitania* on the 7 May 1915 caused riots in cities such as Liverpool and Dublin, making matters ten times worse for *all* aliens, whether friend or foe. It was a volatile time, when many Yiddish-speaking immigrants were attacked. Anything associated with Germany was not trusted and Yiddish was originally a German dialect. It was also the start of the troubles in Ireland with the Easter uprising soon to follow in 1916. So tension was mounting and around the corner, the Irish War of Independence lay in wait. (1919–21)

Philip was a very sick man who was caught up in all this political upheaval. An alien was an alien, no matter how friendly or sick during these tense times; people were afraid and trust was thin on the ground. These were difficult times for the hospital's authorities too, as they were torn between loyalty to the Crown and also to the future of Ireland, being confronted with the possibility that Irish independence could become a reality within a very short space of time. Steven explained that the authorities at Donnybrook were also under tremendous pressure to admit wounded soldiers of the First World War, but they refused, maintaining that it was not the reason that Donnybrook Hospital was founded.

These character references for Philip also held a surprise that we didn't see coming. Some of the records were testimonies by clergymen from the Harcourt Street Baptist chapel in Dublin, and they were each vouching for Philip. The clergymen explained that Philip was a quiet man who had 'converted to Christianity' and had consequently been persecuted by the Jewish community for converting, and also from the Irish community for being an alien. Philip was caught in no-man's land.

The letters also stated that Philip had lived in England *before* settling in Ireland in 1878, which seemed to suggest that Philip had arrived on British soil much earlier than we had first thought. But if Philip, and the rest of the Freeman family arrived in the UK after 1871 and then went to Ireland in 1878, then they would not appear on the 1881 UK census, and they don't show on the bits of Irish censuses that survived the 1922 fire.

There was a wave of conversions at that time, into what were then referred to as Christian-Jews, which sounds like a contradiction in terms. Nevertheless, I found there is such a thing as a Christian-Jew, which, put simply, describes someone who, whilst practicing the culture of Judaism and maintaining kosher rules, believes that Christ was the Messiah. Philip married Sarah at the address of no. 72, Capel Street, according the the Jewish religion. So he must have still practised his religion when he wed in 1880. Until I find descendants, it cannot be confirmed if he later converted or not.

The clergymen put forward a strong case on Philip's behalf. Each of them explained in their letters that Philip was not an *enemy* alien and pointed out that he was in fact an ally from Russia-Poland, and should be treated as such. The Lithuanian area was referred to as Russia-Poland at that time. They explained in great detail that the reason Philip had not become a British subject was simply because, like many, he could not afford to naturalise. Eventually, Philip won his case and remained in Donnybrook for two years.

Philip suffered from chronic arthritis and Bright's disease, an older classification that was given for different forms of kidney disease. As Donnybrook was a hospital for people with incurable illnesses such as these, they did not administer drugs back in those days. Instead, the records gave a detailed account of the various medicinal 'tonics' of beer, brandy, whiskey, port and wine that were included in his diet of vegetables and mutton. I doubt the food would have been kosher in a charity-run hospice, but at least he had a few comforts. And, unthinkable today, patients were allowed to smoke!

Steven also found two moving handwritten letters, written by Philip's wife Sarah. One letter was dated the 10 May 1917. Seemingly, Philip had requested three-month's leave to go home, because his daughter was seriously ill. No name was given for his daughter. With Donnybrook being a charity-run hospital, beds were hard to come by, and so home leave was carefully monitored, because if a patient requested too many periods of home leave, it was thought that he or she was then taking up a bed that could be given to another patient. So the rules for granting leave were strict, and unfortunately Philip had already taken his quota of leave for that year, before his daughter became ill. Sarah's two letters were a plea to the hospital's authorities to reverse their decision and allow her husband to come home to be with his daughter. Permission for leave was refused and the last document Steven found shows that at the end of May 1917, regardless of his failing health, Philip discharged himself.

The admission records for Donnybrook had given Philip's home address as being no. 16 Cuffe Street, Dublin. There was also a side note that said that he had moved there from Windsor House, South Circular Road, Dublin. However, the address on Sarah's two letters to Donnybrook was no. 1 Green Street Green, Orpington, Kent. Descendants from this branch have family names such as; Harris, Russell and Berge.

Wherever Philip and Sarah Freeman's days ended, Sarah's eloquently written letters are now close to a century old. They are handwritten in fountain pen and need to be passed on to Philip and Sarah Freeman's grandchildren who, I am sure will treasure them forever. Contact details are at the back for this book if you think you are a descendant.

30 Never Give Up

Although this book is now drawing to a close, my research will carry on, at least until the day I can hold my grandfather Louis' birth certificate is in my hand and my grandmother Rebecca's son, Abraham, is no longer a mystery. Nothing is certain until you have that proof. In my case, I will never have that piece of paper to prove that I'm Harry Freeman's daughter. DNA is a wonderful way to identify a blood relative. But in my case the test is complicated because my father was male and I am female. A DNA sample would need to be taken from my father's closest male relative, who would be Joyce's son David, my father's great nephew. The results of this test would not be completely reliable, at least not enough to justify the expense, because the results would be diluted at each generation. So what would be the point of the test? No doubt technology will improve. One day I may get that reliable proof to enable me to dot every i and cross every t. Until then, the evidence, albeit all circumstantial, is nevertheless overwhelming, and leaves my heart with not a shadow of doubt that I am the daughter of Harry Freeman, and that's all that matters to me.

Meanwhile, as I drafted the final chapter of my parents' story, I found myself wanting to return to the old neighbourhoods of Little Italy and the Jewish Quarter. So, one afternoon, Brian and I took a drive around the areas where I had spent my childhood and obviously, with the passage of time, I found them much altered.

The old tenement flats that had once flanked Byrom Street, where I lived as a child, had long gone, replaced by modern houses and bungalows, each of them with its own neatly kept garden displaying the pride of every family home. My playground, that soulless brown 'olla of my youth, had now been replaced with grassy areas where children can play.

The area is now dominated by John Moores University, which nestles in the midst of the Byrom Street community. This five story building has since been extended several times, but the original wing that began life as the poly' and which I had watched being built as a child, was still exactly as I remembered it, and I could still picture myself with Joanie, our fingers and toes numb with the cold as we slid down the icy slopes that the bulldozers had created when digging out the foundations. Now the streets were filled with foreign students from all corners of the globe and there was hardly a Liverpool accent to be heard. Of course, Berry's Pawnbroker's had pledged its last ticket long ago and was nowhere to be found.

The old Jewish Quarter around Brownlow Hill has had much the same treatment as Little Italy. Being dominated by John Moores, LIPA (Liverpool Institute for Performing Arts), and Liverpool University, the area was also crowded with students from every nationality. My father's place of birth at no. 34 Pleasant Street, which was the street where his family had lived in 1911 and where my grandmother Rebecca had died, was barely recognisable, and Moon Street, where Louis had lived for over twenty years with his third wife Rosie, was nowhere to be found. Many of the properties in this area are listed buildings, which have been restored to their former glory. They are often used for film sets in period dramas as Liverpool's talent for playwrights and film production continues to grow and gain merit.

It's strange that my Jewish and Catholic family's paths had crossed in so many ways. It was just a coincidence that we moved to a flat overlooking West Derby cemetery in the early 1970s, a stone's throw from the Jewish section of the cemetery where my grandfather Louis and many of his family are buried, and where my mum and John are also resting in the general section of the same cemetery. Those spacious high-rise flats where my mother's washing took flight from her line, are also long gone.

This entire story has unfolded just because my mother fell in love with a Jewish man. They spent twenty-five years meeting secretly, and it seems that for the rest of their lives they had kept in touch with each other. There was no wrong in this, but the times that they lived in, and whatever difficulties my mother had gone through had made her terrified to reveal my Jewish roots and afraid to be with the man who she obviously had loved deeply all her life. Who could have imagined that my very ordinary Liverpool mum had such secrets hidden away? I often wonder how she felt that day when she opened the letter from the warden of Rose Bush Court, giving her the news of Henry Freeman's death.

As for my father, I have no idea why he lost touch with his family or why it was left to United Synagogue to bury him. It appears that he had worked all his life and enjoyed his life. So, what happened to my father? Had he lost his money and had nothing left to pay for his burial? That fifteen-year gap from when he left Liverpool in the mid-fifties until he moved into Rose Bush Court in 1969 holds all his little secrets and could answer these questions.

For my parents, it's a sad ending to a sad story; a story that's by no means uncommon. It has been a privilege for me to have written this book on behalf of my parents, and also on behalf of all the people who have been, and are still, the victims of hatred and bigotry.

There are millions of people in this world, who are dying to know, but scared to find out. If you are one of them, I hope this book has inspired you. If I can do it, so can you.

Wallaby, I'm sure you already know this, but do you realise how exceptionally brave and unusual your own mum was in managing to avoid all the horribleness that went on back then? OC

OC was right. My mum was unusual and, although she always referred to herself as a coward and often buried her head in the sand, I now see another side to her; an exceptionally brave side. But what I had not told OC, or the members of FTF, was that my mum did not manage to avoid *all* the horribleness that went on back then. Regardless of her lack of confidence, my mother stood up to the bigotry and prejudice of the small-minded. As for me, I was lucky. I was kept, and I was loved.

The 1960s brought with it a different mentality: understanding, broadmindedness and tolerance. Women were better educated and confident. With that newfound confidence they were empowered. The pill meant far fewer unplanned pregnancies, fewer unmarried mothers who no longer needed to hide away from a judgmental society.

As for my father, who, for over fifty years of my life had been nothing more than an ink blot on my birth certificate, he now has a name, or names. Henry aka Harry, with Harris, being his name on his school records. Thanks to my cousin Shirley, I can now put a face to that name. And through my cousins Margaret, Joyce, Natalie and Arthur, I have learnt a little more about the father I never knew. With thanks to my maternal cousin Brian Hennessy, I now know that my father did not run away as I had first thought; he wanted to marry my mum, and that mystery telephone call to my business tells me that my father had kept an eye on me from a distance and seemed proud of his secret daughter.

However, my mum had gone through some difficult times, and she did not recognise that times, along with people, had changed. So petrified was she to reveal my father's true identity, that she did not name him on my birth certificate. It's hard to understand such fear. Well, I am not afraid, and I hope this book helps to put the record straight. I am my father's daughter and I am proud to be the daughter of Harry Freeman, who was a Jew.

If you have never known the circumstances of your birth and a heavy veil of mystery completely surrounds your very existence, then your imagination can run riot and you fear the worst. You can easily become torn; torn between dying to know and scared to find out. Whether it's illegitimacy, adoption, or perhaps an unknown mother or father who left the family home, the deeper the secret, the more your imagination can run away with your fears. It's the fear of the unknown and the hurt is too deep. So you wait. You wait until everybody you are close to has died before you begin the search for that mystery part of you. It's far too emotional to ask family who you're close to. You would sooner ask a stranger and discover the facts alone, discreetly, without opening up and telling even your closest friend. Because you have no idea what skeletons you could discover hiding in that wardrobe, and so you would sooner open that wardrobe door alone.

This was my reason for putting my search for my mystery father on to that back-burner for so long – too long. I would try half-heartedly, and then give up far to easily. Of course, twenty-four years ago, when my search first began, I didn't have internet. In fact, back then it never even entered my head to use genealogy to trace him. I was thinking more along the lines of hiring a private detective, which all those years ago was far beyond my purse strings, as every penny we had was ploughed back into our businesses. I was driven by emotion, not logic or common sense. I made stupid, *stupid* mistakes and overlooked the blatantly obvious, the things that were literally staring me in the face. The things that were, in my case, under my nose!

My family secret turned out to be nothing like that which my imagination had caused me to fear as my research has uncovered a heart-warming story that has turned my mum into my hero. And, with the help of the friends I have made along the way, I've now found my father's final resting place and a family to be proud of, with thought-provoking roots that have literally made the hairs on the back of my neck stand on end.

Never give up. There might be family out there who don't know you exist, or a birth mother or father afraid to talk about their secret son or daughter. Harbour no bad feelings. You don't know what they have been through. Perhaps they have tried in vain to find you. Look carefully, they may have left you a trail of breadcrumbs, praying that one day you will find your way home.

I wish you luck in your search.

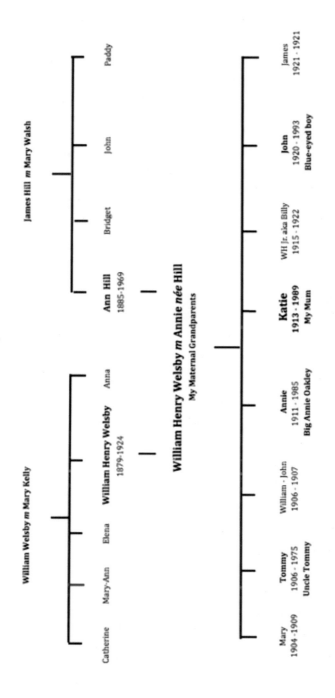

Above: A Small Section of my Maternal Welsby Family Tree.

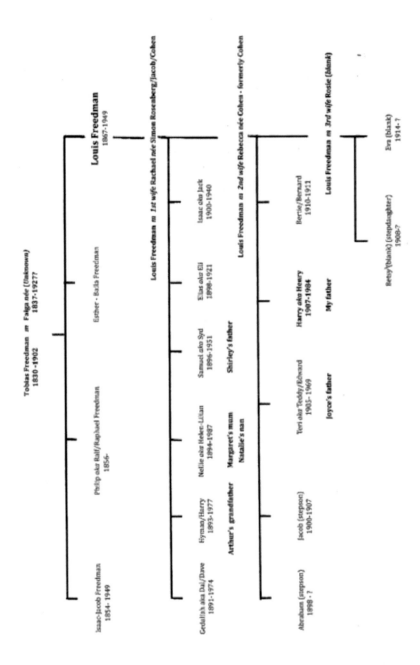

Above: A Section of my Paternal Grandfather's Freeman Family Tree - Louis Freedman.

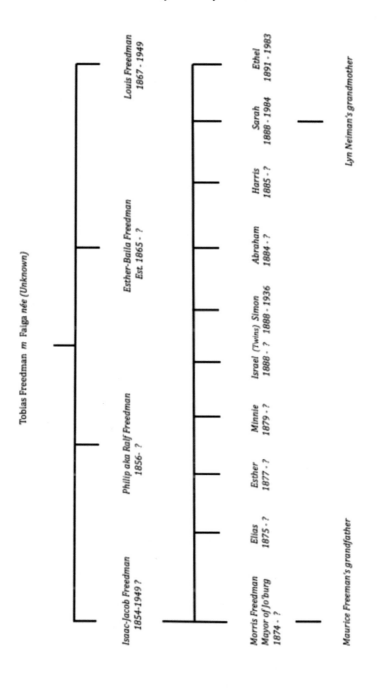

Above: A Section of a Branch of my Paternal Freeman Family Tree. Isaac - Jacob Freedman.

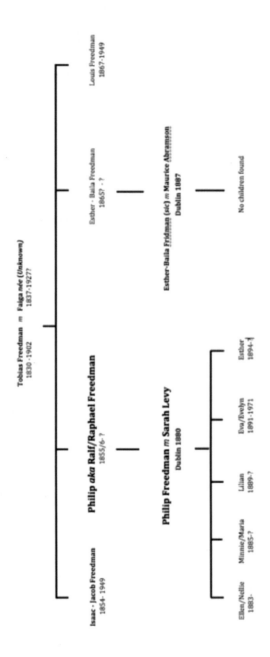

Above: A Section of a Branch of my Paternal Freeman Family Tree - Philip Freedman.

Also Esther - Baila Freedman's Tree.

A word from some of the stars of this research . . .

I was probably the first member of FTF to read Wallaby's introductory post on the night of the 14 February 2009. I typed a reply, then deleted it before posting and left it to someone else to let her down gently. I thought her task was impossible. Freeman is a very common name, there seemed to be no proof that he was her father and overall, there was little real information. I watched the thread, which moved very slowly at first. Then someone found a death and a corresponding birth and at the same time, Wallaby posted more information about her mum. Suddenly, I was convinced she was on the right track and I joined in the hunt.

What followed was the most exciting, frustrating, annoying and difficult search I have ever known. I lived and breathed Freemans for nearly six months and couldn't wait to log on to see what had unfolded each day. It has been a privilege to be involved in this search.
OC

OC: the only thing I know about this great lady, is that she lives in Cornwall and has traced her Holden family back to the 1200s! My tormented imagination could see Jessica Fletcher in; *Murder, She Wrote.* Without OC's help and advice I'd still be looking for Henry Freeman. I am eternally grateful to her for all her help and advice.

Wallaby's plea for help to find her father seemed impossible at first – she knew so little about him. That little bit of information turned out to be enough! Through everyone's hard work - from Wallaby herself, fortunately still in Liverpool and able to access local archives, to those at the other end of the country who helped with visits to London Archives and Libraries to find out about Harry's spell in that area, including my contribution of researching at the National Archives, to those on the other side of the world who ploughed online indexes. Wallaby DID get to know her father, through his family. A hugely satisfying search for us all, but so much more than that - Wallaby gained a whole new family.
Annswaby

Annswaby: Ann is one of the few professional researchers on FTF. Recommended by many regimental museums, such as the King's Own Scottish Boarders, the Worcester Regiment and Sherwood Foresters. She undertakes research for people from all over the world and has been my eyes and ears at the National Archives at Kew. <u>militaryandfamilyresearch.co.uk</u>

Moggie: Mo, as we call her, is retired and lives somewhere in Essex. She had a trained eye for clue-spotting. Often she would follow a wild hunch and astounded us all by producing a vital piece of information. Being too modest to write a small piece for this book, I could not finish this work before I gave her the credit she so deserves and a virtual round of applause. Mo would not give up until I agreed to write this book. She helped with proofreading and had more confidence in me, than I had in myself. If not for her tenacity a seventeen inch laptop would have morphed into a frisbee and this book would never have been written.

When I found Wallaby was a fellow scouser, I felt in touch with her because I'd never met my dad either. So when thread after thread was started in the search for Henry Freeman, I joined in. We found his name was Harry Freedman and he had belonged to the Liverpool Jewish community. He had fallen in love with a Roman Catholic lady, Wallaby's mum. I've cried many tears but I have laughed aloud as well, as I sat in front of my computer, my emotions have been all over the place and yet I have loved every minute of this search.

The determination shown by the members of FTF has been overwhelming. Every poster had something to offer no matter how small, it all helped to find Our Harry, as we called him.
Tilly Mint

Tilly Mint: With the username of Tilly Mint, I knew she had to be from Liverpool. Tilly has been my inspiration in this search, especially at low times when I was sorry I'd ever started! Tilly was there for me: *"Don't give up, there could be family out there that don't know you exist."* How right she was!

I was recruited partway into this tale because my research into my niece's tree had shown me some useful web-links for the kind of material that Wallaby might need in her quest. OC had spotted that my niece's paternal tree included Jewish ancestors with a similar surname, and some with roots in Eastern Europe, echoing Wallaby's family roots.

I have been a dabbler in the project: coming up with esoteric bits of information, for non-Jews, which others have used to move the project forward. I have followed with delight the highs and lows of the emerging story. I have been amazed at the speed of only six months and the dedication with which a team of e-friends started from nothing, to provide Wallaby with a family she never knew she had.
Christine in Herts

Christine in Herts: By day, Christine is an opera singer with the most amazing voice. By night, she is an experienced, amateur family history researcher. Her know-how around family history websites has been invaluable as many websites are not user-friendly.

Wallaby's story touched me more than any that I'd read before because it was similar to mine. I had a 38-year quest to find my father after seeing his name on my birth certificate at the age of 15 when my mother was filling in the 1971 census! That quest finally ended on 14 August 2009 in Dundee when I stood at his grave with his other daughter, my half sister, who is six years younger. But it's not the end of the road, not for me anyway.

I know what it's like not to know your father and the yearning there is to know stuff; anything that can tell you about the other half of your DNA. Who your father was, what he did, where did he come from and . . . where did he go to? Wallaby has now travelled that road too.
*Maggie4_7_*

Maggie4_7_: Maggie knew exactly how I felt. It doesn't matter what you've achieved in life, that void remains empty. People who are rich in family don't understand this. Maggie did.

The Jewish angle is not easy – elation and deflation I call it. I began my search because my grandmother died when she was in her early 30s and my mum knew little about her mother. I managed to trace her back to Bobruisk in Belarus and then got hooked! Decided to look at all my other great grandparents - not easy. Many came to the UK in the late 1800s early 1900s, changed their names, or had their names transcribed incorrectly and there are limited passenger arrival records from outside the Med. Times have changed now of course, and more records are available, but even so, families split up - did they go to the U.S, South America, Australia, Canada, South Africa, somewhere in the U.K or Eire? I've found parallel families who knew nothing about each other; children that passed away with no recognition. Marriages that weren't civil . . . you name it! I'm now looking at Ukraine, Latvia and Lithuania, a big change from the East End of London!

Another problem is that Jewish people rarely spoke of their past for many reasons - fear of reprisal or just too painful. I even remember as a child being told never to look back . . . you don't know who you can hurt.
Naomiatt

Naomiatt: Naomi was an e-friend of Christine in Herts who recruited her help quite late in my research. She has vast experience in Jewish genealogy. Naomi and her friend Watson introduced me to Jewish genealogy websites and gave guidance in Jewish culture. Nothing confused Naomi and she had the same zany humour as me.

I'm writing this purely as an observer as I'm not quick enough to find answers like some people but I have been following this intriguing tale for about a year now on FTF, and the twists and turns of this story and the hard work of those involved have been compelling reading.
Borobabs

I first noticed Wallaby's thread when she joined FTF. I thought she had a hopeless task but was at a loose end and decided to help. One thing lead to another and various researchers came up with bits of information and gradually it all started to slot together
It became a thread that I went to first whenever I logged onto the site and still do.
Margaret in Burton

When I first saw Wallaby's thread asking about how she could get hold of the hospital records for Harry Freeman, I thought, she's got no chance as I knew that medical confidentiality was the most strict of all and she couldn't even prove any relationship to Harry. She then told us her story and what she said was very moving and made me feel I needed to help. I had just started helping my brother-in-law find his birth family so I'd been thinking about people who don't know one or both of their parents and how that must make them feel, something I hadn't personally experienced. I knew from my relative that there were some powerful feelings to be dealt with including those of any family that were found, and Wallaby seemed very 'tuned into' the sensitiveness of the situation for everyone who might be involved. The search was a roller coaster ride of epic proportions, with twists and turns and surprises almost at every point, names changed from one record to another for the same people, making it very hard to determine who was who and how they were related. The fact of the family Jewish immigrants made it all the harder as officialdom wasn't really interested in foreigner's details so the records were Anglicised without a care for us family tree researchers!
But, FTF members triumphed in the end getting Wallaby in touch with her family who have all (bar one) turned out to be warm and friendly people – just like Wallaby!
Margaretmarch

*"You may never know for sure if Harry was your Dad." How **wrong** I was! This has been a very interesting, challenging and at times, emotional, adventure. Initially I thought Wallaby would never confirm her belief that Henry Freeman was her father, there was not enough evidence. But as time went on Wallaby told us more and I, like many others, thought it would be possible, if not probable. The moral of the story is that the smallest piece of information can change everything and shouldn't be ignored, especially when researching a family history.*

It's ironic that Henry/Harry died with no family nearby and now, years later, many people from around the world consider him 'Our Harry'. To the amusement of my husband, I cried when I first set eyes on Our Harry. I'm proud to be part of the team that helped Wallaby, although my part was small, and consisted mainly of being supportive. I wish Wallaby every happiness with her new family.

Kit

On St Valentine's Day 2009, a new member of FTF posted a plea for help in finding out information about her late father. She gave a wonderfully touching account of the love story between her parents, much of which she had only discovered after her mum had sadly died.

There were very few hard facts to go on but the fact that her father was Jewish struck a chord with me as my own grandfather was Jewish. The search for details of Harry's life grew from that first post with many people offering help and advice to Wallaby, which she always willingly followed up. Much of the time I just watched from the sidelines as the facts came flying in. I looked in on the thread nearly every single day to follow the latest developments. There were many times when things were moving so fast that I struggled to keep up but it was still compelling reading. At other times, I laughed out loud at Wallaby's tales of her trips to Records Offices and her little anecdotes of things in her life. I've still not met her, but like many others, I feel like I've adopted her and her family.

The momentous event for me was the day she met some real relatives. We all sat and waited for news about how the meeting went with a lot of banter going on in the meantime. And then the news... Wallaby introduced Harry to us with a photo that her newfound relatives had given her - the first time she had seen him. I'm not ashamed to say that I cried at this point. I know I'm not the only one who was affected like that, so we could only imagine how Wallaby was feeling. I've certainly learnt a lot throughout all this, which in turn has helped with my own family history research.

Night Owl

It's amazing to think one letter and a chance click on an Internet website (FTF) could lead to this book and meeting family members that didn't know each existed. FTF from around the Globe got together to help a stranger. I have so much admiration for all the members and supporters that have given their time and effort to such an astonishing story and helping Wallaby and her new family find each other. It's a lesson to us all. Nothing ventured nothing gained and . . . to never give up hope.

Tralena Mason

It is very seldom that in a world of Family History to find a thread as gripping as this, and watched by so many people. For those who have never contributed to the thread but look in daily, it has become like a soap opera.

The picture of Wallaby's father Harry Freeman was the ultimate experience and those words that she chose to announce to us of his arrival, and to meet her father for the first time brought tears of joy in the hearts of Family Tree Forum members who had lived through this drama from day one. This is a truly exceptional learning curve in Family History especially in the Jewish research experience that will show to others who yearn for the knowledge of their Jewish forefathers.

I feel proud to have had a very small part to play in its evolution and development.

Clematised

I was introduced to Wallaby by Naomiatt. Over the years we have laughed and cried together through elation and deflation into the wee small hours. Jewish Genealogy is difficult to trace for British Jews, let alone a Catholic Scouser! Most Jews have no idea where there roots lay, and give up easily, but not Wallaby.

It's been a privilege and honour to give my time helping research Harry Freeman's family, and giving appropriate advice on Jewish traditions and rituals. I remember Monica emailing to tell me that her and Brian had been invited to Shirley's for Friday night dinner, I replied giving her the full menu and she was surprised that I knew what would be on offer . . . tradition!

My own family originated in Kovna near to the Freemans and it has become instinctive each time I look for records of my own family to make another search for The Freemans. Whilst visiting my grandparents in the same cemetery, I've wandered over and paid my respects to Harry by placing a stone on his grave. Harry is not forgotten.

Watson.

A word from my mum's side, my 2nd Cousin Mary . . .

My Gt. Grandmother was the central character in our family whilst I was growing up. I called her Nin and she lived in the centre of Liverpool with her daughter Catherine, my Gt. Aunt, who I called Auntie Katie, my Gt. Uncle John and a few other relatives, who where the children of my Gt. Grandmother's Brother, who died when he was young. Then, of course my cousin, who we nickname Wallaby. She used this nickname as her username when she joined a website to ask for help in the search for her father. I can't believe after a few short months, she has not only found her father, but the whole story has now turned into this book and I'm sitting here writing my contribution!

It wasn't until I grew up that I realised Wallaby's life wasn't as good as I had thought. Her dear mum had kept her father secret, all her life and she had been brought up in a family of older adults, with no young people like herself who, maybe she could have confided in. It now transpires there were quite a few secrets our family kept, which perhaps one day could fill another book. But I must add, that our family were all hardworking decent people, who were brought up in terrible times due to my Gt. Grandfather dying young, leaving my Nin to bring up her young family in the best way she could.

My mother Mary adored her Auntie Katie. She even lived with the family for a short period in her early twenties. Auntie Katie would never discuss Wallaby's father with anyone. My mum questioned my grandmother about Wallaby's father and eventually found out that he was Jewish. My own mother never told me his origins until after my Auntie Katie died in 1989 and I told my mum she must tell Wallaby.

It was a Christmas morning at my house and my mother phoned Wallaby. After a bit of coaxing by me she blurted out: "your father was Jewish" I now know my mother was hesitant in telling Wallaby about her father, it was the fact she felt she was betraying her aunt by revealing her secret. I must add that our family were very Catholic, in the sense that any other religion i.e. Jewish, Muslim and Protestant would have been cause for a big family crisis, even though they never went to church! Thank God times have changed. It now seems silly and old fashioned in it's reasoning, but in those days- well, it was a different way of thinking and doing things.

I have been following the thread on FTF like many others, Wallaby computerised me and I've been watching with bated breath as each new lead led to another, what a brilliant and kind team all those on FTF are. They have all helped to fulfil a lifetime dream for my cousin to trace her father. Now it is her turn to get to know her father's family and enjoy what she should have had all those years ago. I am very proud to say my cousin has come through all of these trials and tribulations with dignity and of course a great sense of humour! Her mum, I'm sure, would be- absolutely made up. Good luck Wal'... Russia here we come!

With love Mary xx

A word from my father's side, my Cousin Shirley . . .

One day I received a letter from a woman who thought that we might be related. Her name was Monica, you will now know her as Wallaby or Jess. I hear of so many hoaxes these days, but my daughter Linda thought it seemed genuine and suggested that I replied giving my home number and invite her to call. When Monica rang, we talked and the outcome was that her father was my Uncle Harry, who we had not heard from since the mid 1950s!

Monica had never met her father and she explained the entire story about the letter she found when her mother passed away and the information that her late cousin Mary had given her. The following week my partner Monty and I met my new cousin and her husband Brian at their home. I showed her the page in my wedding album where Uncle Harry was standing. It was a traditional 1954 wedding photo of myself, and my late husband Louis, with our families gathered around us. Monica glanced at the photo and immediately she pointed Uncle Harry out to me! Monica said there was something familiar about him.

I am now reunited with family who I had not seen since I was a child and family photos are now being shared via email between Australia, Liverpool, Paris, Wales and Surrey. It's lovely to find a cousin who I never knew existed and a friend who is such a lovely person, I am thrilled that this has happened and to think that all these years we had lived only around the corner from each other. In life, you just never know what or who, is around that corner.
Shirley Bodansky

From my father's side, my Cousin Margaret . . .

A story so strange and to be true is something wonderful. We were going about our lives in the usual manner with quite a small family - until one day, completely out of the blue, we had relations everywhere! This is all because of Monica – our new dear cousin, and her tenacity, with years of hard work, delving into past records.

I have known some of the family for many, many years. Auntie Annie and Uncle Syd were always favourites along with our cousins, Shirley and Raymond and I have warm memories of Uncle Dal. We were always made welcome when we visited them at their home in Knotty Ash. But we didn't get to Liverpool much when we lived in Blackburn in the 1930-40's.

I remember Uncle Harry, Monica's father, was always full of fun and my mother had a soft spot for her younger brother. My sister Renah and I thought he was handsome a good dancer and he dressed so well and with such care. Monica would have really loved him.

On the other side of the world I now have some lovely warm thoughts about all of my family. My husband Fred only met Uncle Harry out of all of my uncles. I dearly would have loved my mother to have been a part of all this. She was truly a special person and I miss her a lot.

Margaret Farrer

From my father's side, my Cousin Joyce . . .

A short time ago I had a visit from my cousin Shirley. Nothing unusual in that, you might think. But there was something unusual, because I hadn't seen Shirley for more than 75 years! She is the daughter of my father's brother, Samuel, who we always called Syd. There was something even more unusual in the reason for Shirley's visit.

Unusual is too ordinary a word for it: more like magical because what brought us back together again was a telephone call completely out the blue, telling us that the person on the line was our 1st cousin Monica. Neither Shirley nor I had ever heard of Monica! The disbelief, then surprise followed by excitement was immense.

I discovered that Monica is the daughter of my Uncle Harry, who was brother to my father Teddy and also to Shirley's father Syd. Monica had been searching and searching for many, many years to find us. Emails and telephone calls then flowed, with Monica giving names dates of births, deaths and details of relationships and we all exchanged photographs, in process of which I learnt a lot more about members of the family I had known and of those I had never heard of. The culmination of all this was the visit from my cousin Shirley, her partner Monty, and bringing with them my new cousin Monica and her husband Brian. We never stopped talking and a lovely day was had by all.

This family story is still ongoing as Monica is a Family History fanatic. There's no other word for it and I have a feeling that she will never give up trying to get further and further back in time to find more ancestors and to discover the origins of the Freeman/Freedman/ Friedman family and to find the roots of our grandfather Louis.

Thank you Monica, for being our lovely new cousin.

Joyce Porter

Further Reading

Jews of Ireland: From Earliest Times to the Year 1910 by Louis Hyman

Jewish Ireland in the Age of Joyce by Cormac O'Grada

The Jews of Lithuania: A History of a Remarkable Community 1316-1945 by Masha Greenbaum

Where Once We Walked: A Guide to the Jewish Communities Destroyed in the Holocaust Revised Edition by Gary Mokotoff and Sallyann Sack with Alexander Sharon.

Ulysses by James Joyce

Jewish Ireland: A Social History by Ray Rivlin.

The Jewish Legion during the First World War by Dr Martin Watts

Pogroms: Anti-Jewish Violence in Modern Russian History
Edited by John Doyle Klier Shlomo Lambroza

Anti-Jewish Violence: Rethinking the Pogrom in East European History Hardcover 7 Dec 2010. Edited by Jonathan L Dekel-Chen, David Gaunt Natan and M. Meir.

A Century of Ambivalence, Second Expanded Edition: The Jews of Russia and the Soviet Union, 1881 to the Present by Zvi Gitelman.

Contact Details:

Follow me on Twitter: Jess Welsby@McWallaby
Facebook: Jess Welsby (Monica)
Email: wallaby999@icloud.com